NORTH AMERICAN
Ducks, Geese, & Swans

NORTH AMERICAN
Ducks, Geese, & Swans

Donald S. Heintzelman

WINCHESTER PRESS

Library of Congress Cataloging in Publication Data

Heintzelman, Donald S.
North American ducks, geese, and swans.

Includes index.
1. Waterfowl—North America. 2. Birds—North America. I. Title.
QL696.A52H44 m 598.4'1'0973 77-26862
ISBN 0-87691-254-4
9 8 7 6 5 4 3 2

Designed by Joseph P. Ascherl

Published by Winchester Press
205 East 42nd Street
New York, N.Y. 10017

Printed in the United States of America

To the memory of the
LABRADOR DUCK
which was last seen alive in 1875

Contents

Preface xi

Checklist of Native and Introduced North American Waterfowl xiii

Chapter 1 Waterfowl Identification 1
- *Cygninae*: Swans 1
- *Anserinae*: Geese 5
- *Dendrocygninae*: Whistling Ducks 14
- *Anatinae*: Surface-Feeding Ducks 16
- *Aythyinae*: Diving Ducks 30
- *Oxyurinae*: Ruddy and Masked Ducks 48
- *Merginae*: Mergansers 50

Chapter 2 Techniques of Waterfowl Study 54
- Binoculars 54
- Telescopes 55
- Decoys and Blinds 56
- Museums and Zoos 57
- Waterfowl Names 58
- The Species Problem 61

Chapter 3 Eclipse Plumage and Hybrids 63
- Eclipse Plumage 63
- Hybrids 63

Chapter 4 Waterfowl Migrations 65
- Flyways 66
- Migration Seasons 72

Chapter 5 Prairie Pothole Waterfowl Breeding Grounds 75

Chapter 6 Local Waterfowl Viewing Areas 79
Ponds and Lakes 79
Reservoirs 79
Rivers, Streams, and Creeks 82
Marshes 82
Seacoasts 82

Chapter 7 Waterfowl Refuges 85
Northeastern States 86
Maine 86
Vermont 88
Massachusetts 90
Rhode Island 92
New York 95
New Jersey 96
Pennsylvania 100
Delaware 102
Maryland 104
Virginia 105
Southeastern States 107
Tennessee 107
North Carolina 110
South Carolina 111
Georgia 113
Alabama 118
Florida 120
Mississippi 124
Arkansas 126
Louisiana 127
Great Lakes States 131
Minnesota 131
Wisconsin 135
Michigan 138
Illinois 138
Indiana 141
Ohio 141
Northcentral States 142
Montana 142

North Dakota 147
South Dakota 151
Wyoming 153
Nebraska 156
Iowa 158
Utah 160
Colorado 162
Kansas 165
Missouri 167
Southwestern States 170
Arizona 170
New Mexico 171
Oklahoma 173
Texas 175
Pacific States 182
Washington 182
Oregon 188
Idaho 195
Nevada 197
California 198
Alaska 206

Appendix 1: Accidental Waterfowl Sightings 213
Appendix 2: National Wildlife Areas in Canada 214
Appendix 3: Waterfowl Conservation Organizations 217
Appendix 4: Homes for Wood Ducks 219

Suggested Reading 229

Index 231

Preface

Ducks, geese, and swans are among the most popular and important wildlife resources in North America. Each year millions of hunters enjoy their sport. Additional millions of people observe and photograph waterfowl in places ranging from small ponds in local parks to some of the splendid national wildlife refuges. Opportunities to see these birds are numerous because of their widespread ecological and geographic distribution.

This book is designed to help hunters and birders, as well as other interested people, to identify the various waterfowl species they see. Another important aim is to provide details about various national wildlife refuges, and a few state-operated waterfowl management areas. Millions of ducks, geese, and swans visit these places every year and the opportunities to observe or photograph these birds are superb. So, too, are the conservation–education opportunities at such locations.

During the preparation of this book, a number of books were consulted including the American Birding Association's *A. B. A. Checklist: Birds of Continental United States and Canada*, the American Ornithologists' Union's *Check-List of North American Birds* (Fifth Edition and Supplements), Bruun and Singer's *Birds of Europe,* Bull's *Birds of New York State*, Delacour's *The Waterfowl of the World*, Heinzel, Fitter and Parslow's *The Birds of Britain and Europe*, Johnsgard's *Waterfowl: Their Biology and Natural History*, Kortright's *The Ducks, Geese, & Swans of North America*, Peterson's *A Field Guide to the Birds* and *A Field Guide to Western Birds*, Reilly's *The Audubon Illustrated Handbook of American Birds*, Robbins' *A Guide to Field Identification: Birds of North America*, Scott's *A Coloured Key to the Wildfowl of the World* and *The Swans*, and Wylie and Furlong's *Key to North American Waterfowl*.

Valuable information also was extracted from files of several periodicals, especially *American Birds, Auk, Birding,* and *Cassinia*.

While writing the sections on national wildlife refuges, extensive reference was made to the information booklets, circulars, leaflets, and checklists issued by the United States Fish and Wildlife Service for their various refuges. The Canadian Wildlife Service also provided preliminary information on Canada's National Wildlife Areas and Migratory Bird Sanctuaries.

A number of individuals also provided helpful information or assistance during various stages of the preparation of this book including Rod Arbogast, Luther M. Ertel, Theodore R. Hake, Sonny Hull, Arthur Neill of Ducks Unlimited, and Ray Sickles and C. L. Strouphser of the Pennsylvania Game Commission. Special thanks also are due Hans Stuart of the United States Fish and Wildlife Service who was extremely helpful in many ways.

Photographs are an important part of this book and I used my own (which are uncredited) whenever possible. Additional photographs were provided by the following agencies, institutions, and organizations: Bushnell Optical Company, Felix Neck Wildlife Trust, Massachusetts Division of Fisheries and Wildlife, Photo Researchers, Inc., San Diego Zoo, Swift Instruments, Inc., United States Fish and Wildlife Service, Wildfowl Museum, Wildfowl Trust, and the Zoological Society of Philadelphia. The names of photographers from these sources appear with their photographs.

Private individuals who also supplied photographs include Alan Brady, Allan D. Cruickshank (with thanks to Helen Cruickshank), Karl H. and Stephen Maslowski, Leonard Lee Rue III, Jan Sosik, Millard Sharp, Larry Stevens, and Michael Wotton.

The drawing of the male Masked Duck was prepared by Rod Arbogast.

Allentown, Pennsylvania Donald S. Heintzelman
5 December 1977

Checklist of Native and Introduced North American Waterfowl

( ) Mute Swan
( ) Whistling Swan
( ) Trumpeter Swan
( ) White-fronted Goose
( ) Snow Goose
( ) Ross' Goose
( ) Emperor Goose
( ) Canada Goose
( ) Brant
( ) Black-bellied Whistling Duck
( ) Fulvous Whistling Duck
( ) Mallard
( ) American Black Duck
( ) Gadwall
( ) Common Pintail
( ) Green-winged Teal
( ) Blue-winged Teal
( ) Cinnamon Teal
( ) American Wigeon
( ) Northern Shoveler
( ) Wood Duck
( ) Redhead
( ) Ring-necked Duck
( ) Canvasback
( ) Greater Scaup
( ) Lesser Scaup
( ) Common Goldeneye
( ) Barrow's Goldeneye
( ) Bufflehead
( ) Oldsquaw
( ) Harlequin Duck
( ) Steller's Eider
( ) Common Eider
( ) King Eider
( ) Spectacled Eider
( ) White-winged Scoter
( ) Surf Scoter
( ) Black Scoter
( ) Ruddy Duck
( ) Masked Duck
( ) Hooded Merganser
( ) Common Merganser
( ) Red-breasted Merganser

Rare North American Visitors

( ) Whooper Swan
( ) Barnacle Goose
( ) Falcated Teal
( ) Eurasian Wigeon
( ) Tufted Duck

Accidental in North America

( ) Bewick's Swan
( ) Bean Goose
( ) Spot-billed Duck
( ) White-cheeked Pintail
( ) Baikal Teal
( ) Garganey
( ) Common Pochard
( ) Smew

NORTH AMERICAN
Ducks, Geese & Swans

Mute swan.

Head of mute swan.

CHAPTER ONE

Waterfowl Identification

The waterfowl of the world form a large and somewhat diverse group, the Family Anatidae, which is further divided into several subfamilies including the swans, geese, and ducks. These are the general groups used in the organization of this book. Most people, even those with only a casual knowledge of waterfowl, already are able to recognize some birds that are representative of these broad categories or subfamilies. This book, however, will help people to identify each of the species native to North America as well as some of the species that visit here on rare occasions.

Anatidae: Swans, Geese, and Ducks
Cygninae: Swans

Swans are the largest species of waterfowl. They are big, white, graceful birds generally seen swimming on ponds, lakes, bays, or large rivers. Three species occur in North America exclusive of rare visitors and accidentals. The whistling and trumpeter swans are native. The mute swan was introduced but now occurs in a wild state in some locations along the Atlantic Coast.

MUTE SWAN *Cygnus olor*

Size: 57 to 60 inches.
Field Recognition: Introduced. A large white swan often seen swimming with its neck held in a prominent S curve and its wings held in an arched or raised position above its back. Its orange bill has a black tip and a large black knob at the base. Individuals not yet fully adult are brownish rather than white and have darker bills unlike those of adults.
Flight Style: In V formations or irregular lines. The powerful wingbeats produce a melodic tone.
Habitat: Ponds, lakes, bays, large rivers, and other aquatic areas.
North American Range: Feral along portions of the East Coast, particularly in the states of New York and New Jersey. Commonly exhibited elsewhere in captivity.

Head of whistling swan.

Whistling swan. Photo by H. C. Oberholser / U.S. Fish and Wildlife Service.

WHISTLING SWAN *Cygnus columbianus columbianus*

Size: 50 to 54 inches.
Field Recognition: A large white swan with a black bill. Many individuals (but not all) have a yellow or orange spot in front of the eye. It holds its neck straight rather than in an S curve as in the mute swan. Birds not yet in adult plumage have light blackish-brown plumage and a bill marked with some pinkish.
Flight Style: In V formations or irregular lines. The wingbeats are powerful and the birds move deceptively fast.
Habitat: Ponds, lakes, large rivers, bays, reservoirs, and other aquatic areas. Corn and other grain fields are used in winter as feeding sites in some areas.
North American Range: Breeds north of the Arctic Circle from Alaska eastward to Hudson Bay and Baffin Land. Winters along the Atlantic Coast from Chesapeake Bay to Currituck Sound, and along the Pacific Coast from southern Alaska south to California. Many occur elsewhere during migration in large flocks.

Whistling swans in flight.

TRUMPETER SWAN *Cygnus cygnus buccinator*

Size: 62 to 66 inches.
Field Recognition: The largest of the North American swans. Sexes similar. White; the bill black with the edge of the mandible marked by a dis-

Head of trumpeter swan.

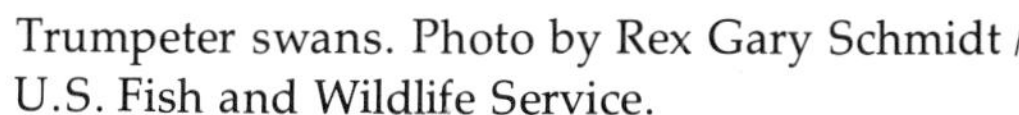

Trumpeter swans. Photo by Rex Gary Schmidt / U.S. Fish and Wildlife Service.

tinctive narrow salmon-red streak (difficult to see except at close range); legs and feet black. Immatures are grayish-white; bill pinkish with a black tip and base; and feet dull yellowish-brown.
Flight Style: Powerful, similar to the mute swan, with a rasping sound produced.
Habitat: Rivers, lakes, and large ponds in wilder areas; during winter it sometimes frequents the ice-free areas around rapids and waterfalls.
North American Range: Breeds locally in southeastern Alaska and the Canadian Rockies, and in isolated colonies in Red Rock Lakes National Wildlife Refuge, Montana, and Yellowstone National Park, Wyoming. Winters largely within its breeding range and in northwestern Washington. Until recently endangered and nearly extinct; now slowly increasing in numbers but still extremely rare and in danger. Rigidly protected.

WHOOPER SWAN *Cygnus cygnus cygnus*

Size: 60 inches.
Field Recognition: A large white swan distinguished by a prominent yellow basal half of the otherwise black bill. The yellow extends at an angle beyond the nostrils. The neck is held upright.
Flight Style: Powerful with the wingbeats producing a whistling sound.
Habitat: Winters on saltwater coastal areas and large rivers and lakes. Summers on lakes, swamps, and islands of northern Europe.
North American Range: Not native to North America. Breeds in northern Eurasia, Iceland, and the southern tip of Greenland. Winters in southern Eurasia, Great Britain, northern Africa, and Japan. Noted on St. Paul Island in Alaska, and in Maine.

Whooper swan.

Head of whooper swan.

Anserinae: Geese

A variety of freshwater and saltwater geese occur in North America. The Canada goose is the most common species exhibited in parks and is the one familiar to most people. In general, geese are intermediate in size between the larger swans and the smaller species of ducks.

WHITE-FRONTED GOOSE *Anser albifrons*

Size: 26 to 34 inches.
Field Recognition: Sexes similar. A medium-size brown goose with a pink bill, conspicuous white band around the face behind the bill, breast speckled with black, flanks and belly white, a white line along the folded wings, and legs and feet yellow. Immatures resemble the adults but lack the conspicuous white face band, speckled breast, and white line along the folded wing.
Flight Style: Generally in large flocks, either in V-formations or irregular formations, the birds using slow, labored wingbeats.
Habitat: Ponds, lakes, coastal marine waters, fields, prairies, and tundra.
North American Range: Breeds in the Alaskan and northwestern Canadian Arctic, and in Greenland. Winters on the Pacific Coast, the western and central Gulf Coast, and central Mexico; rare in the East. The Arctic birds migrate through the Great Plains and the Great Basin, whereas the few birds seen in the East mostly come from Greenland.

White-fronted goose.

Snow goose (white phase).

Snow goose (blue phase).

SNOW GOOSE *Anser caerulescens*

Size: 25 to 31 inches.
Field Recognition: White phase—a medium-size white goose with black wingtips. Individuals not yet fully adult are dusky with black wingtips.

Snow geese in flight.

Blue phase—medium size with dark slaty-bluish body, white neck and head, and white undertail coverts. The bill, legs, and feet are pinkish in both color phases.
Flight Style: Loosely formed lines or imperfect V-formations. The birds usually fly rapidly, often in fairly large flocks.
Habitat: Ponds, lakes, marshes, bays, and grain fields.
North American Range: Breeds in the Arctic from Alaska to Greenland. Winters along the Atlantic Coast from New Jersey to the Carolinas (birds from Greenland), along the Gulf Coast (most blue-phase birds), and along the Pacific Coast as far south as Baja California.

ROSS' GOOSE *Anser rossii*

Size: 20 to 26 inches.
Field Recognition: Sexes similar. The rarest and smallest (mallard size) of the North American geese. Looks like a small edition of the snow goose. White with black wingtips and a pink bill, legs, and feet. The bill of old males is warty at the base and lacks the black edge found on that of the snow goose. In females and young birds, however, the warts are small or absent. Immatures are similar to immature snow geese, but are lighter gray with somewhat pinker legs.

Ross' goose. Photo by David B. Marshall / U.S. Fish and Wildlife Service.

Flight Style: Powerful with deep wingbeats. The large flocks fly rapidly in V-formations or irregular lines but without making much noise.
Habitat: Ponds, lakes, marshes, and grain fields.
North American Range: The breeding grounds are restricted to the Perry River area of central Arctic Canada. Winters in central California, chiefly in the San Joaquin and Sacramento valleys. Frequently joins flocks of snow geese.

EMPEROR GOOSE *Anser canagicus*

Size: 26 to 28 inches.
Field Recognition: A very attractive small goose with a white head and neck, black chin and throat, "scaly" bluish-gray and white body, and white tail. Legs and feet orange; bill flesh color with a white tip. Immatures resemble adults but lack the white head and neck; the bill and feet are darker.
Flight Style: Low and fast with deep, rapid wingbeats. Flocks generally fly abreast in a line.
Habitat: Arctic tundra within 10 miles of the sea during the breeding season. In winter along marine coasts (except for rare appearances on freshwater areas in winter in California).
North American Range: Breeds in northwestern Alaska. Winters in the Aleutian islands; rarely reaches southern Oregon and California.

Emperor goose. Photo by Sigurd T. Olson / U.S. Fish and Wildlife Service.

Canada goose.

CANADA GOOSE *Branta canadensis*

Size: 22 to 40 inches.
Field Recognition: Highly variable in size depending upon which subspecies is seen. A black goose with a brown body and white cheek patches

Canada goose flapping its wings.

Head of Canada goose.

Canada geese flying in V-formation.

and undertail coverts. The bill, legs, and feet are black. Young birds resemble the adults. The race *B. c. hutchinsii,* sometimes known as the Richardson's or Hutchins' goose, is very small.
Flight Style: In V-formations accompanied by loud honking, which suggests the barking of a dog when heard at a distance.
Habitat: Aquatic areas including ponds, lakes, marshes, rivers, streams, creeks, and bays.
North American Range: Breeds in the Arctic south to California, Montana, and southeastern Canada; also widely in the United States where it has been introduced into parks. Winters throughout much of the United States.

Brant (western or black brant form). Photo by Jerry L. Hout / U.S. Fish and Wildlife Service.

Brant (eastern or Atlantic form) in flight. Photo by Alan Brady.

BRANT *Branta bernicla*
Size: 20 to 24 inches.
Field Recognition: A small goose that, in the eastern form, has a brown body, light underparts, white undertail coverts, and a black head, neck, and chest. There is a white mark on each side of the short neck. In the

western form, formerly known as the black brant, the white mark on the neck is much larger and more conspicuous and the belly and sides are dark merging into the black breast. The bill, legs, and feet are black. Immatures resemble the adults but are somewhat darker (particularly in the western form) and lack the white marks on the neck.
Flight Style: Rapid but usually not in a V-formation. Forms loose flocks that fly low in irregular lines.
Habitat: Saltwater bays, inlets, marshes, tidal areas, and ocean.
North American Range: Breeds in the Alaskan and Canadian Arctic and in Greenland. Winters along the Atlantic Coast from Massachusetts southward to North Carolina, and along the Pacific Coast from British Columbia southward to Baja California.

BARNACLE GOOSE *Branta leucopsis*

Size: 24 to 27 inches.
Field Recognition: Sexes similar. Somewhat like the brant, but with the face white and a small black mask between the bill and eyes. Bill, legs, and feet black. Immatures are similar to the adults.
Flight Style: Short, rapid wingbeats.
Habitat: Saltwater marshes, coastal mudflats, and fields.
North American Range: Not native to North America. Breeds in Greenland. Winters in Europe. On rare occasions individuals wander to the Atlantic Coast where they tend to join flocks of Canada geese.

Barnacle geese (pair). Photo by J. B. Blossom / The Wildfowl Trust.

Dendrocygninae: Whistling Ducks

The whistling ducks are an aberrant subfamily that occur mainly in the Southwest. The birds have long legs and appear almost gooselike.

BLACK-BELLIED WHISTLING DUCK *Dendrocygna autumnalis*

Size: 20 to 22 inches.
Field Recognition: Sexes similar. An erect standing duck with a black belly, conspicuous white area on the wings, chestnut forehead, crown,

Black-bellied whistling duck.

chest, neck, and back, and the sides of the head ashy-gray. Bill red; legs and feet pinkish. Immatures are duller and grayer with a dusky bill and dark reddish legs and feet.
Flight Style: Slow, strong wingbeats. Frequently lands and wades into water.
Habitat: Wooded tropical lowlands, lakes, ponds, marshes, and cornfields.
North American Range: Resident in southern Texas.

FULVOUS WHISTLING DUCK *Dendrocygna bicolor*

Size: 18 to 21 inches.
Field Recognition: Tawny brown with a darker brown back and crown, broken horizontal whitish slashes on each side of the body, and whitish undertail coverts. The bill and legs are gray. Sexes similar. Immatures are similar to the adults but are duller.
Flight Style: Strong, slow wingbeats with the birds flying low in a line. Extends the neck down when landing.
Habitat: Lakes, ponds, freshwater marshes, and fields under irrigation.
North American Range: Resident in California, New Mexico, Texas, and southern Louisiana; rare in the East.

Fulvous whistling duck. Photo by Kirke A. King / U.S. Fish and Wildlife Service.

Anatinae: Surface-Feeding Ducks

The surface-feeding ducks, as the name suggests, tip-up or dabble rather than dive underwater for their food. These are the ducks that most people see in small ponds, creeks, or marshes. The mallard is a typical example. In many of these species the male has plumage that is considerably more colorful than that of the female.

MALLARD *Anas platyrhynchos*

North American Ducks, Geese & Swans

Size: 16 to 27 inches.
Field Recognition: The common duck of parks and ponds. *Male*—body gray, head and neck metallic green, and breast chestnut. A white ring divides the neck and breast. Tail black and white. Speculum (band on wings) blue with a narrow border of black then white. Bill yellow, feet orange. *Female*—mottled brown with a darker eye stripe and cap. Speculum as in the male. Bill and feet orange. The form (both sexes) sometimes known as the Mexican duck, of the Rio Grande Valley of New Mexico, is similar to a typical female mallard whereas the form (both sexes) sometimes known as the mottled duck, of Florida and coastal Louisiana and Texas, suggests a pale brownish version of the black duck but has a greenish-blue speculum, instead of purple, and the throat light and unstreaked.

Mallard (male).

Mallards (males and female) in flight.

Flight Style: Powerful and direct as single individuals or in loose groups or V-formations.
Habitat: Ponds, lakes, rivers, creeks, bays, marshes, and grain fields.
North American Range: Widely distributed throughout the continent.

Mallard (female with ducklings). Photo by Hans Stuart / U.S. Fish and Wildlife Service.

American black duck.

American black duck. Photo by Bill Byrne / Massachusetts Division of Fisheries and Wildlife.

AMERICAN BLACK DUCK *Anas rubripes*

Size: 21 to 26 inches.
Field Recognition: A dark brown duck with conspicuous white underwing linings. Speculum purple bordered with black. Bill yellow. Legs and feet reddish to brown. Sexes similar in appearance.

Flight Style: Rapid and direct sometimes in small flocks forming either V-formations or angular lines. Wary.
Habitat: Ponds, lakes, bays, saltwater marshes, and grain fields.
North American Range: Widely distributed throughout the eastern half of the continent.

GADWALL *Anas strepera*

Size: 19 to 23 inches.
Field Recognition: Male—gray, head and neck brownish, belly white, rump black, speculum white with black edges, and white on rear edge of innerwing (in flight). Bill dark. Feet yellow. *Female*—dull brown with a white speculum.
Flight Style: Direct and rapid with quick wingbeats. Flocks are small, compact groups.
Habitat: Ponds, lakes, rivers, freshwater marshes.
North American Range: Southern Canada and the United States.

Gadwall (male). Photo by Alan Brady.

Gadwall (female). Photo by C. J. Henry / U.S. Fish and Wildlife Service.

Common pintail (male). Photo by U.S. Fish and Wildlife Service.

Common pintail (female).

COMMON PINTAIL *Anas acuta*

Size: 20 to 29 inches.
Field Recognition: Male—a gray duck with a long, slender neck, brown head, white breast and sides of neck, and distinctive long, pointed tail. *Female*—mottled brown with a long, slender neck and a somewhat pointed tail. The bill, legs, and feet are grayish-blue (both sexes).
Flight Style: Graceful and rapid, often descending from aloft by zigzagging, then gliding onto the water.
Habitat: Freshwater ponds, lakes, and marshes; also saltwater estuaries and bays.
North American Range: Widespread throughout the continent.

FALCATED TEAL *Anas falcata*

Size: 20 inches.
Field Recognition: Male—head chestnut brown with green sides and a long crest, throat and neck white with a black collar, body gray with elongated wing feathers, speculum green and black. *Female*—brown with a green speculum.
Flight Style: Swift.
Habitat: Riverine swamps, marshes, and lakes.
North American Range: Not native to North America. Breeds in northern Eurasia. Winters from China, Japan, and Indochina south to India. Noted in Pribilof and Aleutian islands in Alaska, British Columbia, and California.

Falcated teal (male). Photo by Leonard Lee Rue III.

GREEN-WINGED TEAL *Anas crecca*

Size: 12 to 16 inches.
Field Recognition: Male—a small gray duck with a vertical white line on each side of the body behind the breast, a brown head with a green stripe, and a green speculum. *Female*—mottled brown with a green speculum. The bill, legs, and feet are grayish. Two subspecies occur in North America of which *A. c. carolinensis* is native. The European form, *A. c. crecca*, is similar to the North American form but lacks the vertical white line on each side of the body having, instead, a white horizontal line above each wing.
Flight Style: Erratic, swift, with rapid wingbeats that produce a whistling

Green-winged teal (male, North American form). Photo by Larry Stevens.

Green-winged teal (female). Photo by Larry Stevens.

Green-winged teal (male, European form).

sound. Flocks land in compact, loose formation and turn as a unit.
Habitat: Smooth shallow waters of ponds, lakes, rivers, streams, marshes, and bays; also brackish waters (rarely).
North American Range: Widespread throughout North America. The European subspecies is a rare but regular visitor along the Atlantic Coast south to the Carolinas.

BLUE-WINGED TEAL *Anas discors*

Size: 14 to 17 inches.
Field Recognition: Male—mottled brown, head bluish with a conspicuous white crescent, forewings light bluish and speculum green. Bill bluish-

Blue-winged teal (male). Photo by Dave McLauchlin / U.S. Fish and Wildlife Service.

Blue-winged teal (female and male). Photo by K. Portman / The Wildfowl Trust.

black. Legs yellow. *Female*—brown with forewings light bluish and speculum green. Bill dusky with pinkish edges. Legs yellow. The bluish wing patches (both sexes) are conspicuous in flight.
Flight Style: Rapid, in tight flocks, with much turning and twisting. They take off vertically.
Habitat: Freshwater ponds, marshes, and slow-moving streams.
North American Range: Widespread throughout the southern half of Canada and the United States.

CINNAMON TEAL *Anas cyanoptera*

Size: 14 to 17 inches.
Field Recognition: Male—head and entire body dark cinnamon-red, the wing coverts cobalt blue. Bill longer than the head and black, eye

Cinnamon teal (male).

Cinnamon teal (female). Photo by K. Portman / The Wildfowl Trust.

orange, legs and feet dull orange-yellow. *Female*—almost identical to the female blue-winged teal. *Immature*—both sexes similar to the adult female during the first autumn.
Flight Style: Similar to that of other teal.
Habitat: Ponds, lakes, streams, sloughs, and marshes.
North American Range: Most of the western United States and a small portion of the southern Canadian Rockies.

EURASIAN WIGEON *Anas penelope*

Size: 17 to 20 inches.
Field Recognition: Male—gray with a light brownish breast, a dark cinnamon head and conspicuous cream-colored crown. Bill bluish-gray. *Female*—brown, head somewhat reddish when seen in good light. Both

Eurasian wigeon (male).

Eurasian wigeon (female).

sexes have blackish axillaries (underarm feathers). Eurasian wigeons commonly associate with flocks of American wigeons that should be examined carefully for this species.

Flight Style: Rapid and erratic with rustling wingbeats. Flocks (not normally seen in North America) form loose lines or blunt wedges.

Habitat: Freshwater ponds, lakes, and marshes; also coastal bays and marshes.

North American Range: Not native to this continent. A rare but regular visitor to the Atlantic and Pacific coasts and occasionally inland.

AMERICAN WIGEON *Anas americana*

Size: 18 to 23 inches.

Field Recognition: Male—brown, head grayish with a white crown and a large green patch behind each eye, forewings white, speculum green,

American wigeon (male).

American widgeon (female). Photo by Larry Stevens.

belly white, and tail gray. *Female*—mottled brown with a grayish head. Bill and feet bluish-gray (both sexes).
Flight Style: The flocks are small and compact but fly rapidly in irregular formations.
Habitat: Freshwater ponds, lakes, bays, and marshes; also seen commonly on fields under irrigation and occasionally in aquatic areas that are brackish or marine. Flocks frequently appear in city and town parks.
North American Range: Distributed widely throughout the continent.

NORTHERN SHOVELER *Anas clypeata*

Size: 17 to 22 inches.
Field Recognition: The large spatulate-shaped bill in both sexes is distinctive; no other North American species has a bill shaped similarly. *Male*

Northern shoveler (male).

Northern shovelers (female and male). Photo by Dave McLauchlin / U.S. Fish and Wildlife Service.

—body white with dark brown sides and belly, head greenish-black, back greenish-black, breast white, and light blue area on forward edge of each wing. Eye vivid yellow. *Female*—mottled brown with the bill shaped as in the male. Eye brown.
Flight Style: Generally direct and slow.
Habitat: Shallow ponds, slowly moving creeks, and freshwater marshes; also the shallow portions of saltwater bays as well as in tidal mudflats (in winter).
North American Range: Widespread throughout the United States and southern and western Canada.

WOOD DUCK *Aix sponsa*

Size: 17 to 21 inches.
Field Recognition: The most vividly colored of all North American ducks (males only). *Male*—a spectacular combination of metallic purples, blues, browns, and whites. Head crested. Bill red and white. Unlike any other duck in North America. *Female*—brown, belly white, head with a crest and white spectacles. Feet dull yellow (both sexes).
Flight Style: Direct and swift with the head held higher than the level of the body.
Habitat: Rivers, ponds, marshes, and swamps with a forest edge.
North American Range: The eastern half of the United States and extreme southern Canada; also central British Columbia southward to central California.

Wood duck (male).

Wood duck (female and male).

Aythyinae: Diving Ducks

The diving ducks, so-called because they dive beneath the surface of the water for food, frequently are found on freshwater ponds, lakes, and rivers. Some of the species are also found on saltwater bays, inlets, and other sheltered marine areas.

REDHEAD *Aythya americana*

Size: 18 to 22 inches.
Field Recognition: Male—a gray duck with a rounded red head, black chest, and white belly. Bill bluish with a black tip and a white ring

Redhead (male).

Redhead (female). Photo by Alan Brady.

immediately behind it. *Female*—brown with a white breast, and grayish speculum. Bill similar to that of the male but duller.
Flight Style: Rapid with quick wingbeats; often in V-formations.
Habitat: Ponds, lakes, bays, and marshes.
North American Range: Widespread throughout the United States, wintering on the Atlantic and Pacific coasts, and distributed in southwestern Canada.

RING-NECKED DUCK *Aythya collaris*

Size: 14 to 18½ inches.
Field Recognition: Male—back dark, chest black, head dull purple (frequently appearing black) and peaked toward the back, underparts white, speculum gray, and a conspicuous white crescent on each side of the body behind the chest. Bill gray with a black tip, and two conspicuous white rings (one at the base, the other behind the black tip) that are important field marks. *Female*—brown, eye-ring white, speculum gray, underparts white, and bill similar to that of the male.
Flight Style: In small, open flocks swiftly and directly.
Habitat: Ponds, lakes, bays, rivers, marshes, and marine waters that are sheltered.
North American Range: Widespread from the Canadian Rockies, prairie provinces, and eastern Canada south along the Atlantic and Pacific coasts, the Gulf Coast, and the southeastern part of the United States. Breeds in Canada, parts of the West, and northern New England.

Ring-necked duck (male).

Ring-necked duck (female). Photo by Allan D. Cruickshank.

CANVASBACK *Aythya valisineria*

Size: 19 to 24 inches.
Field Recognition: Male—a light gray duck with a black chest, dull reddish head distinguished by a sloping forehead and bill. Eye red (adults) or clear yellow (immatures). *Female*—light grayish with a buffy neck and

Canvasback (male).

Canvasbacks (female and male). Photo by Rex Gary Schmidt / U.S. Fish and Wildlife Service.

head and sloping forehead and bill similar to the male. Eye brown. Bill black (paler in female). Feet grayish- or yellowish-blue (both sexes).
Flight Style: Swift on long, pointed wings. Usually migrates in V-formations.
Habitat: Freshwater ponds, lakes, potholes, and marshes. Also saltwater marshes, and bays.
North American Range: Widespread throughout the United States and western Canada. Breeds in the western Canadian provinces and in northwestern United States. Winters along the Atlantic, Gulf, and Pacific coasts and inland from these coasts to some extent.

GREATER SCAUP *Aythya marila*

Size: 15 to 21 inches.
Field Recognition: Male—light gray on the back, white below, chest and rear black, head rounded with dull greenish gloss (in good light), and

Greater scaup (male).

Greater scaup (female). Photo by Alan Brady.

long white stripe on the wing (when extended). Bill blue. *Female*—brown with a prominent white area at the base of the bill, and white wing stripe as in the male. Bill blue.
Flight Style: Erratic and swift with much turning and twisting. Frequently forms large, tight flocks.
Habitat: Freshwater ponds, lakes, and rivers in summer; coastal marine waters and the Great Lakes in winter.
North American Range: Most of North America, breeding in Alaska and northwestern Canada. Winters along the Atlantic, Gulf, and Pacific coasts and the Great Lakes.

LESSER SCAUP *Aythya affinis*

Size: 14 to 19 inches.
Field Recognition: Male—a smaller version of the Greater Scaup but with a dull purple head (in good light) the top of which is slightly peaked in-

Lesser scaup (male). Photo by Allan D. Cruickshank.

Lesser scaup (female). Photo by Allan D. Cruickshank.

stead of being rounded as in the Greater Scaup. The white wing stripe is restricted to the inner wing (secondaries). *Female*—brown with the top of the head slightly peaked as in the male and a conspicuous white area at the base of the bill. A white wing stripe as in the male. Bill blue with a black tip (both sexes).
Flight Style: Similar to the greater scaup.
Habitat: Inland ponds, lakes, rivers, and marshes; also sheltered saltwater areas in winter.
North American Range: Widespread through the continent. Breeds from the West northward through western Canada to much of Alaska. Winters along the Atlantic, Gulf, and Pacific coasts and inland from these areas. Migrates over much of the continent.

TUFTED DUCK *Aythya fuligula*

Size: 17 inches.
Field Recognition: Male—head dull purple with a distinctive drooping rear

Tufted duck (male).

tuft of feathers, a black chest and back, sides and underparts white. *Female*—brown, similar to female scaup, but with a tuft on the rear of the head.
Flight Style: Fast, in irregular formations.
Habitat: Winters in flocks in bays and lakes but seldom on salt water. Breeds on ponds and lakes.
North American Range: Not native to North America. Breeds in Iceland and northern Eurasia. Winters in southern Eurasia and portions of Africa. Noted in Alaska, California, and Massachusetts.

COMMON GOLDENEYE *Bucephala clangula*

Size: 15 to 21 inches.
Field Recognition: Male—white with a black back, dull greenish head, and a conspicuous round white spot behind the bill on each side of the face. Eye bright yellow. Bill black. *Female*—body gray, white neck and underparts, head dull brownish. Eye and bill as in the male. Both sexes have large white wing patches.

Common goldeneye (male). Photo by Ducks Unlimited.

Common goldeneye (female).

Flight Style: The wingbeats produce a whistling sound that is distinctive. The flight is unusually strong and swift with the birds sometimes collecting into small flocks.
Habitat: Ponds, lakes, and rivers; also saltwater areas in winter.
North American Range: Breeds in the Canadian and Alaskan Arctic southward in eastern Canada to the United States, winters in the United States and the Atlantic Coast of Canada along with the Pacific Coast of Canada and southern Alaska.

BARROW'S GOLDENEYE *Bucephala islandica*

Size: 16 to 20 inches.
Field Recognition: Similar to the common goldeneye but with several important differences. *Male*—head purplish (rather than greenish in the

Barrow's goldeneyes (female and male). Photo by Kirke A. King / U.S. Fish and Wildlife Service.

Barrow's goldeneye (male).

common goldeneye) marked by a large white crescent on each side of the face behind the bill. The back and sides also show more black than the common goldeneye. *Female*—similar to the female common goldeneye but with a shorter bill (a poor field mark).
Flight Style: Much the same as the common goldeneye.
Habitat: Ponds and lakes surrounded by forest.
North American Range: Northwestern United States, extreme western Canada, and southern Alaska; rare in the East, usually appearing along the New England Coast, especially in Massachusetts.

BUFFLEHEAD *Bucephala albeola*

Size: 12 to 16 inches.
Field Recognition: Male—a small duck with a white body, black back, and dark purplish head with a large white patch extending around the back from each eye. Also has large, conspicuous white patches on the wing (in flight). *Female*—brown, a white spot on each cheek, and white wing patches (in flight).
Flight Style: In small flocks close to the water with rapid wingbeats.
Habitat: Ponds, rivers, lakes; protected marine areas in winter.
North American Range: Widespread from the Arctic southward. Breeds largely in Canada and Alaska and winters mainly in the United States and the Pacific Coast area of Canada.

Bufflehead (male). Photo by Alan Brady.

Bufflehead (female).

Oldsquaw (male in winter plumage; mounted specimen). Photo by Karl H. Maslowski.

Oldsquaw (female, in summer plumage, with ducklings). Photo by Karl H. Maslowski.

OLDSQUAW *Clangula hyemalis*

Size: 14 to 23 inches.
Field Recognition: Male (winter)—a white duck with a long, pointed black tail, dark wings, black breast and back, and a dark brown patch on each cheek. Bill pink with a dark tip and base. *Male (summer)*—head, neck and chest black offset by a large white patch around each eye, wings

dark, back dark brown, underparts white, tail black, long and pointed. *Female (winter)*—brown, white below and on the sides of the head with a dark patch on each cheek and a dark crown and nape. Wings dark. Bill and legs gray. *Female (summer)*—similar to the winter plumage but with more dark brown on the head.
Flight Style: In small flocks low over the water with short, quick wingbeats. The birds frequently turn and twist showing their backs and breasts.
Habitat: Tundra ponds in summer; coastal and other large expanses of water in winter (rarely seen on small bodies of water).
North American Range: Breeds in Arctic Canada and Alaska. Winters along the Atlantic and Pacific coasts, sometimes far out at sea, and in the Great Lakes.

Harlequin ducks (male and female). Photo by San Diego Zoo.

HARLEQUIN DUCK *Histrionicus histrionicus*

Size: 14½ to 21 inches.
Field Recognition: Male—an unusual duck with a grayish-blue body offset by brown sides and bold white markings. The head is darker than the body and also has bold white markings. Bill, legs, and feet bluish-gray (both sexes). Sometimes holds its tail erect like a ruddy duck. *Female*—brown with three small white spots on each side of the head.
Flight Style: Swift, with quick wingbeats, in compact groups above the water. Also tends to turn quickly.

Habitat: Coastal waters and tumbling mountain streams.
North American Range: Breeds from Alaska south to the mountains of California and Colorado and in northern Quebec and Labrador. Winters along the Pacific Coast from Alaska south to California and along the Atlantic Coast south to Maryland. Rare in the East but fairly common in the West.

Steller's eider (male on left; female on right). Photo by Paul Johnsgard / National Audubon Society and Photo Researchers, Inc.

STELLER'S EIDER *Polysticta stelleri*

Size: 17 to 19 inches.
Field Recognition: Male—an uncommon Asian eider with a white head and body offset by a black eye-ring, chin, collar, and back; tail black; breast, sides, and underparts brown; a small yellowish-green patch on the back of the head and another in front of each eye; bold white wing coverts; bill, legs, and feet gray. *Female*—dark brown with a blue speculum bordered with white bars.
Flight Style: Swift with the wings making a sound not unlike that of goldeneyes.
Habitat: Offshore waters and coastal shores.
North American Range: Breeds on the Arctic coast and islands of northwestern Alaska. Winters in Alaska's Aleutian and Pribilof islands.

COMMON EIDER *Somateria mollissima*

Size: 21 to 27 inches.
Field Recognition: Male—a beautiful duck with black underparts and tail, a white back and chest, some white on the wings, and a white head offset by a large black area through and above each eye, a pale lemon

Common eider (male).

Common eider (female on nest). Photo by O. J. Murie / U.S. Fish and Wildlife Service.

nape, and a pale yellow streak between the bill and each eye. Bill yellowish-orange. Feet grayish-green. *Female*—brown with darker bars on the body. Bill grayish.

Flight Style: Just above the water with steady wingbeats and head extended low. Much different than other ducks.

Habitat: Coastal and other marine waters.

North American Range: Breeds around the Arctic edge of North America and southward on the Atlantic Coast to Maine. Winters along the southern edge of the Arctic ice packs, sometimes reaching as far south as coastal Washington and North Carolina. Very large rafts occur in winter in Alaskan waters and off coastal Massachusetts.

KING EIDER *Somateria spectabilis*

Size: 18 to 24 inches.
Field Recognition: A large, colorful duck. *Male*—body black, part of wings and chest white, head pale grayish on top with pale greenish cheeks marked by some black lines around the bill and eyes. Bill and knob behind it vivid orange. Immatures are grayish-black with a light chest and a pinkish bill. *Female*—reddish-brown with heavy black bars.
Flight Style: Similar to the common eider.
Habitat: Coastal waters in winter; rare on large inland waters.
North American Range: Breeds on the Arctic coasts of North America from northwestern Alaska eastward to Labrador. Winters along the Atlantic and Pacific coasts as far south as California and New Jersey, and sometimes on the Great Lakes.

King eider (male). Photo by Ron Garrison / San Diego Zoo.

King eider (female on nest). Photo by Karl H. and Stephen Maslowski.

SPECTACLED EIDER *Somateria fischeri*

Size: 20 to 23 inches.

Field Recognition: A rare bird in the North American Arctic. *Male*—head pale green with a large white patch (edged with black) around each eye, white throat, neck, and upperparts, and black breast and underparts. *Female*—brown with notable pale brown spectacles around the eyes, and feathers extending farther down the mandible than in the common eider.

Spectacled eider (male). Photo by J. B. Blossom / The Wildfowl Trust.

Spectacled eider (female at nest). Photo by Michael Wotton.

Flight Style: Similar to the common eider.
Habitat: Marine coasts of northwestern Arctic Alaska.
North American Range: Breeds along the northwestern coast of Arctic Alaska. Winters off Alaska's Pribilof and Aleutian islands, and rarely off Kodiak Island.

WHITE-WINGED SCOTER *Melanitta deglandi*

Size: 19 to 23 inches.
Field Recognition: Male—black with a white patch on the wings and a white eye-ring. Bill orange with a black knob. *Female*—dark brown, two white patches on each side of the head, and a white wingpatch. Bill bluish-gray. The white areas on the head are not always clearly visible. White-winged scoters frequently are seen swimming in flocks in coastal waters.
Flight Style: Direct and strong, commonly flying in lines over the surf.
Habitat: Coastal waters and large lakes.
North American Range: Breeds in a strip from west-central Alaska south-

White-winged scoter (male). Photo courtesy Felix Neck Wildlife Trust.

White-winged scoter (female). Photo by Allan D. Cruickshank.

ward to northern North Dakota. Summers from eastern Canada south to Massachusetts. Winters along the Pacific Coast from Alaska south to Baja California, on the Great Lakes, and along the Atlantic Coast from Gulf of St. Lawrence south to South Carolina.

SURF SCOTER *Melanitta perspicillata*

Size: 17 to 21 inches.
Field Recognition: Male—black with two large white patches on the head (forehead and rear). Bill reddish and yellow, with a black circle on each side surrounded by white. Eye white. *Female*—brown, darker on the back, with two white patches on each side of the head and another at the rear (the latter missing in immatures). Bill blackish. Eyes brown.
Flight Style: Similar to the black scoter. In large, loosely formed flocks. The wingbeats produce a loud humming sound that can be heard at a distance.
Habitat: Saltwater bays and inlets; also large lakes.
North American Range: Summers in Alaska and northern Canada. Winters along the Pacific Coast from Alaska south to Baja California, and along the Atlantic Coast from Nova Scotia south to North Carolina (rare along Florida and the Gulf Coast).

Surf scoter (male: only one white patch on head showing). Photo by Alan Brady.

Surf scoter (female). Photo by Franklin Williamson / Zoological Society of Philadelphia.

Black scoter (male). Photo courtesy Felix Neck Wildlife Trust.

Black scoter (female). Photo by J. B. Blossom / The Wildfowl Trust.

BLACK SCOTER *Melanitta nigra*

Size: 17 to 21 inches.
Field Recognition: Male—all black. Bill bright orange. *Female*—brown, darker above, with a large light area on each side of the head and neck. Bill bluish-gray.
Flight Style: Similar to the other scoters.
Habitat: Coastal saltwater areas and large freshwater lakes. Smaller inland waters in summer.
North American Range: Breeds in Alaska. Winters along the Pacific Coast from Alaska south to southern California, along the Atlantic Coast from Newfoundland south to South Carolina, and on the Great Lakes.

Oxyurinae: Ruddy and Masked Ducks

RUDDY DUCK *Oxyura jamaicensis*

Size: 14 to 17 inches.
Field Recognition: A small, chunky duck. *Male (summer)*—body brownish-red, underparts whitish, head blackish with large white cheeks, tail blackish, and flight feathers blackish. Bill vivid blue. *Male (winter)*—similar to the female but with the bold white cheeks more prominent. *Female*—brown, darker above with light cheeks divided by a dark brown horizontal streak. Undersides whitish with much dark marking on the lower breast. Bill grayish.
Flight Style: Patters along the water surface before rising with difficulty, then moves in a tail-heavy flight style. Noisy flight.
Habitat: Ponds, lakes and marshes; also marine areas in winter.
North American Range: Breeds in western North America and is extending the range eastward to the Great Lakes area, Quebec, and New Eng-

Ruddy duck (male). Photo by Alan Brady.

Ruddy duck (females). Photo by Jan Sosik.

land. Winters along the Pacific Coast from southern British Columbia southward, along the Atlantic Coast from Massachusetts southward, and in the southcentral United States.

MASKED DUCK *Oxyura dominica*

Size: 13 to 14 inches.
Field Recognition: Male—head reddish-brown with a bold black face mask, back reddish-brown with dark spots, chest and underparts lighter brown with dark spots on the sides, tail dark, wings dark with a white speculum. *Female*—brown, darker on the back and head, with light cheeks divided by two dark brown horizontal streaks. A white speculum on the wings. Difficult to detect, and the most inconspicuous of all ducks.
Flight Style: Similar to the ruddy duck, but with flocks consisting of small groups or pairs.
Habitat: Dense aquatic vegetation on ponds, lakes, marshes, and swamps.
North American Range: A tropical species that barely reaches the United States. Occurs casually in the Rio Grande Valley of southern Texas.

Masked duck (male). Drawn by Rod Arbogast.

Masked ducks (female with young). Photo by D. Hagemeyer / U.S. Fish and Wildlife Service.

Merginae: Mergansers

Mergansers are fish-eating ducks whose bills have special teethlike edges useful for grasping and holding fish. Their general outline is somewhat different from the profiles of other species of waterfowl.

HOODED MERGANSER *Mergus cucullatus*

Size: 16 to 20 inches.
Field Recognition: The smallest of the mergansers in North America. *Male*—head black with a large white crest, back black with several white stripes, sides of body brown, underparts white, chest and breast white with two vertical black stripes, and tail black with a white tip. Bill black. Eye bright yellow. *Female*—grayish above, lighter below. Head reddish-gray with a reddish crest. Bill dusky yellow. Eyes yellow.
Flight Style: The crest is depressed and the birds use direct and rapid flight. Generally found in small flocks or pairs.
Habitat: Ponds, lakes, and rivers in wooded areas.
North American Range: Breeds in a wide, coast-to-coast band across the United States (except the Southwest) and southern Canada. Winters along the Atlantic, eastern Gulf, and Pacific coasts of the United States and inland from these areas to some extent.

Hooded merganser (male). Photo by Bill Byrne / Massachusetts Division of Fisheries and Wildlife.

Hooded merganser (female and male). Photo by B. A. Crosby / The Wildlife Trust.

COMMON MERGANSER *Mergus merganser*

Size: 21 to 27 inches.
Field Recognition: A merganser without a crest. *Male*—body white, back black, and head dull greenish. Bill vivid red. Feet orange. *Female*—gray, darker above, with a brown head (with a light crest). Throat, chest, and underparts white. Wings gray and black with a white speculum. Bill dull red.

Common merganser (male and female). Photo by Larry Stevens.

Common merganser (female). Photo by Larry Stevens.

Flight Style: Direct, strong, and swift in linelike formations.
Habitat: Lakes and rivers in forested areas in summer. Ponds, lakes, rivers, and other places with open water in winter. Also protected marine bays and brackish areas on rare occasions in winter.
North American Range: Breeds along southern coastal Alaska, the southern half of Canada, and portions of the northern United States. Winters southward in most of the United States except the southern and southeastern third.

RED-BREASTED MERGANSER *Mergus serrator*

Size: 19 to 26 inches.
Field Recognition: The larger of the two crested mergansers. *Male*—head greenish-black with a double-pointed crest, throat and underparts white, a wide brownish band across the chest, sides grayish, back black, wings black with a white speculum, and tail dark gray. The bill, legs, feet, and eyes all are bright red. *Female*—gray above, white below. Crested head rich brownish. Throat whitish blending into the surrounding brownish areas of the head. Wings dark with a white speculum as in the male. Bill dullish red. Eye red or yellowish.
Flight Style: Similar to the common merganser but with less white showing on the body and wings (male).
Habitat: Lakes and rivers in summer; saltwater areas in winter.
North American Range: Breeds through large portions of Alaska, Canada, and the northcentral and eastern part of the United States. Winters along the Pacific Coast from southern Alaska south to Baja California and, in the East, on the Great Lakes and New England Coast southward to the Gulf Coast.

Red-breasted merganser (male). Photo by J. B. Blossom / The Wildfowl Trust.

Red-breasted mergansers (male and female). Photo by E. E. Jackson / The Wildfowl Trust.

CHAPTER TWO

Techniques of Waterfowl Study

Looking at wild ducks, geese, and swans is both enjoyable and educational. Some people will use this book at a pond or lake in a local park. To them it is simply fun to watch the various ducks and geese feeding and swimming and to try to identify the different species.

Other people may travel to important government wildlife refuges that were established for the protection and preservation of waterfowl, where they may watch the birds more carefully. Some may even become interested in waterfowl behavior. If so, they are on their way toward exploring the mystery and fascination of bird behavior in general. They are in good company. Some of the first studies on animal behavior were done on waterfowl and even today many of the most comprehensive studies are those that describe waterfowl behavior patterns.

Those interested in this aspect of looking at waterfowl will want to refer to some of the books listed in the Suggested Reading section for fuller details. Knowing why ducks, geese, and swans act as they do gives us a fuller and richer appreciation of these important wildlife resources.

Regardless of where one looks at waterfowl, however, some basic equipment and techniques are helpful. This section of the book will assist you with these and other considerations.

Binoculars

In many city parks it is unnecessary to use binoculars to see many of the ducks, geese, and swans clearly. Most of these birds are fed regularly by the public and are accustomed to being approached closely. However, wild waterfowl also uses many such ponds and lakes during some seasons of the year and these birds generally are shy and far more difficult to approach.

In general, a pair of binoculars is very helpful to people

Center-focus binoculars are essential for serious waterfowl observation and study. Photo courtesy of Swift Instruments, Inc.

looking at waterfowl. The most popular types (all of which should have center focusing) are 7×35, 7×50, and 8×40, but some observers and birders use instruments up to 10X in magnification. People seriously interested in looking at waterfowl, or becoming active in birding generally, should buy binoculars with coated lenses that help reduce glare from water surfaces and provide brighter and clearer images.

Telescopes

Many active birders who watch waterfowl regularly also use a telescope to see birds resting far out on lakes or marshes beyond the distance at which binoculars are effective. A variety of types, styles, and brands is available. Some have fixed magnifications that may be altered by changing the eyepiece, whereas others have zoom features that allow the user to quickly change magnifications by turning a small wheel on the scope. Regardless of the type used, a minimum magnification of 20X is necessary and

A telescope, mounted on a tripod or gunstock for support, is a valuable aid in watching ducks at a distance. Photo courtesy of Bushnell Optical Company.

many birders prefer 30X or higher for studying ducks at a distance.

Since it is difficult to hold telescopes steady with such high magnifications, they should be mounted on a special bracket for your car window, on a small photographic tripod, or some other firm support. Most birders use a tripod. Some people mount telescopes on gunstocks that then enable them to follow flying ducks, geese, and swans easily when they pass overhead or at other awkward angles.

Decoys and Blinds

Hunters have long used duck and geese decoys to lure birds within shooting range. Blinds or hides are helpful also because they allow one to remain out of sight. Photogra-

A pair of common pintail decoys in the collection of the Wildfowl Museum at Salisbury State College, Maryland. The birds were carved by Tan Brunet of Louisiana and won "Best in World" in 1977 in the decorative decoy category in competition at Salisbury, Maryland. Photo by Orlando Wootten / Wildfowl Museum.

phers can use decoys and blinds effectively when trying to take close-up photos of these birds. Birders, however, generally do not use decoys, although they do commonly use their autos as blinds while driving close to waterfowl ponds and marshes in various national wildlife refuges. The birds generally do not become alarmed if you remain inside an auto.

Museums and Zoos

People interested in seeing antique waterfowl decoys, and in studying the history and current trends in decoy carving, can do no better than to visit the Ward Foundation's Wildfowl Museum located in Holloway Hall on the campus of Salisbury State College, Salisbury, Maryland. This museum has an excellent and extensive display of an-

The Wildfowl Museum, operated by the Ward Foundation, is housed at Salisbury State College, Salisbury, Maryland. Photo by Orlando Wootten / Wildfowl Museum.

The administrative building and visitors center at the Middle Creek Wildlife Management Area in eastern Pennsylvania.

tique hunting decoys as well as outstanding examples of modern decorative decoys.

Another effective way to become familiar with all of the waterfowl of a region at any time of the year is by visiting natural history museums. These institutions usually have preserved specimens of local waterfowl that can be studied carefully and leisurely. Alternatively, one can visit zoos, many of which have fine displays of live, captive waterfowl from various parts of the world.

Waterfowl Names

The names of ducks, geese, and swans are currently in a state of change, but those used in this book are the most up-to-date generally recommended for these birds by leading waterfowl authorities. However, some of the names used in this book may not agree with those used elsewhere. For example, waterfowl authorities now prefer to name *Dendrocygna bicolor* the fulvous whistling duck whereas the

One of the waterfowl displays in the visitors center at the Middle Creek Wildlife Management Area in eastern Pennsylvania.

species generally is referred to as fulvous tree duck in many older books. Some other name changes include black-bellied whistling duck for black-bellied tree duck, American black duck for black duck, common pintail for pintail, Eurasian wigeon for European wigeon, and northern shoveler for shoveler.

Many zoos display fine collections of live waterfowl including rare and common species. These trumpeter swans are displayed at the National Zoological Park in Washington, D.C. Photo by Rex Gary Schmidt / U.S. Fish and Wildlife Service.

In addition to the more or less standard names used for waterfowl, there are hundreds (perhaps thousands) of local or colloquial names used by hunters and others for some of the different species. For example, the lesser scaup frequently is referred to as "bluebill" or "little bluebill," whereas the canvasback sometimes is called "canvas" or "can" in some parts of the country. It is impossible to include these colloquial names here, but people interested in the subject will find many of the unofficial names included in *The Ducks, Geese & Swans of North America* by Francis H. Kortright (Stackpole Company, 1953). Additional details are provided in *The Dictionary of American Bird Names* by Ernest A. Choate (Gambit, 1973).

The scientific names of waterfowl are subject to change as new research produces more complete and accurate understanding of the relationships of genera, species, and subspecies. Listed below are some new and old scientific names for North American waterfowl.

SPECIES	NEW SCIENTIFIC NAME	OLD SCIENTIFIC NAME
Whistling swan	*Cygnus columbianus columbianus*	*Olor columbianus*
Trumpeter swan	*Cygnus cygnus buccinator*	*Olor buccinator*
Snow goose	*Anser caerulescens*	*Chen hyperborea*
Ross' goose	*Anser rossii*	*Chen rossii*
Emperor goose	*Anser canagicus*	*Philacte canagica*
Green-winged teal	*Anas crecca*	*Anas carolinensis*
Eurasian wigeon	*Anas penelope*	*Mareca penelope*
American wigeon	*Anas americana*	*Mareca americana*
Northern shoveler	*Anas clypeata*	*Spatula clypeata*
Spectacled eider	*Somateria fischeri*	*Lampronetta fischeri*
Black scoter	*Melanitta nigra*	*Oidemia nigra*
Hooded merganser	*Mergus cucullatus*	*Lophodytes cucullatus*

The Species Problem

In most cases the species of waterfowl in North America are readily recognized as such, but in a few instances authorities differ regarding what is a "good" species and what is merely a subspecies. Among swans, for example, some ornithologists recognize the whistling, Bewick's, trumpeter, and whooper swans as four distinct species. Other authorities (with whom I agree) consider whistling and Bewick's swans merely as two well-marked and geographically isolated subspecies of *Cygnus columbianus,* and trumpeter and whooper swans as two well-marked and geographically isolated subspecies of *Cygnus cygnus.* Similarly, the so-called Mexican duck and the mottled duck, sometimes considered as two distinct species, are now considered subspecies of the mallard by many leading waterfowl authorities. The so-called blue goose, once recognized as a distinct species, now is known to be only a color phase of the snow goose.

The question of what constitutes a distinct species can be very complex among some forms of waterfowl and is mainly of interest to ornithologists and other scientists. However, in some cases hunting regulations can be affected as can the number of species birders are able to count.

CHAPTER THREE

Eclipse Plumage and Hybrids

Eclipse Plumage

One of the curious features of male ducks in the Northern Hemisphere is the so-called eclipse plumage that these birds wear for about two months beginning when the female starts to incubate her eggs and continuing during the summer. The males form flocks, become shy, and quickly loose their flight feathers making them flightless for the duration of the molt. They also assume a duller brown plumage similar to the females in most cases. By autumn, however, the eclipse plumage usually is molted again and the drakes (males) are in full nuptial (breeding) plumage that is retained for the duration of the winter and spring.

The eclipse plumage occurs mostly in ducks of the Northern Hemisphere, but some examples are known from Southern Hemisphere waterfowl and from certain other families of birds elsewhere.

Hybrids

Hybrids result from the interbreeding of two different species and are known among many families of birds. Ducks and geese exhibit an unusually high rate of hybridism; indeed more than 400 different kinds of waterfowl hybrids are known including examples among wild birds (hybrids occur most readily among captive ducks and geese). Mallards, for example, are known to interbreed with about forty other species, wood ducks with about twenty other species.

Some typical and fairly common crosses include mallard × black duck, mallard × pintail, mallard × American wigeon, mallard × northern shoveler, and mallard × green-winged teal.

Anyone observing and studying waterfowl, or hunting these birds, should not be surprised if they happen to see an odd-looking duck or goose that seems to show some of the features of two different species. Such birds may be encountered from time to time at ponds in local parks as well as in a completely wild state.

CHAPTER FOUR

Waterfowl Migrations

The migrations of waterfowl in spring and autumn are known to almost everybody. This is particularly true of the large flocks of Canada geese that cross overhead twice each year. But millions of other ducks, geese, and swans also migrate, although their movements may not be as well known to many people. These birds do not spread at random over the landscape; rather, they have fairly well-established migration routes that, in turn, blend into fairly well-defined flyways. There are four such flyways in North America: Atlantic, Mississippi, Central, and Pacific. They were discovered by waterfowl biologists by plotting on maps the origin and recovery points of thousands of banded migratory ducks and geese.

These flyways are not just of academic interest. They form part of the basis of modern waterfowl-management programs in North America. By carefully monitoring the breeding success or failure of each species on its major nesting ground, and the overall population levels of the birds likely to use each of the flyways, it is possible to establish yearly hunting regulations and bag limits for each species for each flyway. Sometimes hunting of some species is prohibited on some flyways where the populations are low but allowed on another flyway if populations of the same species are high enough to sustain hunting pressure.

Waterfowl flyways also play important roles in determining where many of our national wildlife refuges are located. Many are carefully planned and established at key locations along each of the flyways in order to provide ducks, geese, and swans with feeding and resting places as they migrate from their breeding grounds to their wintering grounds or vice versa. Other refuges are established on the wintering grounds to further assure that the birds will have the necessary habitat, food, and protection to survive there. Still other refuges are established to preserve the vital breeding grounds in the northern United States and Canada. Both countries cooperate fully in this effort.

In recent years many of the national wildlife refuges located on flyways between the breeding and wintering grounds have taken on added importance to the birds that use them. Many birds now stop at such places and remain there to feed and rest for periods of time far longer than they have ever done in the past.

Atlantic Flyway

As its name suggests, the Atlantic Flyway is a major migratory route for large numbers of waterfowl along the East Coast of Canada and the United States. Pictured on a map, one quickly sees that the waterfowl breeding grounds that produce the birds that use the flyway extend far west of Hudson Bay and eastward to the coasts of Greenland. Various migration routes, therefore, serve this large geographic area and combine to form the flyway. However, by the time the birds reach the Atlantic Coast south of New Jersey, the flyway becomes very narrow and extends south as far as Puerto Rico.

A great variety of birds use the Atlantic Flyway. At Brigantine National Wildlife Refuge in New Jersey, for example, one sees thousands of American black ducks. Thousands of snow geese also spend about two months there in autumn and early winter before continuing farther south to their traditional wintering grounds along the Atlantic Coast. These birds, greater snow geese, nest in eastern Arctic Canada and along the coast of Greenland.

Many Canada geese observed on the Atlantic Flyway nest along the eastern side of Hudson Bay whereas others nest in the Maritime Provinces and New England; canvasbacks and redheads, however, may come from the area around the Pas and the Delta marshes in Canada. In contrast, marshes along Lake Erie and in southern Ontario doubtless produce many Atlantic Flyway American black

Opposite:
The Atlantic Flyway and the breeding grounds producing waterfowl using it. Map courtesy of U.S. Fish and Wildlife Service.

ATLANTIC FLYWAY

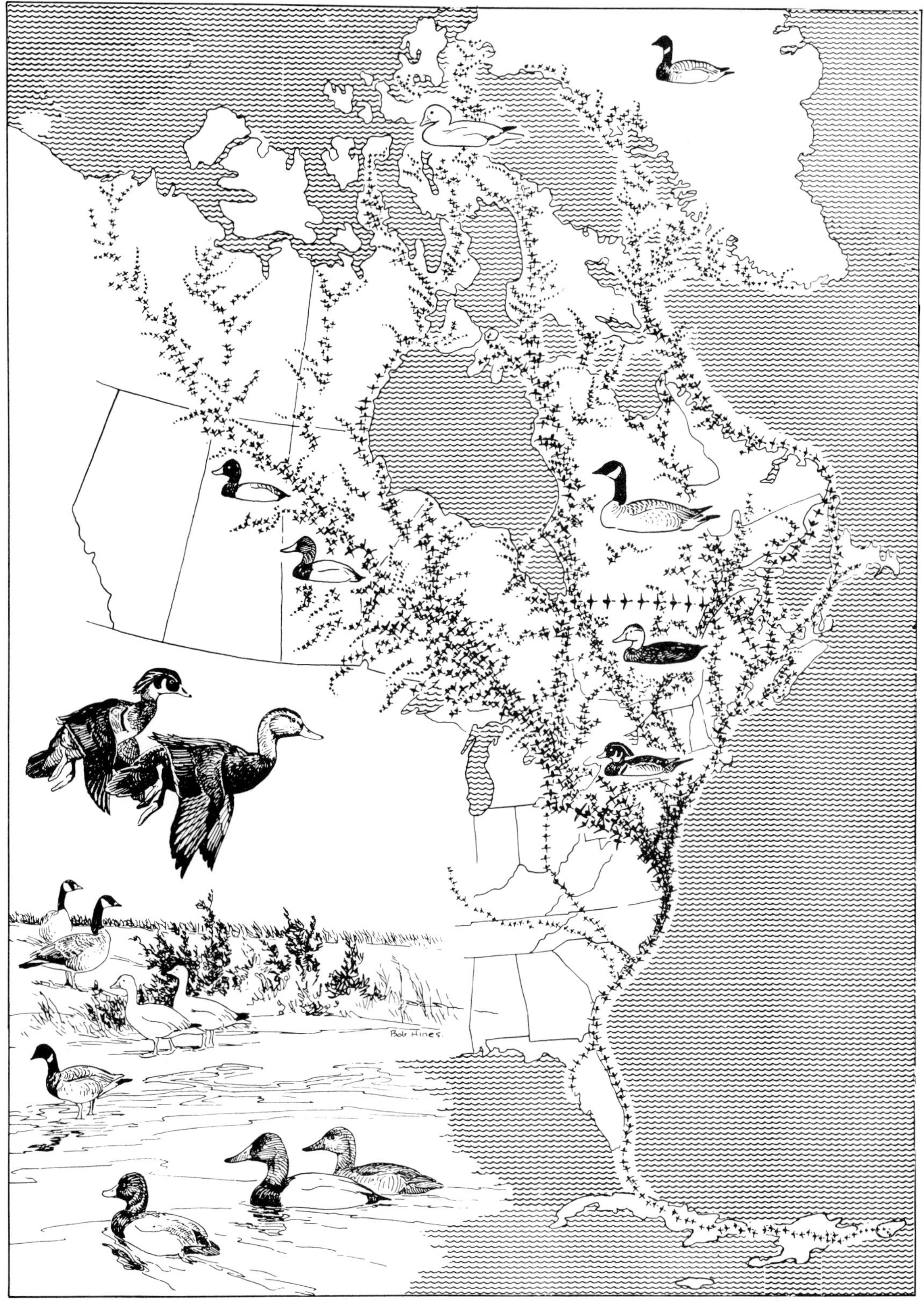

UNITED STATES DEPARTMENT OF THE INTERIOR • FISH AND WILDLIFE SERVICE

ducks. Occasionally a few birds from the West even appear along the flyway—white-fronted geese and Barrow's goldeneyes are two examples. There is, of course, considerable geographic and yearly variation in respect to the origins of the birds that use any of the four flyways.

Mississippi Flyway

The Mississippi Flyway looks like a giant funnel placed over the face of North America. The mouth of the funnel is extremely wide and extends from Alaska eastward to Baffin Island. The funnel's neck then converges onto the Mississippi River, which collects tremendous concentrations of waterfowl and channels them to the Gulf Coast where the birds spread out east and west along the coast.

Mallards are particularly common users of this flyway and gather by the thousands along the bottomlands of the Illinois River, in pools along the Mississippi River, and in Arkansas swamps and rice fields. Wood ducks also are common nesting birds along the flyway, and large numbers of ring-necked ducks use this route, too. Blue phase snow geese from various northern migration routes also move down the Mississippi Flyway and form impressive concentrations of birds in Louisiana and Texas marshes. Some now stop for a while at various refuges along the way. Canada geese also make extensive use of this flyway and winter from the Gulf Coast northward to Wisconsin. Clearly, the Mississippi Flyway is one of North America's great waterfowl areas!

Opposite:
The Mississippi Flyway and the breeding grounds producing waterfowl using it. Map courtesy of U.S. Fish and Wildlife Service.

MISSISSIPPI FLYWAY

UNITED STATES DEPARTMENT OF THE INTERIOR • FISH AND WILDLIFE SERVICE

Central Flyway

Unlike the two eastern flyways, the Central Flyway more or less forms a broad, straight line from northeastern Alaska diagonally southward across the Northwest Territories and the Continental Divide to the Texas coast. Some birds even continue beyond into Mexico, Central America, and northern South America.

A great variety of species use this flyway—mallards, northern shovelers, common pintails, redheads, and teal of several species. Canada geese and white-fronted geese also are abundant. However, because of weather and other factors in the prairie pothole waterfowl production areas, the numbers of birds that occur on this flyway vary somewhat more than on some of the others. During favorable years large numbers of birds are seen; at other times the populations of the various species are reduced—sometimes reduced severely.

Opposite:
The Central Flyway and the breeding grounds producing waterfowl using it. Map courtesy of U.S. Fish and Wildlife Service.

CENTRAL FLYWAY

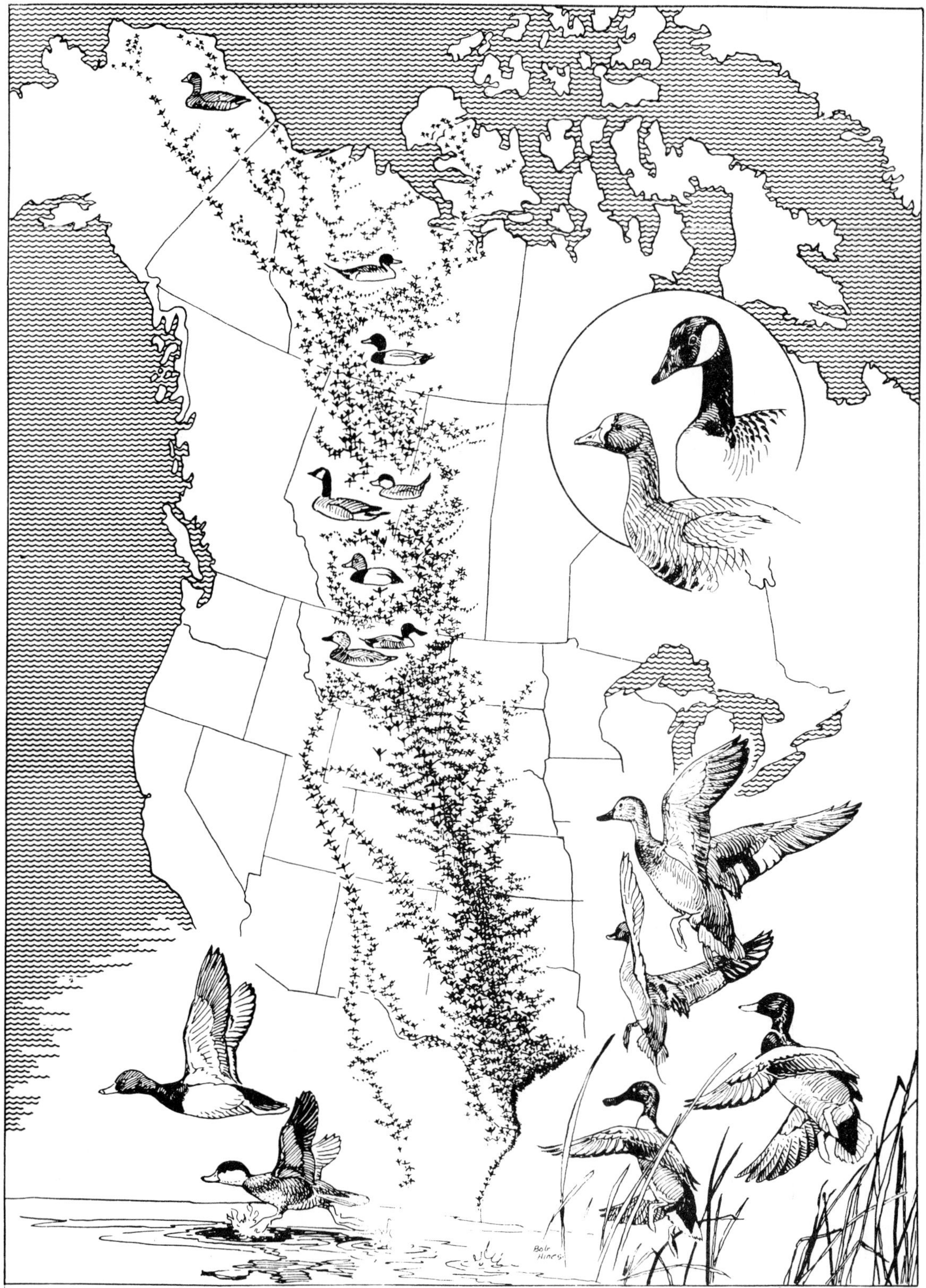

UNITED STATES DEPARTMENT OF THE INTERIOR • FISH AND WILDLIFE SERVICE

INT: 4038-73

Pacific Flyway

From Alaska and western Canada, waterfowl funnel southward in the Pacific Flyway in a band extending between the Pacific Coast and the western slopes of the Rocky Mountains. While many birds winter in the United States, many also continue southward and winter in western Mexico. Some even reach northern South America.

Geese—white-fronted, Canada, brant, Ross', and snow—all use the Pacific Flyway as do large numbers of mallards, common pintails, American wigeon, and northern shovelers. The great Bear River marshes in Utah, for example, supply many redheads that winter in California, and the little Ross' goose that nests in the Perry River area of Arctic Canada also joins the migrants on the Pacific Flyway to reach the wintering grounds it uses in central California. Thus like its counterpart on the Atlantic Coast, the Pacific Flyway is a major migration route for the waterfowl of western North America.

Migration Seasons

Ducks, geese, and swans begin migrating northward between February and May from their wintering grounds, with a few birds of some species occasionally appearing in late January and early June. Each species, of course, has its own temporal period that can vary somewhat depending upon where in North America one sees the birds.

The various waterfowl species also have more or less well-defined periods during autumn when they migrate southward to their wintering grounds. September through November or early December is the period when most of the species engage in these southward migrations.

Opposite:
The Pacific Flyway and the breeding grounds producing waterfowl using it. Map courtesy of U.S. Fish and Wildlife Service.

PACIFIC FLYWAY

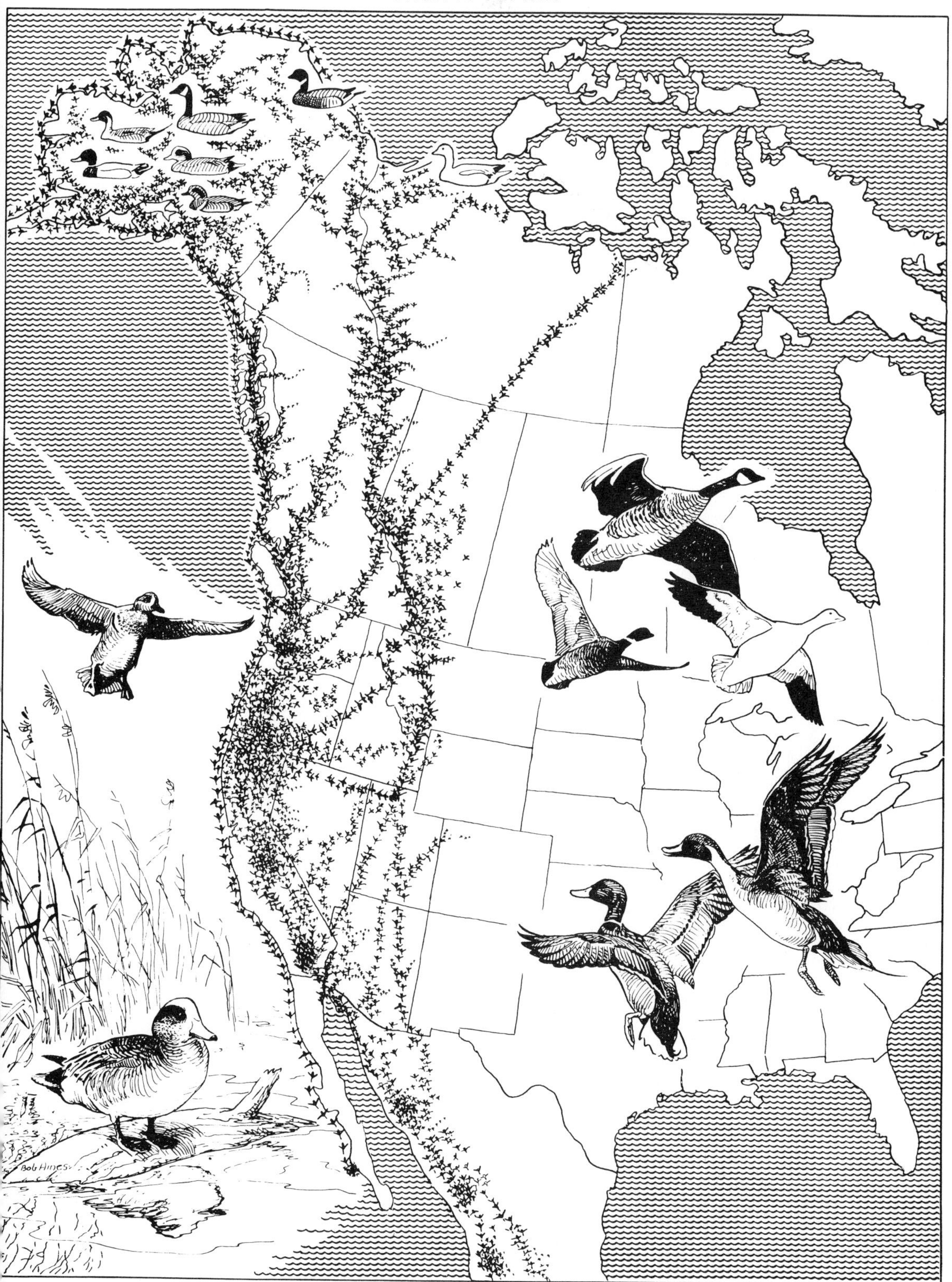

UNITED STATES DEPARTMENT OF THE INTERIOR • FISH AND WILDLIFE SERVICE

The "prairie pothole country" is a major breeding ground for millions of ducks including redheads such as these birds.

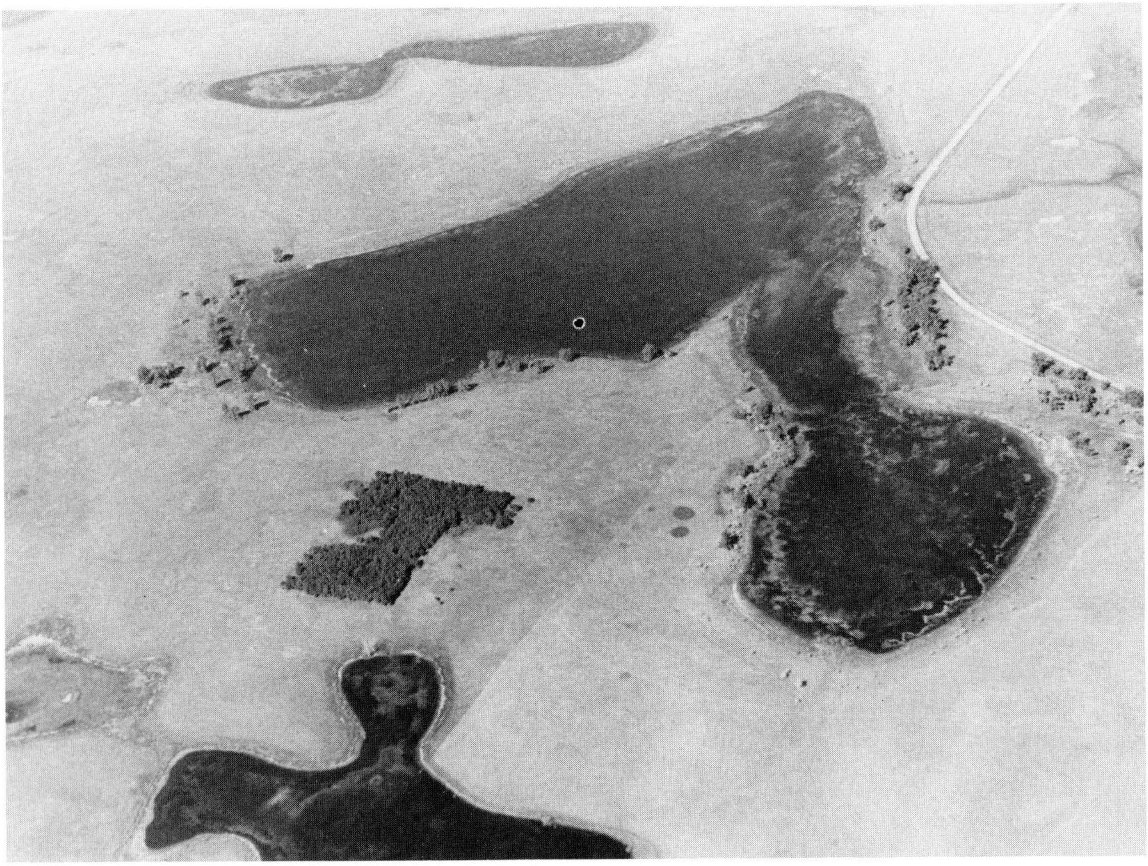

A typical waterfowl production area in the prairie pothole country of the Dakotas. Photo by U.S. Fish and Wildlife Service.

CHAPTER FIVE

Prairie Pothole Waterfowl Breeding Grounds

Although some species of waterfowl breed widely throughout North America, and other species such as whistling swans restrict their breeding grounds to the Arctic, the most important and productive duck breeding area on the continent is the so-called "prairie pothole country" of parts of Montana, North and South Dakota, Minnesota, and the Canadian provinces of Alberta, Saskatchewan, and Manitoba. In these states and provinces countless thousands of wetlands—marshes, sloughs, ponds, lakes, and potholes—provide essential nesting habitat for millions of ducks of various species.

Earlier in this century many of these wetlands were destroyed or threatened by drainage, development, droughts, and floods, and the future of waterfowl looked dark. Fortunately conservationists and government wildlife authorities in the United States and Canada recognized the problem in time to preserve many of the most important wetlands. In the prairie pothole country of the Dakotas, for example, major wetlands were purchased and set aside as national wildlife refuges and waterfowl production areas by the United States Fish and Wildlife Service. Additional smaller, scattered, or temporary wetlands were secured through easements whereby a landowner is paid a lump sum to assure perpetual wetland protection. Ducks benefit and landowners still retain most property rights. Various educational and recreational opportunities are available at some sites. Similar wetland preservation programs are operated by provincial and state wildlife agencies.

In addition to government efforts to preserve and protect wetlands in the prairie pothole country, various private con-

Federal waterfowl production areas in the prairie pothole country of the United States are identified by U.S. Fish and Wildlife Service signs. Photo by U.S. Fish and Wildlife Service.

servation organizations have contributed millions of dollars to augment governmental activities. The most notable and extensive program is that of Ducks Unlimited, and its affiliate Ducks Unlimited (Canada), which now manages over 1,300 "duck factories" or wetland areas covering over 2.5 million acres of vital habitat and over 12,000 miles of shoreline. Some of these sites are small, less than 50 acres, but one is huge—the 512,000-acre Mawdesley Wildlife Development project near the Pas in Manitoba. The majority of the Ducks Unlimited wetland projects are in the prairie pothole

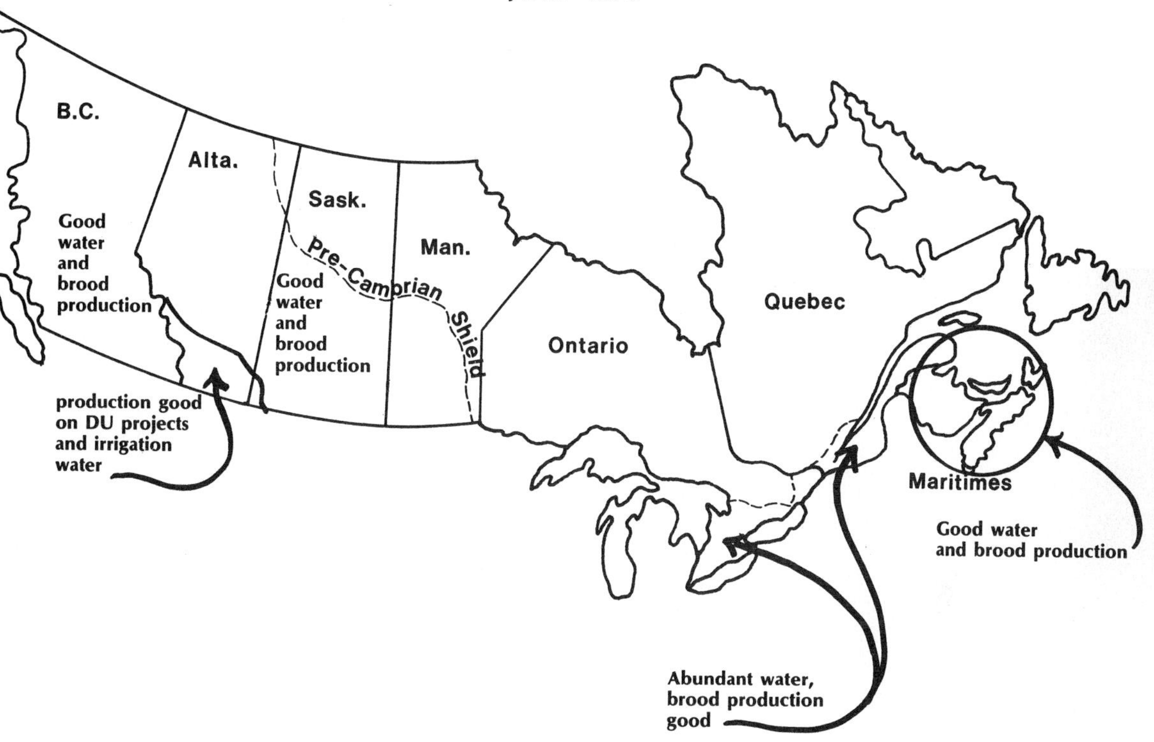

The status of waterfowl production in Canada during July 1976. Map courtesy of Ducks Unlimited (Canada).

country, but some include sites in British Columbia and others extend eastward to New Brunswick and Nova Scotia. Recently a new branch of the organization was established in Mexico—Ducks Unlimited de Mexico.

Outside the prairie pothole country, other government waterfowl-management areas have been created in some states. In Pennsylvania, two notable examples are the Pymatuning Waterfowl Area and the Middle Creek Wildlife Management Area—both owned and operated by the Pennsylvania Game Commission. In addition to waterfowl hunting and management, both sites offer excellent educational and recreational opportunities. Small museums exist at both locations.

Lake Muhlenberg in the Allentown, Pennsylvania, park system offers local residents excellent opportunities for viewing waterfowl.

CHAPTER SIX

Local Waterfowl Viewing Areas

Anyone wishing to observe ducks, geese, and swans has almost unlimited opportunities to do so in North America. Indeed, there often are numerous places near one's home where these birds can be seen without difficulty. Common species are most frequently seen at such places, but sometimes rarer birds appear for brief periods of time, especially during the spring and autumn migration seasons.

Ponds and Lakes

Local ponds and lakes in parks or on farms frequently attract a varied assortment of waterfowl and offer excellent viewing opportunities because some of the birds tend to become very tame. For example, several small lakes in the Allentown, Pennsylvania, park system support large populations of tame and wild ducks and geese. Canada geese and mallards are the typical species seen, but black ducks, American wigeon, pintails, green-winged teal, and various other species are commonly seen in winter. Occasionally rare birds, such as Eurasian wigeon, also appear to the delight of local bird watchers.

As a result of these wildlife attractions, thousands of people visit these lakes every year to feed the birds, which is discouraged and unnecessary, and watch them. At one of the sites, Lake Muhlenberg, special signs are even placed along nearby roads warning motorists of waterfowl crossing areas.

Reservoirs

Municipal and other water reservoirs are attractive to waterfowl and frequently are excellent spots to watch these birds. For example, ornithologists and bird watchers have been studying Lake Ontelaunee (the municipal reservoir for the City of Reading, Pennsylvania) for decades and list no

Feeding waterfowl at local parks is a popular activity but often unnecessary.

American wigeons are seen frequently in winter at Lake Muhlenberg in Allentown, Pennsylvania.

MUTE SWAN

TRUMPETER SWAN

SNOW GOOSE (Blue Phase)

ROSS' GOOSE (*Photo by Glen Smart/U.S. Fish and Wildlife Service*)

EMPEROR GOOSE

BRANT

BARNACLE GOOSE

MALLARD

COMMON PINTAIL (*Photo by Glen Smart/U.S. Fish and Wildlife Service*)

CINNAMON TEAL (*Photo by Glen Smart/U.S. Fish and Wildlife Service*)

RING-NECKED DUCK (*Photo by Millard H. Sharp*)

CANVASBACK (*Photo by Robert House/U.S. Fish and Wildlife Service*)

COMMON GOLDENEYE (*Photo by Glen Smart/U.S. Fish and Wildlife Service*)

RUDDY DUCK (*Photo by Millard H. Sharp*)

HOODED MERGANSER

COMMON MERGANSER (*Photo by Millard H. Sharp*)

The movement of whistling swans from the Susquehanna River to nearby fields to feed is spectacular.

Signs such as this warn motorists of waterfowl crossing areas near Lake Muhlenberg in Allentown, Pennsylvania.

less than thirty waterfowl species seen there over the years. Included are such interesting species as oldsquaws, white-winged scoters, and surf scoters. Occasionally whistling swans stop there briefly during migration.

Rivers, Streams, and Creeks

The running waterways—rivers, streams, and creeks—in the vicinity of one's home are likely to attract a variety of species of waterfowl from time to time. One river near my home sometimes attracts mergansers and other river ducks during winter. I need merely drive along the river and look for the birds with binoculars or a telescope.

Sometimes concentrations of waterfowl on rivers can be impressive. In early to mid-March, for example, thousands of whistling swans gather on the lower Susquehanna River in southeastern Pennsylvania prior to migrating north to their Arctic breeding grounds. Birders gather from far and wide to watch these spectacular concentrations and enjoy the movement of the birds as they fly from the river to nearby fields to feed. In recent years an added attraction has been an effort to spot swans marked with numbered neck collars placed there (under authority of federal permit) by Dr. William Sladen of Johns Hopkins University who is conducting an extensive research program on the birds. One observer, Theodore R. Hake of York, Pennsylvania, uses a large astronomical telescope to look for marked birds and read the numbers of the neck collars. He has been very successful and has contributed much valuable information to the project.

Marshes

Local marshes and other wetlands are important waterfowl areas and many productive hours can be spent exploring such places looking for ducks and other waterfowl. Such sites certainly should not be overlooked as local waterfowl viewing areas.

Seacoasts

Those people fortunate enough to live near seacoasts, or who can visit them easily, are in a position to enjoy still another important waterfowl area. In some places large concentrations of scoters and eider gather in offshore waters.

Rafts of common eiders gather in winter off the Massachusetts coast and sometimes can be seen from shore. Photo by Bill Byrne / Massachusetts Division of Fisheries and Wildlife.

Sometimes these birds can be seen from shore or from atop cliffs or bluffs overlooking the sea. They are well worth looking for. Indeed, the sight of enormous concentrations of sea ducks can be among the most interesting of all waterfowl efforts. At other places brant gather, and sometimes harlequin ducks appear off rock jetties or rocky coastlines in northern areas.

Most national wildlife refuges have visitor information centers where free literature and bird checklists are available.

CHAPTER 7

Waterfowl Refuges

In addition to local waterfowl viewing areas, the network of national wildlife refuges owned and operated by the United States Fish and Wildlife Service provides major viewing, propagation, and conservation areas for millions of ducks, geese, and swans. In the following pages those federal refuges that are especially important for waterfowl are described, and the most abundant or common waterfowl species (but by no means all of the species) likely to be seen at each refuge are mentioned. Most of these areas can be visited readily; exceptions are most of the Alaskan refuges. Many have basic visitor facilities (information centers, rest rooms, nature trails, auto tour routes, and occasionally small museums), and some offer special conservation programs to organized groups by prior arrangements. Before visiting one of these refuges you may wish to write to the refuge manager, at the address provided in this book, and request an information circular and map, bird checklist, and other publications. Almost all of the refuges have such literature available for free distribution. This information will permit you to prepare for your visit and will give you directions and maps for visiting the refuge, or you can pick up copies of such material at the refuge visitor center or headquarters upon your arrival there. Keep in mind, however, that many headquarters are closed on weekends, but most visitor centers are open daily.

In a few instances descriptions of several important state waterfowl management areas with excellent visitor facilities are included, but no effort is made to include all of these or even most of them. Specific details and information on the important roles that state wildlife agencies play in waterfowl conservation can be obtained by contacting each state agency directly.

Northeastern States

Maine

FRANKLIN ISLAND NATIONAL WILDLIFE REFUGE

Waterfowl: Nesting common eiders.
Wildlife: Mammals, birds, reptiles, and fish.
Habitats: Rocky shoreline, white spruce timber, open areas.
Size: 12 acres.
Location: An island in Muscongus Bay south of Friendship, Maine. Public use is permitted from August 1st through March 31st.
Literature Available: General information booklet.
Address: Refuge Manager, Moosehorn National Wildlife Refuge, Calais, Maine 04619.

MOOSEHORN NATIONAL WILDLIFE REFUGE

Waterfowl: Canada geese, black ducks, and ring-necked ducks.
Wildlife: Mammals (39 species), birds (207 species), reptiles (9 species), amphibians (16 species), and fish (28 species).
Habitats: Lakes, bogs, marshes, streams, rocky outcroppings, forested areas, farmland, and rocky coastline.
Size: 22,665 acres in two units.
Location: In northeastern Maine. The northern Baring Unit is located adjacent to U.S. Route 1 approximately 3 miles northwest of Calais. The southern Edmunds Unit, also along U.S. Route 1, is located near Dennysville on Cobscook Bay.
Literature Available: General information sheet and map, and checklists for mammals, birds, reptiles, amphibians, and fish.
Address: Refuge Manager, Moosehorn National Wildlife Refuge, Calais, Maine 04619.

PETIT MANAN NATIONAL WILDLIFE REFUGE

Waterfowl: Black ducks and green-winged teal.
Wildlife: Mammals, birds, reptiles, amphibians, and fish.
Habitats: Bogs, rocky outcroppings, freshwater ponds, beaver flowages.
Size: 1,991 acres of coastal peninsula and a 9-acre island.
Location: In northeastern coastal Maine. Use of the island is restricted to wildlife studies and research. The two coastal peninsula parcels are open to limited public use from April 15th through November 15th.
Literature Available: General information booklet.
Address: Refuge Manager, Moosehorn National Wildlife Refuge, Calais, Maine 04619.

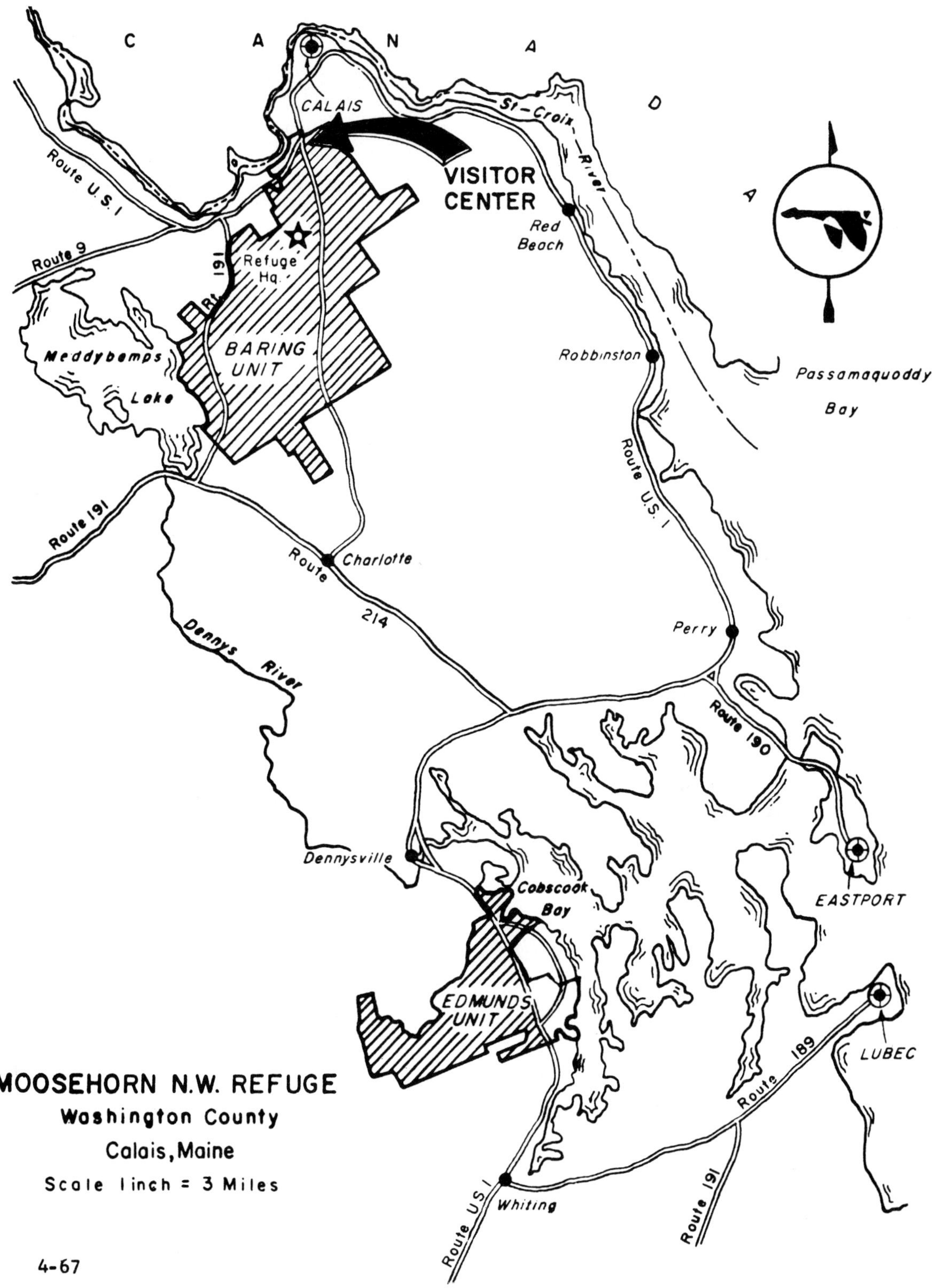
C A N A D A
CALAIS
St-Croix River
VISITOR
CENTER
Red
Beach
Route U.S. I
Route 9
Refuge
Hq.
Rt. 191
BARING
UNIT
Meddybemps
Lake
Robbinston
Passamaquoddy
Bay
Route U.S. I
Route 191
Route
Charlotte
214
Dennys River
Perry
Route 190
Dennysville
Cobscook
Bay
EASTPORT
EDMUNDS
UNIT
LUBEC
Route 189
MOOSEHORN N.W. REFUGE
Washington County
Calais, Maine
Scale 1 inch = 3 Miles
Route U.S. I
Whiting
Route 191
4-67

POND ISLAND NATIONAL WILDLIFE REFUGE

Waterfowl: Common eiders and other sea ducks.
Wildlife: Birds, reptiles, and fish.
Habitat: A treeless rock base island.
Size: 10 acres.
Location: In the Atlantic Ocean, 16 miles northeast of Portland, near Popham Beach, Maine.
Literature Available: General information booklet.
Address: Refuge Manager, Parker River National Wildlife Refuge, Newburyport, Massachusetts 01950.

RACHEL CARSON NATIONAL WILDLIFE REFUGE

Waterfowl: Canada geese, black ducks, and green-winged teal.
Wildlife: Mammals, birds, reptiles, amphibians, and fish.
Habitats: Coastal marshes and bays.
Size: 4,000+ acres.
Location: Southeastern Maine. A series of units within a 45-mile-long area between Brave Boat Harbor northeast of Kittery and the Spurwink River south of Portland.
Literature Available: General information sheet.
Address: Refuge Manager, Parker River National Wildlife Refuge, Newburyport, Massachusetts 01950.

Vermont

MISSISQUOI NATIONAL WILDLIFE REFUGE

Waterfowl: Canada geese, black ducks, wood ducks, and common goldeneyes.
Wildlife: Mammals (24 species), birds (185 species), reptiles, amphibians, and fish.
Habitats: Marshes, river, lake, wooded areas, and farmland.
Size: 4,226 acres.
Location: Extreme northwestern Vermont. The refuge headquarters is about 2½ miles west of Swanton on State Route 78.
Literature Available: General information sheet and map, and bird and mammal checklists.
Address: Refuge Manager, Missisquoi National Wildlife Refuge, Swanton, Vermont 05488.

RACHEL CARSON NATIONAL WILDLIFE REFUGE

YORK & CUMBERLAND COUNTIES, MAINE

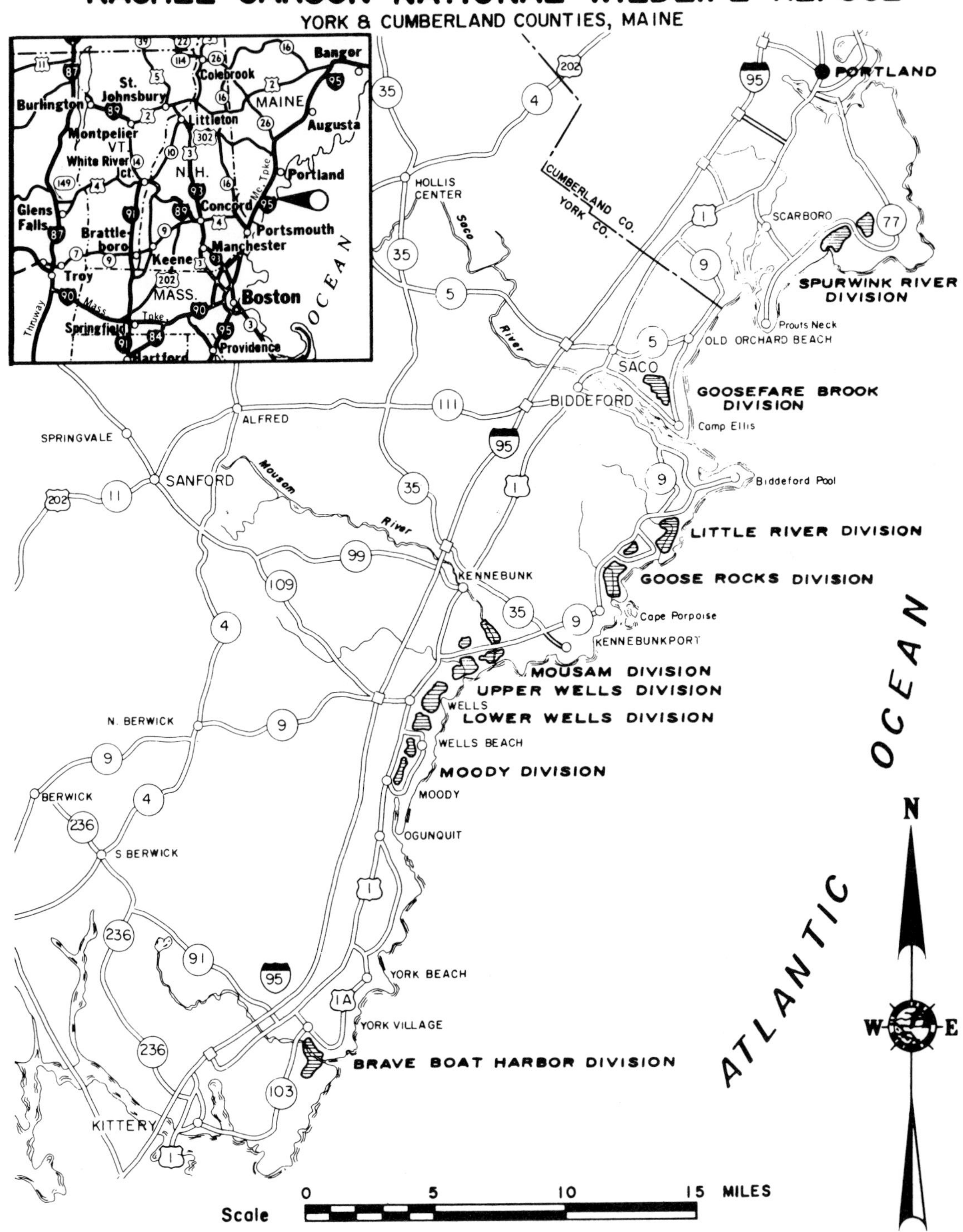

Massachusetts

GREAT MEADOWS NATIONAL WILDLIFE REFUGE

Waterfowl: Mallards, black ducks, wood ducks, and teal.
Wildlife: Mammals, birds (209 species), reptiles, amphibians, and fish.
Habitats: Marshes, rivers, wooded areas, and fields.
Size: 4,000 acres.
Location: Northeastern Massachusetts near Concord, about 20 miles west of Boston. Two units, one north and one south of Concord.
Literature Available: General information sheet and map, and checklist of birds.
Address: Refuge Manager, Great Meadows National Wildlife Refuge, 191 Sudbury Road, Concord, Massachusetts 01742.

MONOMOY NATIONAL WILDLIFE REFUGE

Waterfowl: Canada goose, black duck, green-winged teal, scoters, and eiders.
Wildlife: Mammals, birds (249 species), and fish.
Habitat: Coastal barrier beach with sand dunes, marshes, and ponds. The refuge consists of two islands—Monomoy and Morris.
Size: 3,300+ acres.
Location: Eastern Massachusetts on Cape Cod, 1 mile south of Chatham.
Literature Available: General information sheet and map, and checklist of birds.
Address: Refuge Manager, Great Meadows National Wildlife Refuge, 191 Sudbury Road, Concord, Massachusetts 01742.

NANTUCKET NATIONAL WILDLIFE REFUGE

Waterfowl: Canada geese, black ducks, and migrating sea ducks.
Wildlife: Mammals, birds, reptiles, amphibians, and fish.
Habitats: Shoreline and maritime island areas.
Size: 40 acres.
Location: About 25 miles south of Cape Cod at the northern tip of Nantucket Island.
Literature Available: General information booklet.
Address: Refuge Manager, Great Meadows National Wildlife Refuge, 191 Sudbury Road, Concord, Massachusetts 01742.

PARKER RIVER NATIONAL WILDLIFE REFUGE

Waterfowl: Canada geese, black ducks, and green-winged teal.
Wildlife: Mammals, birds (268 species), reptiles, amphibians, and fish.
Habitat: A barrier beach-dune complex on Plum Island containing ocean beach, sand dunes, salt marshes, freshwater marshes, pasture, rivers.
Size: 4,650 acres.

GREAT MEADOWS NATIONAL WILDLIFE REFUGE

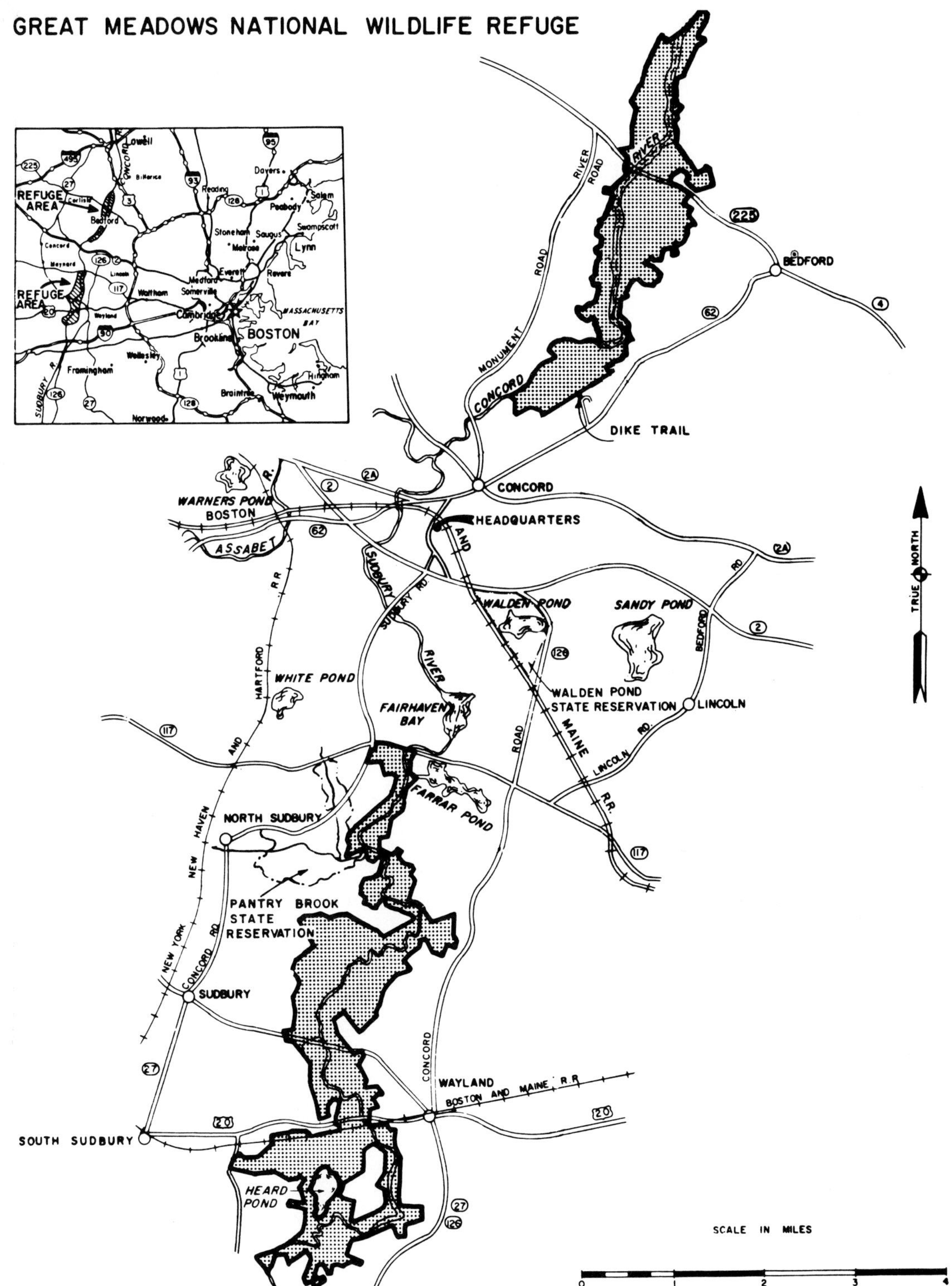

Location: In extreme northeastern Massachusetts, 3 miles east of Newburyport and 35 miles north of Boston.
Literature Available: General information about map, wildlife trail guide, and bird checklist.
Address: Refuge Manager, Parker River National Wildlife Refuge, Newburyport, Massachusetts 01950.

Rhode Island

SACHUEST POINT NATIONAL WILDLIFE REFUGE

Waterfowl: Canada geese, snow geese, mallards, black ducks, gadwalls, pintails, blue-winged teal, buffleheads, oldsquaws, common eiders, white-winged scoters, surf scoters, black scoters, and ruddy ducks.
Wildlife: Mammals, birds, reptiles, amphibians, and fish.
Habitats: Beaches, tidal marshes, uplands, and grassy areas.
Size: 228 acres.
Location: Five miles east of Newport, near Middletown, at the southeastern corner of Aquidneck Island on a peninsula extending into the Atlantic Ocean.
Literature Available: Map.
Address: Refuge Manager, Ninigret National Wildlife Refuge, Box 307, Charlestown, Rhode Island 02813.

TRUSTOM POND NATIONAL WILDLIFE REFUGE

Waterfowl: Canada geese, mallards, black ducks, pintails, blue-winged teal, redheads, canvasbacks, greater scaup, and ruddy ducks.
Wildlife: Mammals, birds, reptiles, amphibians, and fish.
Habitats: Shallow brackish pond, barrier beach, upland woodland and scrubland, and open fields.
Size: 350 acres.
Location: On the southern coast of Rhode Island, near Wakefield, about 10 miles west of Narragansett Bay.
Literature Available: Map.
Address: Refuge Manager, Ninigret National Wildlife Refuge, Box 307, Charlestown, Rhode Island 02813.

SACHUEST POINT NATIONAL WILDLIFE REFUGE

NEWPORT COUNTY, RHODE ISLAND

UNITED STATES DEPARTMENT OF THE INTERIOR

UNITED STATES FISH AND WILDLIFE SERVICE

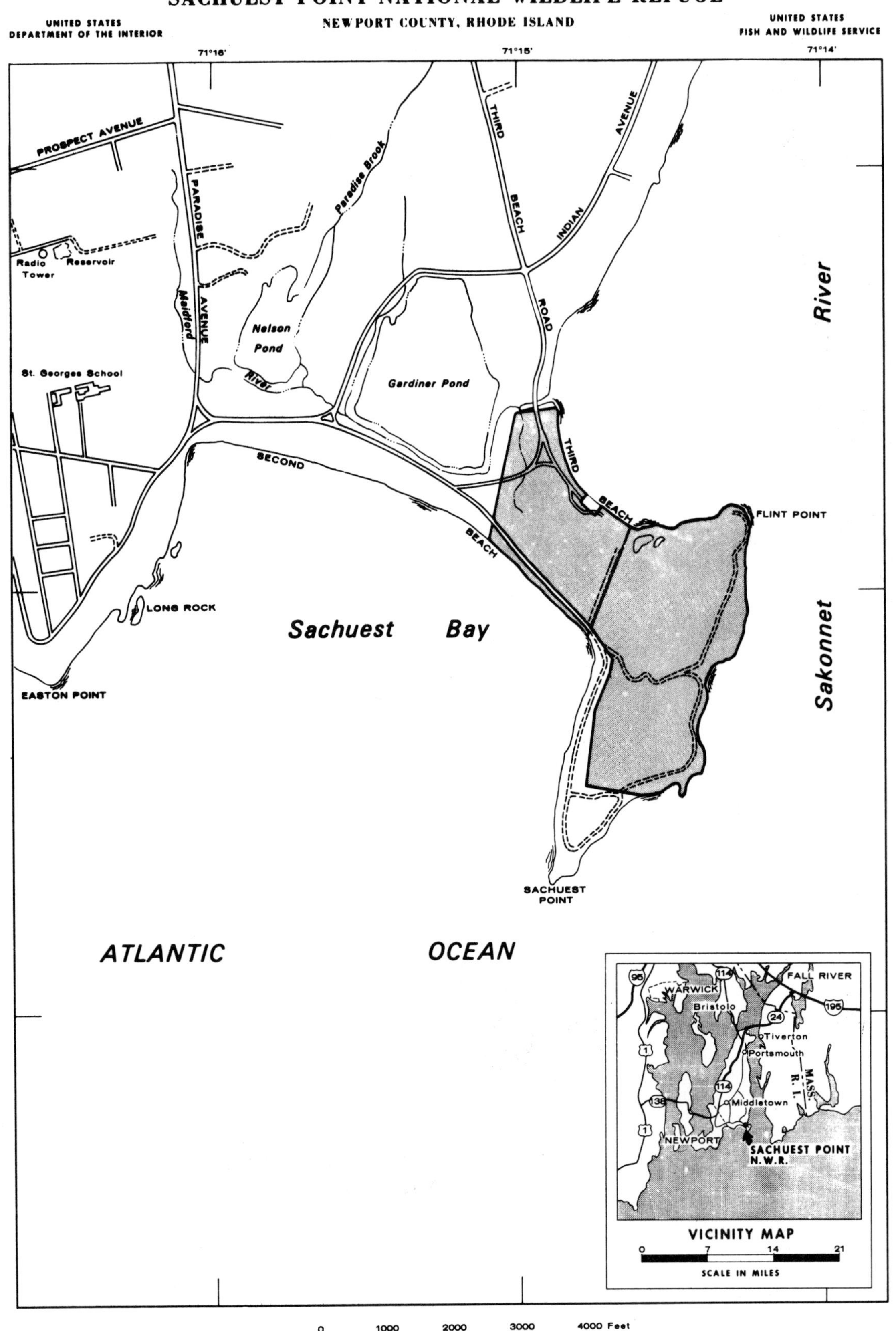

TRUSTOM POND NATIONAL WILDLIFE REFUGE

WASHINGTON COUNTY, RHODE ISLAND

UNITED STATES
DEPARTMENT OF THE INTERIOR

UNITED STATES
FISH AND WILDLIFE SERVICE

71°36'00"
71°35'00"
Perryville State
Trout Hatchery
Route 1
Route 1
Mill
Pond
Factory Pond
Green
Hill
Road
Matunuck
Schoolhouse
Moonstone
Road
Green Hill Swamp
10
Beach
Card Road
Road
Green Hill
Card Pond
Gull Island
POND
Flat Meadow
Cove
TRUSTOM
Moonstone Beach
Green Hill Point
SOUND
ISLAND
BLOCK

VICINITY MAP
138
95
112
Kingston
Ashway
216
Narragansett
1
Westerly
Point Judith
TRUSTOM POND N.W.R.
Ninigret N.W.R.
Sound
Island
Block
Block Island N.W.R.
Scale 0 2 4 6 Miles
SCALE IN MILES

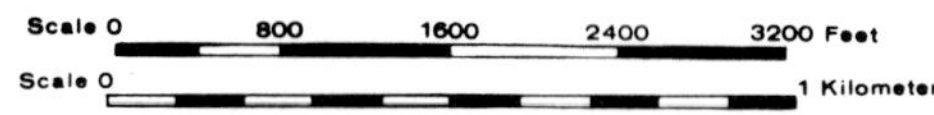

New York

IROQUOIS NATIONAL WILDLIFE REFUGE

Waterfowl: Canada geese, mallards, black ducks, pintails, and American wigeons.
Wildlife: Mammals, birds, reptiles, amphibians, and fish.
Habitats: Marshes, swamp woodland, wet meadows, pastures, and farmland.
Size: 10,800 acres.
Location: In western New York, about 8 miles north of Oakfield and 7 miles south of Medina.
Literature Available: General information sheet and map, and bird checklist.
Address: Refuge Manager, Iroquois National Wildlife Refuge, Basom, New York 14013.

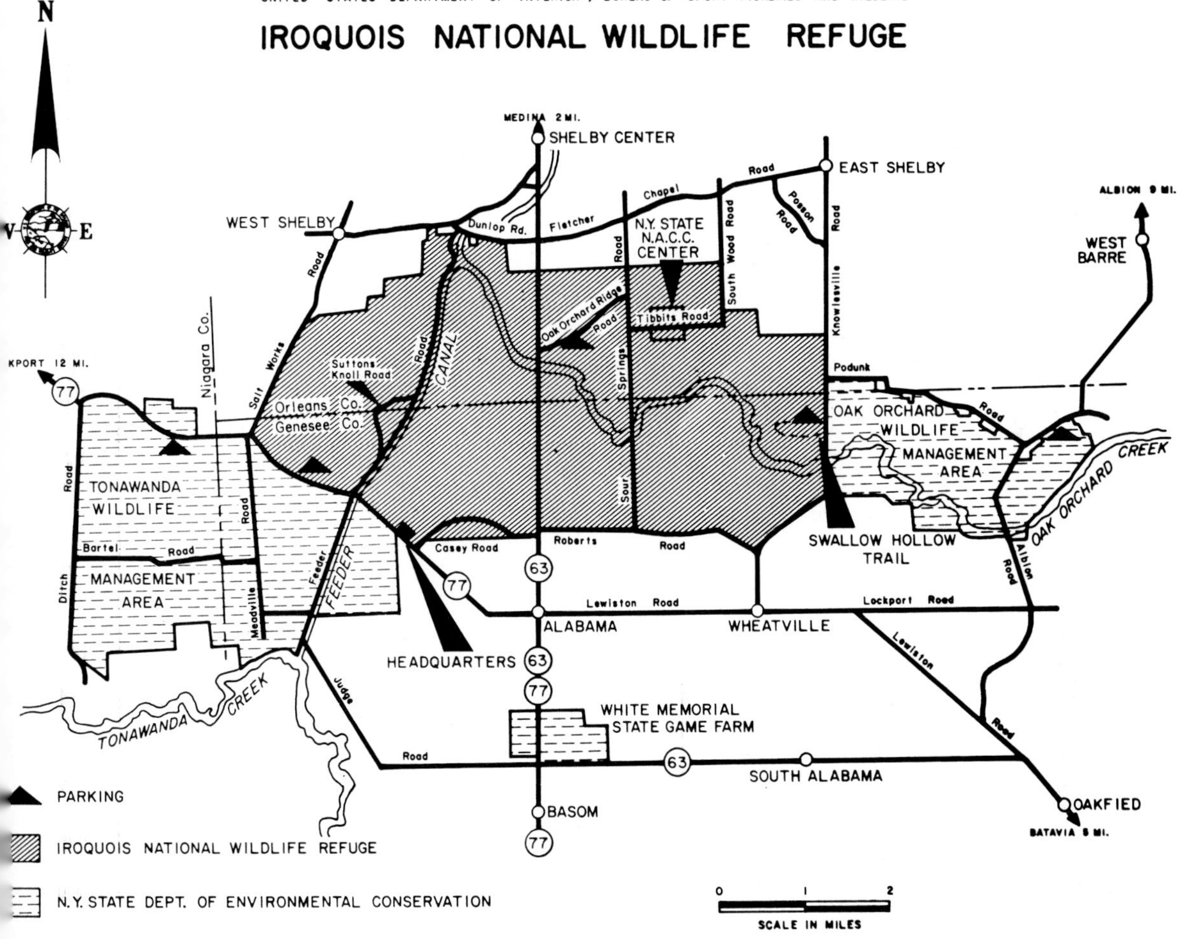

MONTEZUMA NATIONAL WILDLIFE REFUGE

Waterfowl: Canada geese, mallards, blue-winged teal, and wood ducks.
Wildlife: Mammals, birds (236 species), reptiles, amphibians, and fish.
Habitats: Upland woodland, swamp woodland, and freshwater marshes.
Size: 6,433 acres.
Location: Central New York, at the northern end of Cayuga Lake, about 5 miles east of Seneca Falls.
Literature Available: General information sheet and map, tour guide leaflets, and bird checklist.
Address: Refuge Manager, Montezuma National Wildlife Refuge, R.D. 1, Box 1411, Seneca Falls, New York 13148.

MORTON NATIONAL WILDLIFE REFUGE

Waterfowl: Black ducks, common goldeneyes, oldsquaws, and red-breasted mergansers.
Wildlife: Mammals, birds (221 species), reptiles, amphibians, and fish.
Habitats: Beaches, brackish pond, wooded bluffs, woodland, and open fields.
Size: 187 acres.
Location: On eastern Long Island overlooking Noyack Bay just west of Sag Harbor.
Literature Available: Information circular and map, and bird checklist.
Address: Refuge Manager, Morton National Wildlife Refuge, RD-359, Noyack Road, Sag Harbor, New York 11963.

New Jersey

BRIGANTINE NATIONAL WILDLIFE REFUGE

Waterfowl: Mute swans, Canada geese, brant, snow geese, black ducks, pintails, gadwalls, and northern shovelers.
Wildlife: Mammals (38 species), birds (269 species), reptiles, amphibians, and fish.
Habitats: Saltwater inlets and bays, freshwater and saltwater marshes, ponds, and pools, meadows, pastures, and wooded areas.
Size: 20,229 acres.
Location: Coastal New Jersey, about 11 miles north of Atlantic City. The headquarters is about 1 mile east of Oceanville off U.S. Route 9.
Literature Available: General information circular and map, bird and mammal checklists, and calendar of wildlife events.
Address: Refuge Manager, Brigantine National Wildlife Refuge, P.O. Box 72, Oceanville, New Jersey 08231.

BRIGANTINE NATIONAL WILDLIFE REFUGE

ATLANTIC AND OCEAN COUNTIES, NEW JERSEY

UNITED STATES
DEPARTMENT OF THE INTERIOR

FISH AND WILDLIFE SERVICE
BUREAU OF SPORT FISHERIES AND WILDLIFE

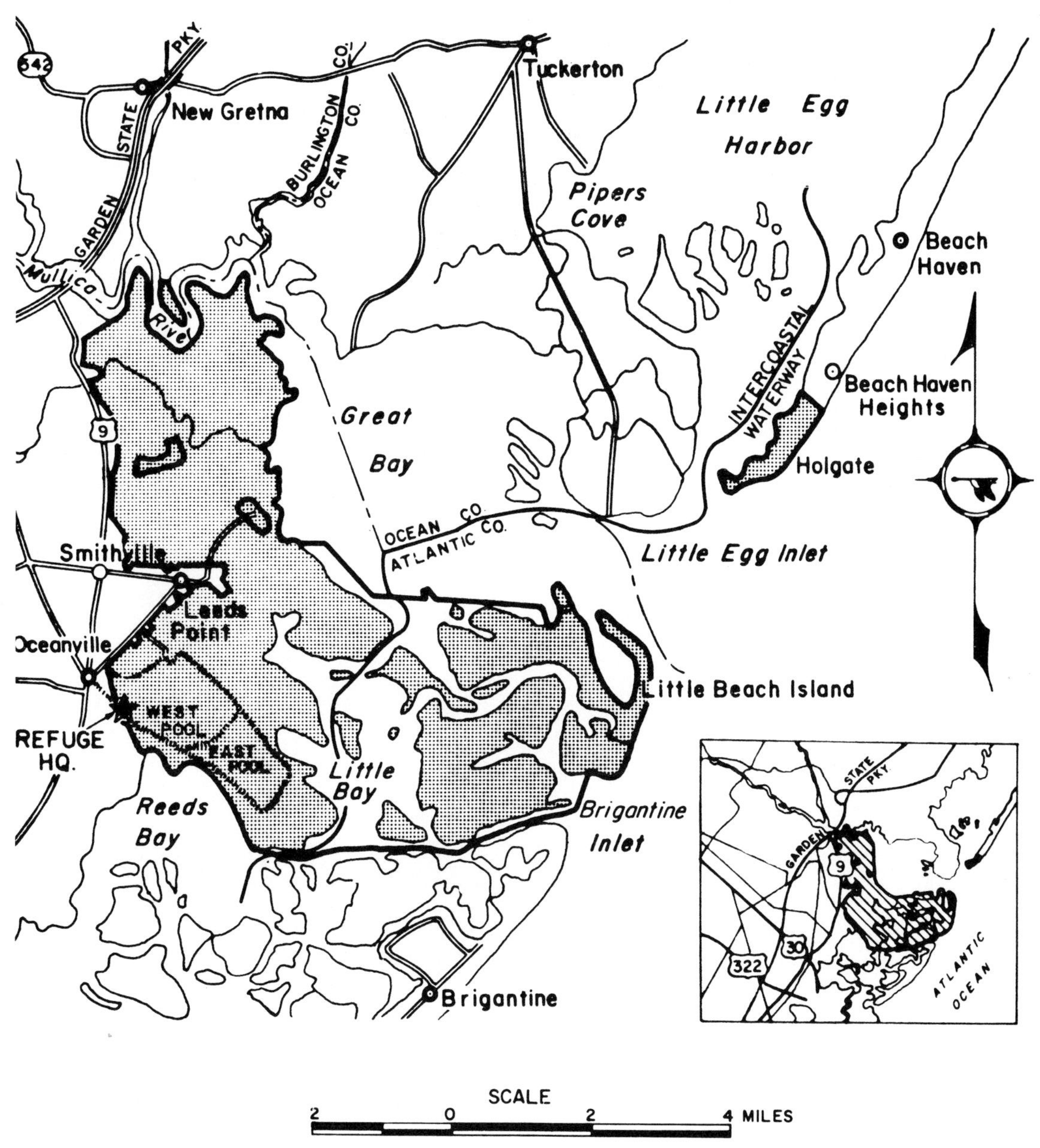

Birders studying waterfowl at Brigantine National Wildlife Refuge, New Jersey.

Large numbers of snow geese gather at Brigantine National Wildlife Refuge, New Jersey, in late autumn and early winter.

Small numbers of feral mute swans can be seen at Brigantine National Wildlife Refuge, New Jersey.

GREAT SWAMP NATIONAL WILDLIFE REFUGE

Waterfowl: Canada geese and various ducks.
Wildlife: Mammals (30 species), birds (more than 207 species), reptiles (21 species), amphibians (18 species), and fish (19 species).
Habitats: Swamp woodland, forested ridges, marshes, pastures, and meadows.
Size: 5,800 acres.
Location: Northern New Jersey, about 7 miles south of Morristown. The refuge headquarters is on Pleasant Plains Road near Basking Ridge.
Literature Available: General information circular and map, checklists of mammals, birds, reptiles, amphibians, and fish.
Address: Refuge Manager, Great Swamp National Wildlife Refuge, R.D. 1, Box 148, Basking Ridge, New Jersey 07920.

Pennsylvania

ERIE NATIONAL WILDLIFE REFUGE

Waterfowl: Canada geese and various ducks.
Wildlife: Mammals (32 species), birds (more than 223 species), reptiles, amphibians, and fish.
Habitats: Marshes, pools, beaver ponds, forested slopes, meadows, woodlots, and pastures.
Size: 5,000 acres.
Location: Northwestern Pennsylvania. The refuge headquarters is about 14 miles east of Meadville and 2 miles south of Mt. Hope on State Route 173.
Literature Available: General information sheet, map, and bird and mammal checklists.
Address: Refuge Manager, Erie National Wildlife Refuge, R.D. 2, Box 167, Guys Mills, Pennsylvania 16327.

MIDDLE CREEK WILDLIFE MANAGEMENT AREA

Waterfowl: Swans, Canada geese, mallards, and wood ducks.
Wildlife: Mammals, birds (229 species), reptiles, amphibians, and fish.
Habitats: Lake, swamp, meadows, pastures, and woodland.
Size: 5,000 acres.
Location: Eastern Pennsylvania, just south of Kleinfeltersville, Lebanon County. This refuge is owned and operated by the Pennsylvania Game Commission.
Literature Available: General information sheet and map, bird checklist, and conservation trail guide.
Address: Resident Manager, Middle Creek Wildlife Management Area, R.D. 1, Newmanstown, Pennsylvania 17073.

The Middle Creek Wildlife Management Area in eastern Pennsylvania is being developed as an important waterfowl area by the Pennsylvania Game Commission.

PYMATUNING WATERFOWL AREA

Waterfowl: Canada geese, mallards, black ducks, wood ducks, blue-winged teal, and gadwalls.
Wildlife: Mammals, birds, reptiles, amphibians, and fish.
Habitats: Lake, ponds, marshes, fields, and wooded areas.
Size: 11,000 acres.
Location: In northwestern Pennsylvania, just south of Linesville. This refuge is owned and operated by the Pennsylvania Game Commission, which also operates an excellent Waterfowl Museum on Ford Island where visitors can look at exhibits of ducks and other birdlife of the area.
Literature Available: General information sheet, map, and other printed materials dealing with the history of the area.
Address: Waterfowl Management Coordinator, Pymatuning Waterfowl Area, R.D. #1, Hartstown, Pennsylvania 16131.

TINICUM NATIONAL ENVIRONMENTAL CENTER

Waterfowl: Canada geese, mallards, black ducks, pintails, green-winged teal, blue-winged teal, American wigeon, ruddy ducks, and common mergansers.
Wildlife: Mammals, birds (more than 268 species), reptiles, amphibians, and fish.
Habitats: Tidal marshes, ponds, dikes, and fields.
Size: 1,200 acres.
Location: In Philadelphia, near the International Airport.
Literature Available: General information booklet.
Address: Center Manager, Tinicum National Environmental Center, Suite 104, Scott Plaza 2, Philadelphia, Pennsylvania 19113.

Delaware

BOMBAY HOOK NATIONAL WILDLIFE REFUGE

Waterfowl: Canada geese, snow geese, mallards, black ducks, gadwalls, pintails, green-winged teal, blue-winged teal, American wigeon, northern shovelers, wood ducks, ring-necked ducks, greater scaup, lesser scaup, buffleheads, ruddy ducks, hooded mergansers, and common mergansers.
Wildlife: Mammals (33 species), birds (256 species), reptiles (18 species), amphibians (9 species), and fish.
Habitats: Brackish tidal marshes, freshwater pools, swamps, meadows, pastures, and wooded areas.
Size: 16,280 acres.
Location: 9 miles southeast of Smyrna.
Literature Available: General information circular and map, calendar of nature events, and checklists for mammals, birds, reptiles, and amphibians.
Address: Refuge Manager, Bombay Hook National Wildlife Refuge, R.D. 1, Box 147, Smyrna, Delaware 19977.

LITTLE CREEK STATE WILDLIFE AREA

Waterfowl: Canada geese, snow geese, mallards, black ducks, gadwalls, pintails, green-winged teal, blue-winged teal, northern shovelers, American wigeon, ring-necked ducks, greater scaup, buffleheads, ruddy ducks, and hooded mergansers.
Wildlife: Mammals, birds, reptiles, amphibians, and fish.
Habitats: Delaware Bay, tidal marshes, freshwater marshes, pools, and dikes.
Size: 733 acres.
Location: Near Little Creek along Route 9, 4 miles east of Dover.
Literature Available: None.
Address: Delaware Division of Fish and Wildlife, Edward Tatnall Building, Legislative Avenue and William Penn Street, Dover, Delaware 19901.

Several of the waterfowl pools at Bombay Hook National Wildlife Refuge, Delaware.

PRIME HOOK NATIONAL WILDLIFE REFUGE

Waterfowl: Canada geese, snow geese, and various ducks.
Wildlife: Mammals (33 species), birds, reptiles, amphibians, and fish.
Habitats: Open water, ponds, marshes, scrub and wooded areas, meadows, and pastures.
Size: 10,700 acres.
Location: About 22 miles southeast of Dover along Delaware Bay.
Literature Available: General information sheet and map, and wildlife checklists.
Address: Refuge Manager, Prime Hook National Wildlife Refuge, Box 195, Milton, Delaware 19968.

Maryland

BLACKWATER NATIONAL WILDLIFE REFUGE

Waterfowl: Canada geese, mallards, and various other ducks.
Wildlife: Mammals, birds (more than 250 species), reptiles, amphibians, and fish.
Habitats: Freshwater ponds, marshes, scrub areas, timbered swamps, farmland, and rivers.
Size: 11,216 acres.
Location: The Eastern Shore of Maryland, about 10 miles south of Cambridge.
Literature Available: General information sheet and map, waterfowl management circulars, auto tour guide, and bird checklist.
Address: Refuge Manager, Blackwater National Wildlife Refuge, Route 1, Box 121, Cambridge, Maryland 21613.

Waterfowl on a wetland portion of Blackwater National Wildlife Refuge, Maryland. Photo by W. H. Julian / U.S. Fish and Wildlife Service.

EASTERN NECK NATIONAL WILDLIFE REFUGE

Waterfowl: Whistling swans, Canada geese, and various ducks.
Wildlife: Mammals, birds (153 species), reptiles, amphibians, and fish.
Habitats: Ponds, marshes, coves, fields, hedgerows, and forested areas.
Size: 2,285 acres.
Location: The Eastern Shore of Maryland in Kent County.
Literature Available: Trail guides, bird checklist, and general information circular and map.
Address: Refuge Manager, Eastern Neck National Wildlife Refuge, Route 2, Box 225, Rock Hall, Maryland 21661.

MARTIN NATIONAL WILDLIFE REFUGE

Waterfowl: Geese and various ducks.
Wildlife: Mammals, birds, reptiles, amphibians, and fish.
Habitats: Marshes, estuary, tidal creeks, and uplands.
Size: 4,423 acres.
Location: Southwestern Maryland, about 11 miles west of Crisfield.
Literature Available: General information sheet and map.
Address: Refuge Manager, Blackwater National Wildlife Refuge, Route 1, Box 121, Cambridge, Maryland 21613.

Virginia

BACK BAY NATIONAL WILDLIFE REFUGE

Waterfowl: Whistling swans, Canada geese, snow geese, and various ducks.
Wildlife: Mammals, birds (240 species), reptiles, amphibians, and fish.
Habitats: Ocean beach, sand dunes, marshes, wooded areas, and cultivated fields.
Size: 4,600 acres.
Location: Southeastern Virginia near Norfolk and Virginia Beach. Access to the refuge is by boat, jeep, or beach buggy.
Literature Available: Information sheet and map, and bird checklist.
Address: Refuge Manager, Back Bay National Wildlife Refuge, Box 6128, Virginia Beach, Virginia 23456.

CHINCOTEAGUE NATIONAL WILDLIFE REFUGE

Waterfowl: Whistling swans, Canada geese, snow geese, and various ducks.
Wildlife: Mammals (including the famous Chincoteague ponies), birds (278 species), reptiles, amphibians, and fish.
Habitats: A barrier island with dunes, salt marshes, wooded areas, and freshwater ponds.
Size: 9,000 acres.
Location: Northeastern Virginia and partly in southeastern Maryland near Chincoteague, Virginia.

Literature Available: General information sheet and map, bird checklist, and fish list.
Address: Refuge Manager, Chincoteague National Wildlife Refuge, P.O. Box 62, Chincoteague, Virginia 23336.

MASON NECK NATIONAL WILDLIFE REFUGE

Waterfowl: Whistling swans, Canada geese, mallards, black ducks, wood ducks, and lesser scaup.
Wildlife: Mammals, birds (210 species), reptiles, amphibians, and fish. The refuge is a special bald eagle sanctuary.
Habitats: Marshes, river, upland forest, and ponds.
Size: 2,436 acres.
Location: Northeastern Virginia, about 18 miles south of Washington, D.C.
Literature Available: General information sheet and map, and bird checklist.
Address: Refuge Manager, Mason Neck National Wildlife Refuge, P.O. Box A, Woodbridge, Virginia 22191.

PRESQUILE NATIONAL WILDLIFE REFUGE

Waterfowl: Canada geese, snow geese, and puddle ducks.
Wildlife: Mammals, birds (199 species), reptiles, amphibians, and fish.
Habitat: An island in the James River containing marshes, hardwood swamp, and farmland.
Size: 1,329 acres.
Location: Southeastern Virginia near Hopewell. Access to the refuge is by boat or a refuge-owned ferry. Advance arrangements must be made with the refuge manager prior to a visit.
Literature Available: General information sheet and map, and bird checklist.
Address: Refuge Manager, Presquile National Wildlife Refuge, P.O. Box 658, Hopewell, Virginia 23860.

Southeastern States

Tennessee

CROSS CREEKS NATIONAL WILDLIFE REFUGE

Waterfowl: Canada geese, and wood ducks.
Wildlife: Mammals, birds (204 species), reptiles, amphibians, and fish.
Habitats: Ponds, marshes, fields, and wooded areas.
Size: 9,892 acres.
Location: Northwestern Tennessee, several miles from Dover.
Literature Available: General information sheet and map, and bird checklist.
Address: Refuge Manager, Cross Creeks National Wildlife Refuge, Route 1, Box 113-B, Dover, Tennessee 37058.

HATCHIE NATIONAL WILDLIFE REFUGE

Waterfowl: Mallards, wood ducks, and various other ducks.
Wildlife: Mammals, birds (200 species), reptiles, amphibians, and fish.
Habitats: Forested bottomlands, streams, ponds, oxbow lakes, uplands, and the Hatchie River.
Size: 11,056 acres.
Location: In western Tennessee, along the south side of the Hatchie River south of Brownsville.
Literature Available: Information circular and map, bird checklist, and other materials.
Address: Refuge Manager, Hatchie National Wildlife Refuge, Box 187, Brownsville, Tennessee 38012.

REELFOOT NATIONAL WILDLIFE REFUGE

Waterfowl: Canada geese, mallards, pintails, ring-necked ducks, and other species.
Wildlife: Mammals, birds (259 species), reptiles, amphibians, and fish.
Habitats: Reelfoot Lake (in part), marshes, swamp forest, cypress forest, and wooded bluffs.
Size: 9,586 acres.
Location: Extreme northwestern Tennessee near Samburg.
Literature Available: Information sheet and map, bird checklist, and other materials.
Address: Refuge Manager, Reelfoot National Wildlife Refuge, Box 295, Samburg, Tennessee 38254.

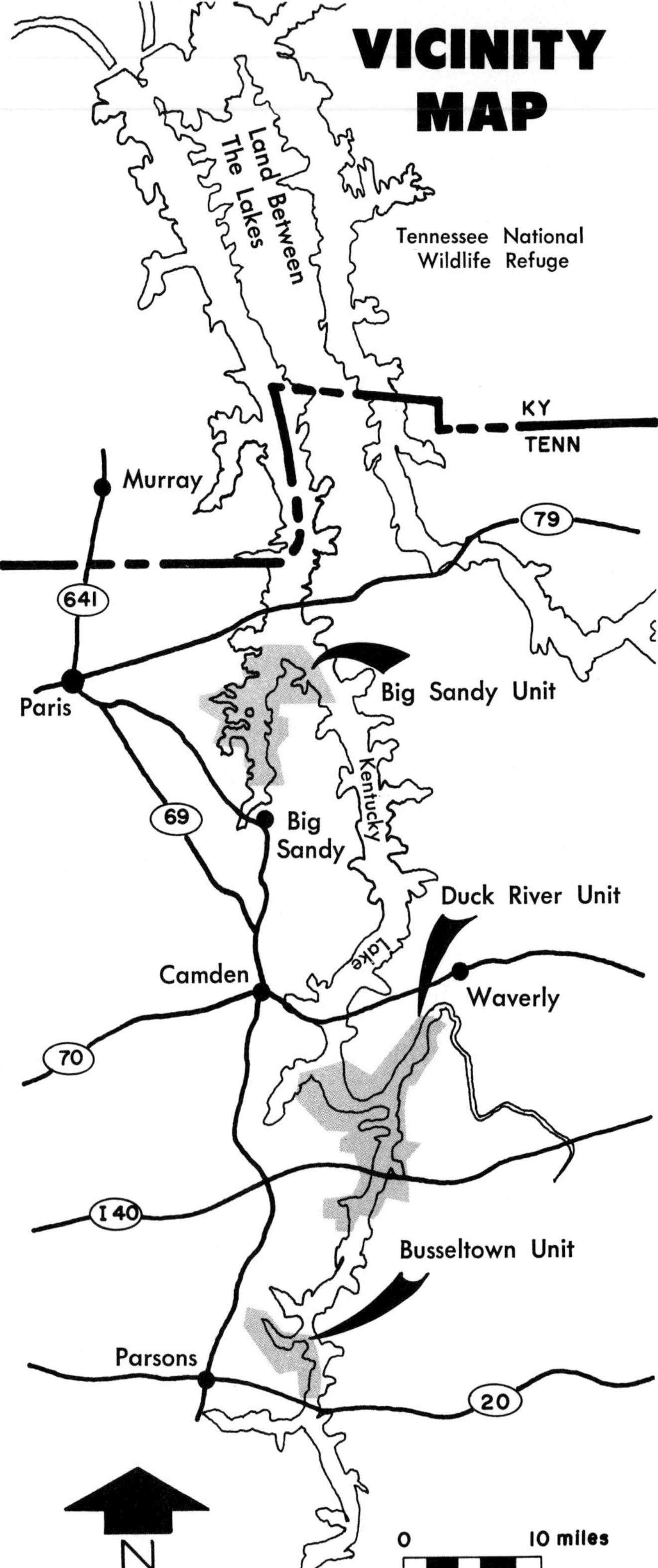
VICINITY
MAP
Land Between
The Lakes
Tennessee National
Wildlife Refuge
KY
TENN
Murray
79
641
Paris
Big Sandy Unit
Kentucky
69
Big
Sandy
Duck River Unit
Lake
Camden
Waverly
70
I 40
Busseltown Unit
Parsons
20
N
0
10 miles

CROSS CREEKS NATIONAL WILDLIFE REFUGE

Scale 0 2000 4000 8000 12000 16000 FEET
0 1/2 1 1½ 2 3 MILES

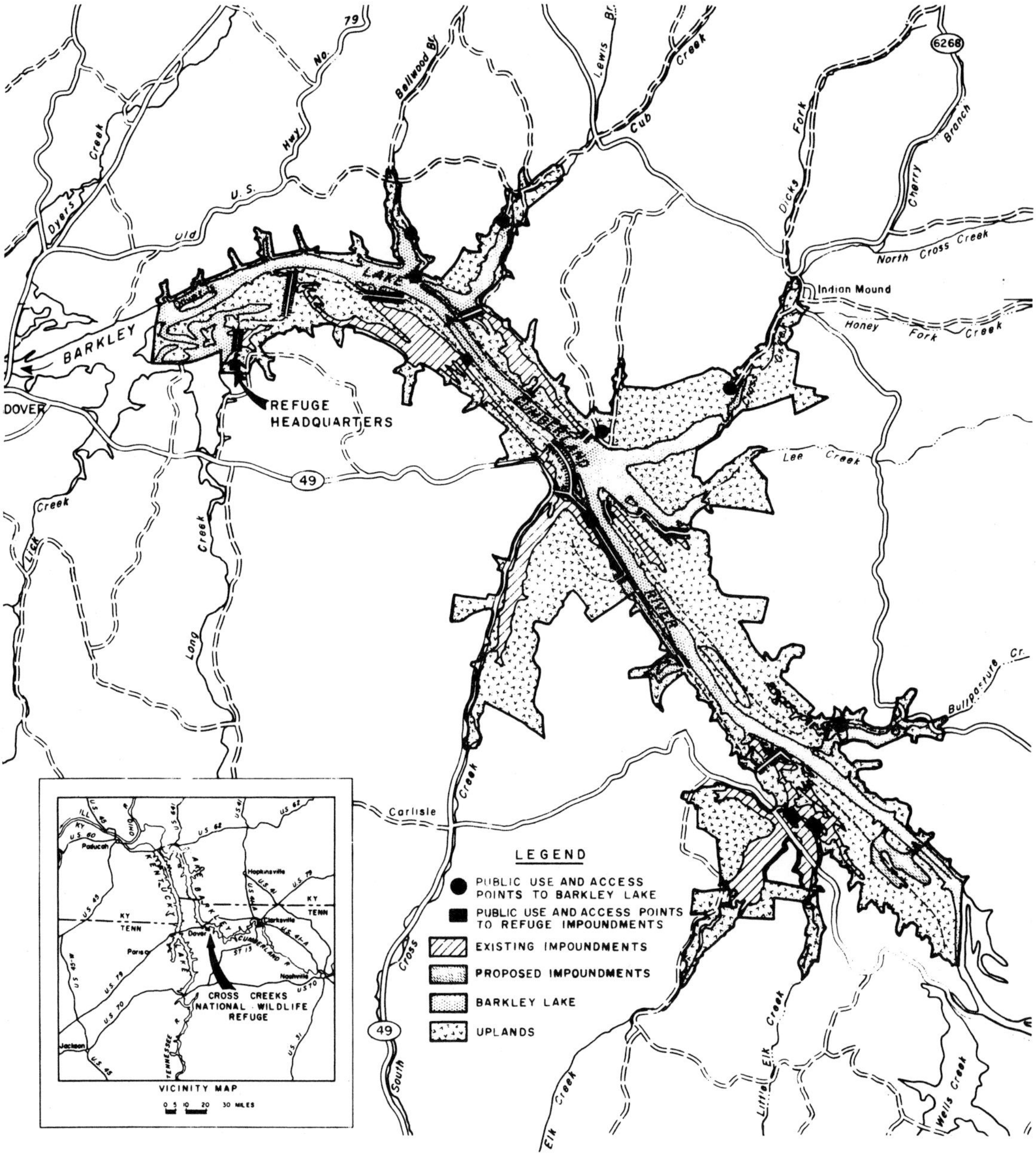

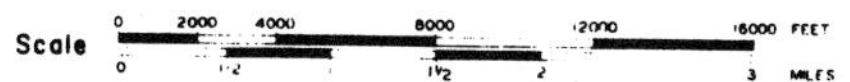

TENNESSEE NATIONAL WILDLIFE REFUGE

Waterfowl: Canada geese, mallards, American wigeon, and wood ducks.
Wildlife: Mammals, birds (211 species), reptiles, amphibians, and fish.
Habitats: River, lakes, forests, fields, and farmland.
Size: 51,347 acres separated into three units.
Location: In western Tennessee. The Big Sandy Unit is just north of Big Sandy, the Duck River Unit is just south of Waverly, and the Busseltown Unit is just east of Parsons.
Literature Available: General information circular and map, separate information sheets and maps for each of the units, self-guiding tour route leaflets, and bird checklists.
Address: Refuge Manager, Tennessee National Wildlife Refuge, P.O. Box 849, Paris, Tennessee 38242.

North Carolina

MATTAMUSKEET NATIONAL WILDLIFE REFUGE

Waterfowl: Whistling swans, Canada geese, snow geese, mallards, black ducks, and pintails.
Wildlife: Mammals, birds, reptiles, amphibians, and fish.
Habitats: Large lake, marshes, farmland, and woodland.
Size: 50,000 acres.
Location: In eastern North Carolina, about 23 miles south of Columbia.
Literature Available: General information circular and map, and bird checklist.
Address: Refuge Manager, Mattamuskeet National Wildlife Refuge, New Holland, North Carolina 27885.

PEA ISLAND NATIONAL WILDLIFE REFUGE

Waterfowl: Whistling swans, Canada geese, snow geese, and various ducks.
Wildlife: Mammals, birds (265 species), reptiles, amphibians, and fish.
Habitats: Beach, ocean dunes, tidal marshes, ponds, and fields.
Size: 5,915 acres.
Location: On the Outer Banks at the northern tip of Hatteras Island, south of Nags Head.
Literature Available: General informaton circular and map, calendar of wildlife events, and bird checklist.
Address: Refuge Manager, Pea Island National Wildlife Refuge, P.O. Box 1026, Manteo, North Carolina 27954.

PUNGO NATIONAL WILDLIFE REFUGE

Waterfowl: Canada geese, mallards, black ducks, and pintails.
Wildlife: Mammals, birds, reptiles, amphibians, and fish.

Habitats: Farmland, wooded areas, freshwater marshes, and a lake.
Size: 12,229 acres.
Location: Eastern North Carolina, south of Plymouth.
Literature Available: Information sheet and map, and bird checklist.
Address: Refuge Manager, Pungo National Wildlife Refuge, P.O. Box 116, Plymouth, North Carolina 27962.

SWANQUARTER NATIONAL WILDLIFE REFUGE

Waterfowl: Whistling swans, Canada geese, mallards, black ducks, and pintails.
Wildlife: Mammals, birds, reptiles, amphibians, and fish.
Habitats: Marshland, islands, and parts of Pamlico Sound.
Size: 15,500 acres.
Location: Coastal North Carolina in Hyde County, bordering Pamlico Sound.
Literature Available: Information sheet and map, and bird checklist.
Address: Refuge manager, Mattamuskeet National Wildlife Refuge, New Holland, North Carolina 27885.

South Carolina

CAPE ROMAIN NATIONAL WILDLIFE REFUGE

Waterfowl: Canada geese, mallards, black ducks, gadwalls, teal, ring-necked ducks, scaup, and buffleheads.
Wildlife: Mammals, birds, reptiles, amphibians, and fish.
Habitats: Sea islands, sandy beaches, salt marshes, and wooded areas. Bulls Island, an outstanding barrier reef within the refuge, is an excellent wildlife area.
Size: 60,000 acres.
Location: Along the South Carolina coast, about 20 miles northeast of Charleston. The refuge headquarters is at Moore's Landing on See Wee Road. Daily boat trips to Bulls Island leave from Moores Landing.
Literature Available: General information sheet and map, and Bulls Island information sheet and map.
Address: Refuge Manager, Cape Romain National Wildlife Refuge, Route 1, Box 191, Awendaw, South Carolina 29429.

CAROLINA SANDHILLS NATIONAL WILDLIFE REFUGE

Waterfowl: Canada geese, mallards, black ducks, and wood ducks.
Wildlife: Mammals, birds (184 species), reptiles, amphibians, and fish.
Habitats: Wooded uplands, hardwood creek bottoms, farmland, ponds, and lake.
Size: 46,000 acres.
Location: Northeastern South Carolina, 4 miles northeast of McBee.
Literature Available: General information sheet and map, and bird checklist.

CAROLINA SANDHILLS NATIONAL WILDLIFE REFUGE

CHESTERFIELD COUNTY, SOUTH CAROLINA

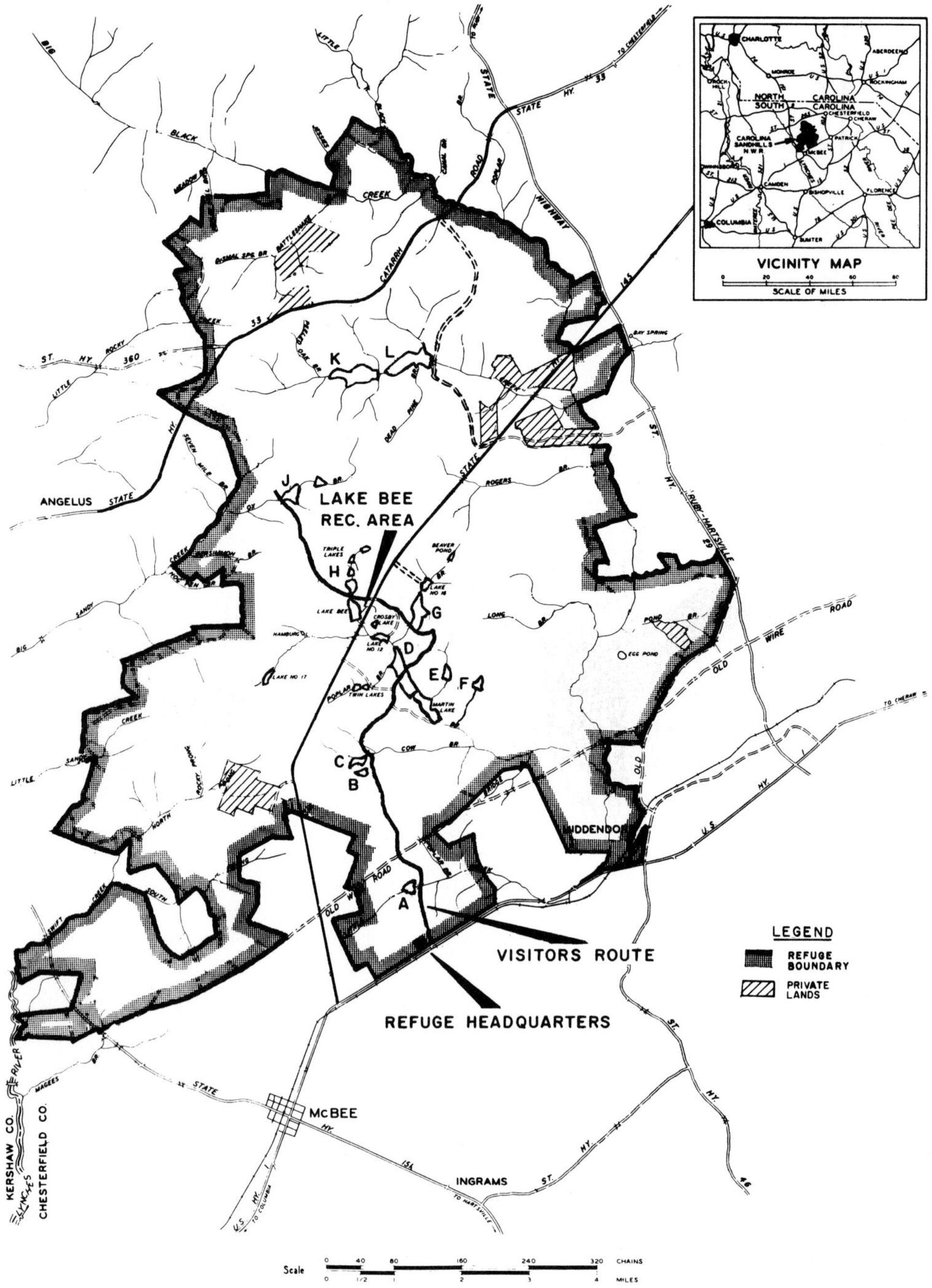

Opposite: The use of nest platforms has established a resident flock of Canada geese on the Harris Neck National Wildlife Refuge, Georgia. Photo by D. W. Pfitzer / U.S. Fish and Wildlife Service.

Address: Refuge Manager, Carolina Sandhills National Wildlife Refuge, McBee, South Carolina 29101.

SANTEE NATIONAL WILDLIFE REFUGE

Waterfowl: Canada geese and various ducks.
Wildlife: Mammals, birds, reptiles, amphibians, and fish.
Habitats: Lakes and fields.
Size: 74,350 acres.
Location: Southcentral South Carolina, about 7 miles south of Summerton.
Literature Available: Information sheet and map, and bird checklist.
Address: Refuge Manager, Santee National Wildlife Refuge, P.O. Box 158, Summerton, South Carolina 29148.

Georgia

HARRIS NECK NATIONAL WILDLIFE REFUGE

Waterfowl: Canada geese and various species of ducks.
Wildlife: Mammals, birds (204 species), reptiles, amphibians and fish.
Habitats: Creeks, marshes, ponds, woodlands, and farmland.
Size: 2,687 acres.
Location: In coastal Georgia between Savannah and Brunswick, along State Route 131.
Literature Available: Information sheet and map, and bird checklist.
Address: Refuge Manager, Savannah National Wildlife Refuge, Route 1, Hardeeville, South Carolina 29927.

HARRIS NECK NATIONAL WILDLIFE REFUGE

MC INTOSH COUNTY, GEORGIA

UNITED STATES
DEPARTMENT OF THE INTERIOR

FISH AND WILDLIFE SERVICE
BUREAU OF SPORT FISHERIES AND WILDLIFE

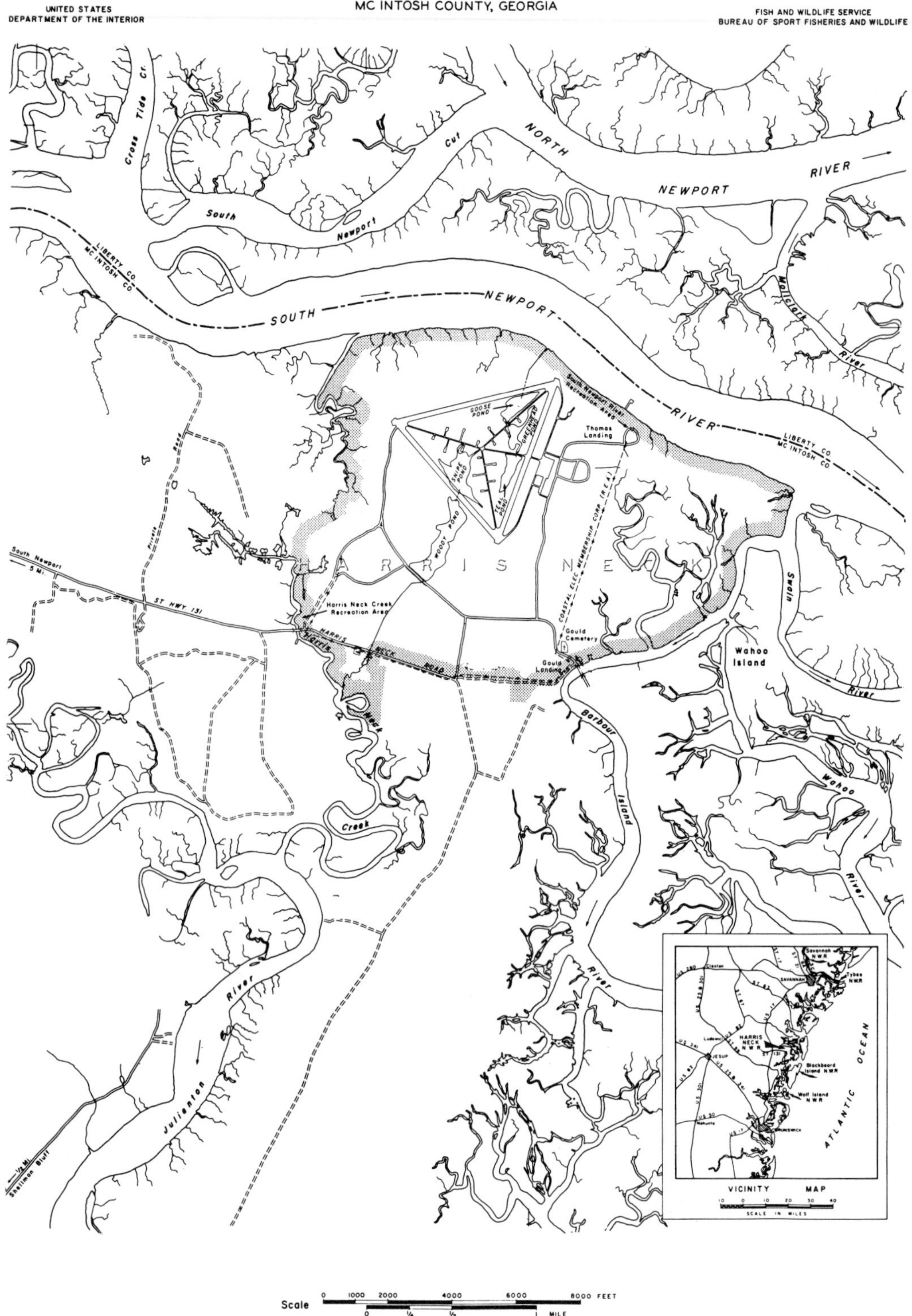

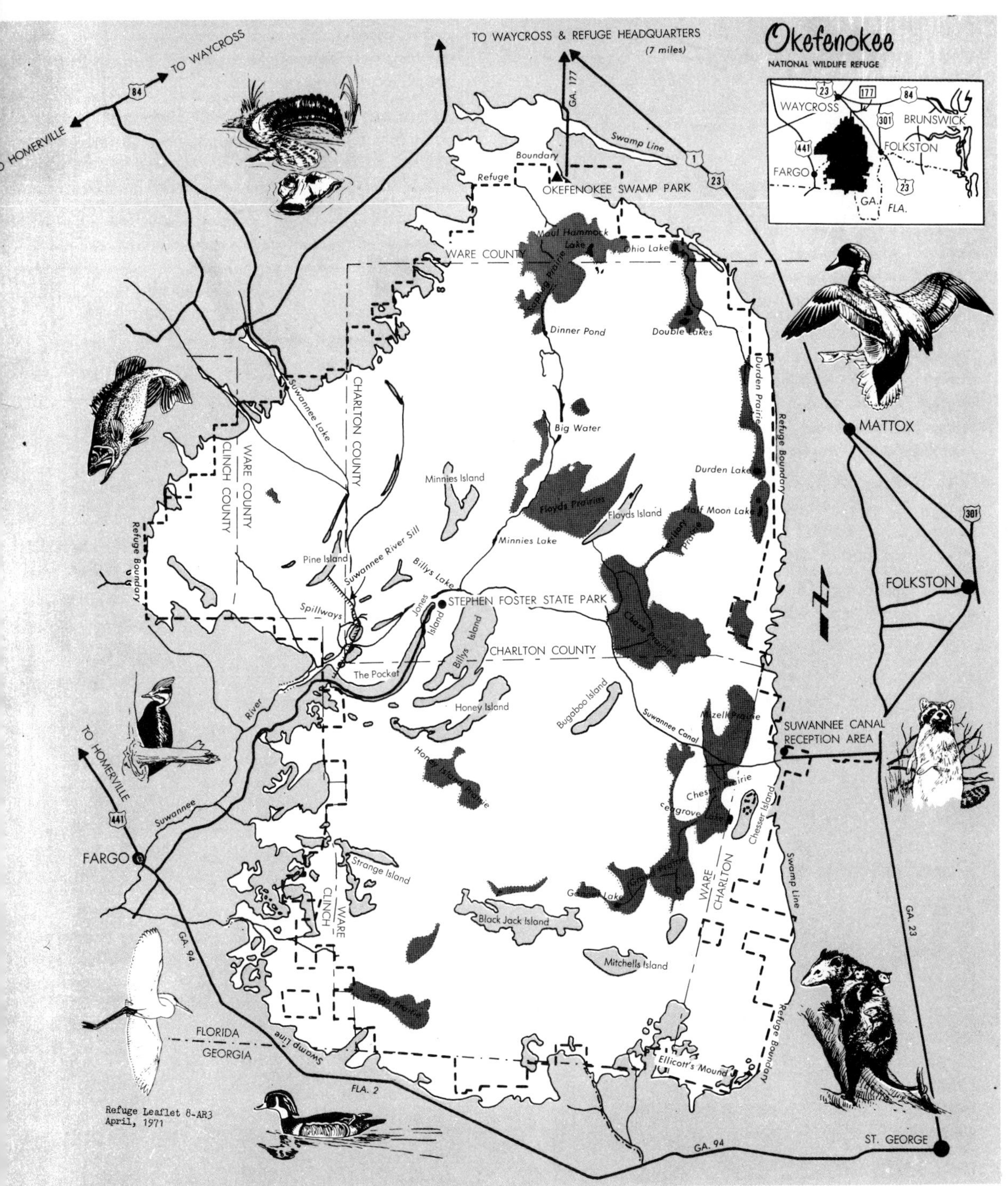
Okefenokee
NATIONAL WILDLIFE REFUGE
TO WAYCROSS & REFUGE HEADQUARTERS
(7 miles)
TO WAYCROSS
TO HOMERVILLE
WAYCROSS
BRUNSWICK
FOLKSTON
FARGO
GA.
FLA.
Swamp Line
Boundary
Refuge
OKEFENOKEE SWAMP PARK
WARE COUNTY
Ohio Lake
Dinner Pond
Double Lakes
Durden Prairie
Refuge Boundary
MATTOX
Big Water
Minnies Island
Durden Lake
Floyds Prairies
Floyds Island
Half Moon Lake
Minnies Lake
CHARLTON COUNTY
WARE COUNTY
CLINCH COUNTY
Suwannee Lake
Pine Island
Suwannee River Sill
Billys Lake
STEPHEN FOSTER STATE PARK
Spillways
Jones Island
Billys Island
CHARLTON COUNTY
Chase Prairie
FOLKSTON
The Pocket
Honey Island
Bugaboo Island
Suwannee Canal
Mizell Prairie
SUWANNEE CANAL
RECEPTION AREA
Chesser Prairie
Chesser Island
TO HOMERVILLE
Suwannee
River
Honey Island Prairie
FARGO
Strange Island
Black Jack Island
WARE
CLINCH
WARE
CHARLTON
Swamp Line
GA. 23
Mitchells Island
GA. 94
FLORIDA
GEORGIA
Swamp Line
FLA. 2
Ellicott's Mound
Refuge Boundary
GA. 94
ST. GEORGE
Refuge Leaflet 6-AR3
April, 1971

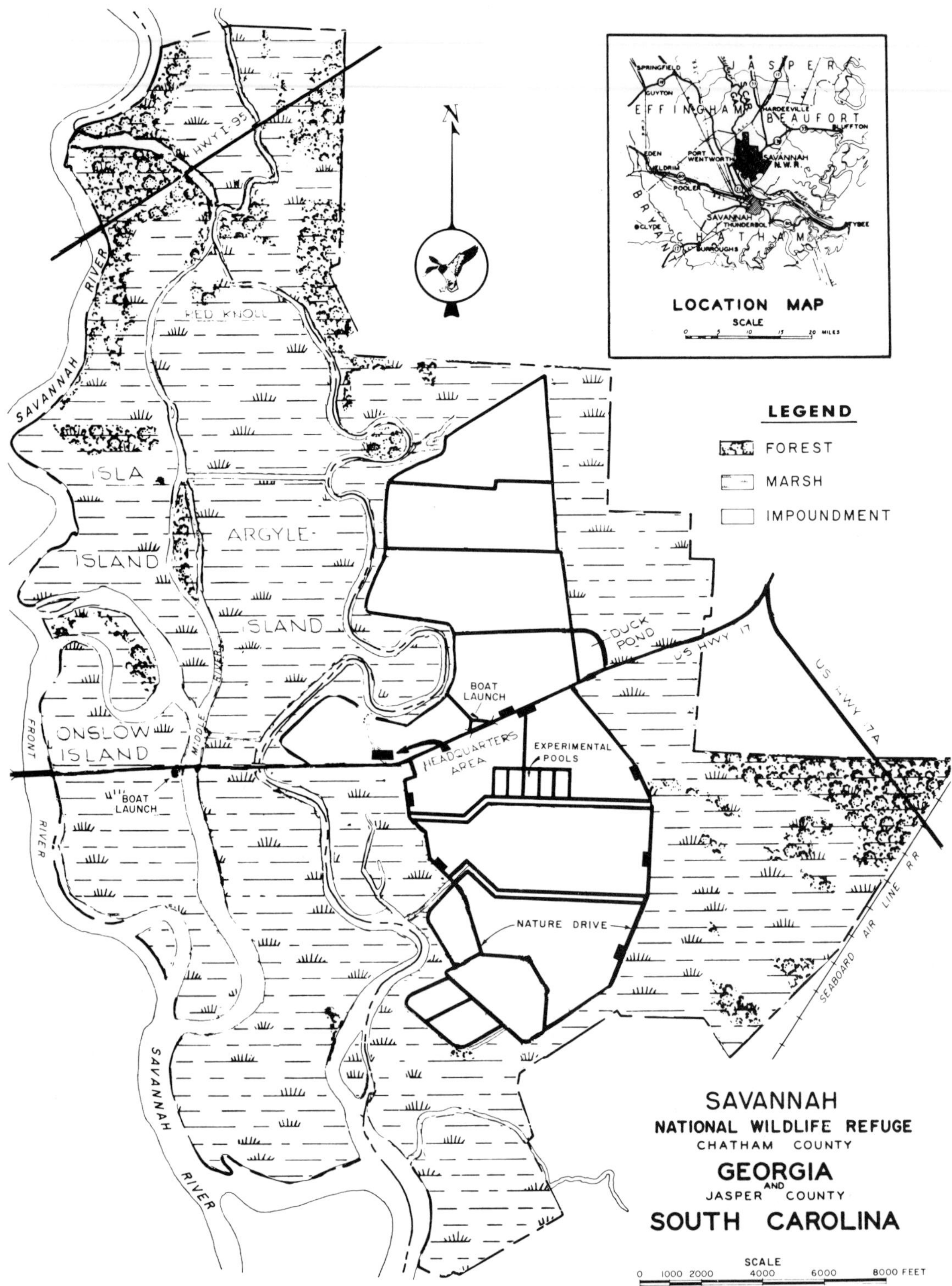

Opposite: A view of wetlands on the Savannah National Wildlife Refuge, Georgia. Photo by U.S. Fish and Wildlife Service.

OKEFENOKEE NATIONAL WILDLIFE REFUGE

Waterfowl: Wood ducks and various other ducks.
Wildlife: Mammals (42 species), birds (225 species), reptiles (58 species including large alligator populations), amphibians (32 species), and fish (34 species).
Habitat: A vast peat bog consisting of lush swamp vegetation, cypress forests, lakes, and slowly moving waterways.
Size: 379,302 acres.
Location: Southeastern Georgia near the Florida border. There are three primary entrances into Okefenokee Swamp plus one secondary entrance. The Suwannee Canal Recreation Area entrance (known locally as Camp Cornelia) is 12 miles southeast of Folkston off State Route 121; the Stephen C. Foster State Park entrance is 18 miles northeast of Fargo via State Route 177; the Okefenokee Swamp Park entrance is 13 miles south of Waycross on U.S. Routes 1 and 23; and the Kingfisher Landing secondary (undeveloped) entrance is about 12 miles north of Folkston and a mile off U.S. Route 1.
Literature Available: Information circulars and maps, canoeing trails map, bird and wildlife checklists, and other literature.
Address: Refuge Manager, Okefenokee National Wildlife Refuge, P.O. Box 117, Waycross, Georgia 31501.

SAVANNAH NATIONAL WILDLIFE REFUGE

Waterfowl: Mallards, black ducks, gadwalls, green-winged teal, pintails, ring-necked ducks, and wood ducks.
Wildlife: Mammals, birds (213 species), reptiles (including a sizable alligator population), amphibians, and fish.

Habitats: Savannah River, rice fields, marshes, swamps, and wooded islands.
Size: 13,136 acres.
Location: Southeastern Georgia, about 10 miles north of Savannah.
Literature Available: Information circular and map, and bird checklist.
Address: Refuge Manager, Savannah National Wildlife Refuge, Route 1, Hardeeville, South Carolina 29927.

Alabama

CHOCTAW NATIONAL WILDLIFE REFUGE

Waterfowl: Mallards, black ducks, pintails, wood ducks, and various other ducks.
Wildlife: Mammals, birds (139 species), reptiles, amphibians, and fish.
Habitats: Lakes, ponds, sloughs, farmland, and wooded areas.
Size: 4,218 acres.
Location: Southwestern Alabama, on the Tombigbee River, between Butler and Jackson.
Literature Available: Information circular and map, and bird checklist.
Address: Refuge Manager, Choctaw National Wildlife Refuge, Box 325, Jackson, Alabama 36545.

EUFAULA NATIONAL WILDLIFE REFUGE

Waterfowl: Canada geese, snow geese, mallards, American wigeons, and ring-necked ducks.
Wildlife: Mammals (35 species), birds (204 species), reptiles, amphibians, and fish.
Habitats: Large reservoir, river, harbor, marshes, and woodland.
Size: 11,160 acres.
Location: In southeastern Alabama and southwestern Georgia, about 7 miles north of Eufaula, Alabama.
Literature Available: Information circular and map, auto tour guide leaflets, and mammal and bird checklists.
Address: Refuge Manager, Eufaula National Wildlife Refuge, Box 258, Eufaula, Alabama 36027.

WHEELER NATIONAL WILDLIFE REFUGE

Waterfowl: Canada geese and various species of ducks.
Wildlife: Mammals (49 species), birds (252 species), reptiles (48 species), amphibians (26 species), and fish.
Habitats: Streams, shorelines, backwater sloughs, and embayments, pine plantations, hardwood bottoms, fields, and pastures.
Size: 34,500 acres.
Location: Northern Alabama extending for 15 miles along the Tennessee River between Decatur and Huntsville.

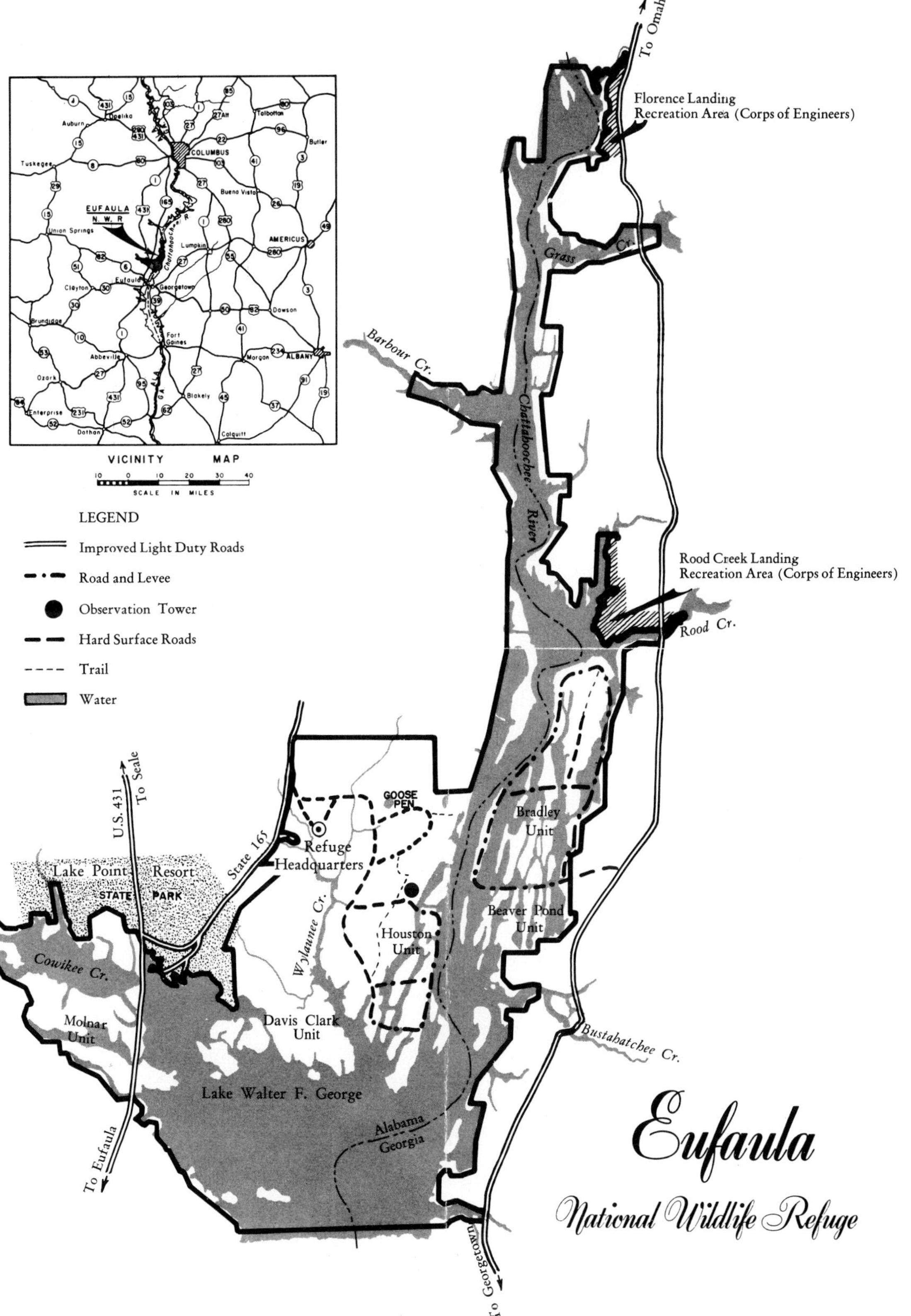

To Omaha
Florence Landing
Recreation Area (Corps of Engineers)
Grass Cr.
Barbour Cr.
Chattahoochee River
Rood Creek Landing
Recreation Area (Corps of Engineers)
Rood Cr.
VICINITY MAP
SCALE IN MILES
LEGEND
Improved Light Duty Roads
Road and Levee
Observation Tower
Hard Surface Roads
Trail
Water
To Scale
U.S. 431
State 165
GOOSE PEN
Refuge Headquarters
Bradley Unit
Lake Point Resort
STATE PARK
Wylaunee Cr.
Houston Unit
Beaver Pond Unit
Cowikee Cr.
Molnar Unit
Davis Clark Unit
Bustahatchee Cr.
Lake Walter F. George
Alabama
Georgia
To Eufaula
To Georgetown
Eufaula
National Wildlife Refuge

Literature Available: Information circular and map, checklists for mammals, birds, reptiles, amphibians, trees, shrubs, and woody vines.
Address: Refuge Manager, Wheeler National Wildlife Refuge, Box 1643, Decatur, Alabama 35601.

Florida

CHASSAHOWITZKA NATIONAL WILDLIFE REFUGE

North American Ducks, Geese & Swans

Waterfowl: Mallards, black ducks, gadwalls, pintails, American wigeon, redheads, and canvasbacks.
Wildlife: Mammals, birds (234 species), reptiles (including alligators), amphibians, and fish.
Habitats: Salt bays and estuaries, brackish marshes, hardwood swamps, ponds, and sections of the Homosassa River.
Size: 30,000 acres.
Location: The Gulf Coast of Florida, about 65 miles north of St. Petersburg, and 4 miles south of Homosassa Springs on U.S. Route 19.
Literature Available: Information circular and map, bird checklist, and other literature.
Address: Refuge Manager, Chassahowitzka National Wildlife Refuge, Route 1, Box 153, Homosassa, Florida 32646.

J. N. "DING" DARLING NATIONAL WILDLIFE REFUGE

Waterfowl: Mottled ducks, pintails, lesser scaup, and red-breasted mergansers.
Wildlife: Mammals, birds (267 species), reptiles (40 species), amphibians (11 species), fish, and seashells (400 species).
Habitat: A tropical island with dry ridges, wet sloughs, mangroves, and shallow bays.
Size: 4,000 acres.
Location: Off the southwestern coast of Florida, about 15 miles west of Fort Myers.
Literature Available: Information circular and map, and checklists for birds, reptiles, and amphibians.
Address: Refuge Manager, J. N. "Ding" Darling National Wildlife Refuge, P.O. Drawer B, Sanibel, Florida 33957.

LAKE WOODRUFF NATIONAL WILDLIFE REFUGE

Waterfowl: Wood ducks, pintails, blue-winged teal, ring-necked ducks, and scaup.
Wildlife: Mammals (23 species including black bear, mountain lion, bobcat, and manatee), birds (192 species), reptiles, amphibians, and fish.
Habitats: Lake Woodruff, marshes, and hardwood swamps.
Size: 18,810 acres.

LAKE WOODRUFF NATIONAL WILDLIFE REFUGE

VOLUSIA COUNTY, FLORIDA

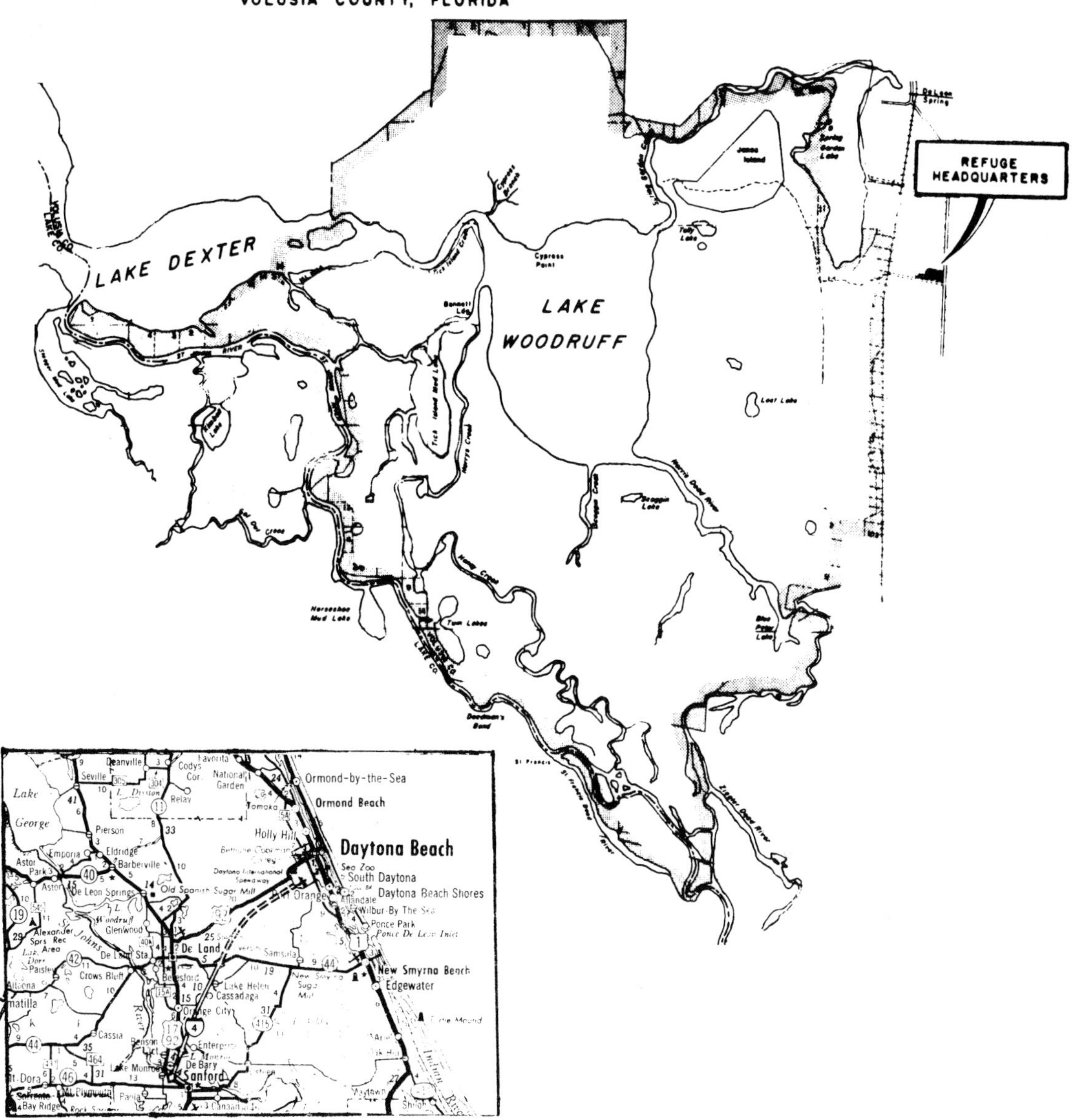

Location: On the East Coast along the St. Johns River near DeLeon Springs. The refuge headquarters is on Route 40-A, ½ mile southwest of DeLeon Springs.

Literature Available: Information sheet and map, bird and mammal checklists, and other materials.

Address: Refuge Manager, Lake Woodruff National Wildlife Refuge, P.O. Box 488, DeLeon Springs, Florida 32028.

LOXAHATCHEE NATIONAL WILDLIFE REFUGE

Waterfowl: Mottled ducks, wood ducks, ring-necked ducks, pintails, blue-winged teal, green-winged teal, American wigeon, and northern shovelers.
Wildlife: Mammals (22 species including mountain lion and bobcat), birds (245 species including the endangered snail kite), reptiles (33 species including alligators), amphibians (15 species), and fish (51 species).
Habitat: A portion of the Everglades including sawgrass marsh, wet prairies, tree islands, and sloughs.
Size: 145,635 acres.
Location: Southeastern Florida, 12 miles west of Delray Beach.
Literature Available: Information circular and map, checklists for mammals, birds, reptiles, amphibians, and fish, and boating and fishing regulations.
Address: Refuge Manager, Loxahatchee National Wildlife Refuge, Box 278, Delray Beach, Florida 33444.

MERRITT ISLAND NATIONAL WILDLIFE REFUGE

Waterfowl: Mottled duck, gadwalls, pintails, lesser scaup, and teal.
Wildlife: Mammals (20 species), birds (280 species), reptiles, amphibians, and fish. The refuge provides vital habitat for at least eight species or subspecies of endangered wildlife.
Habitats: Barrier beaches and sand dunes, marshes and swamps (saltwater and freshwater), wooded hammocks and flatwoods, and saltwater lagoons.
Size: 134,143 acres.
Location: Along the Atlantic Coast of central Florida, about 6 miles east of Titusville on State Route 402. The refuge is adjacent to the Kennedy Space Center.
Literature Available: Information circular and map, tour guide leaflets, and bird checklist.
Address: Refuge Manager, Merritt Island National Wildlife Refuge, P.O. Box 6504, Titusville, Florida 32780.

ST. MARKS NATIONAL WILDLIFE REFUGE

Waterfowl: Canada geese, pintails, American wigeons, redheads, ring-necked ducks, and buffleheads.
Wildlife: Mammals, birds (263 species), reptiles, amphibians, and fish.
Habitats: Marshes, freshwater impoundments, brackish bays, tidal flats, hardwood swamps, pine woodlands, shoreline, and tidal creeks.
Size: 96,700 acres.
Location: Along northwestern Florida's Gulf Coast just south of St. Marks.
Literature Available: Information circular and map, bird checklist, and trail guide.
Address: Refuge Manager, St. Marks National Wildlife Refuge, P.O. Box 68, St. Marks, Florida 32355.

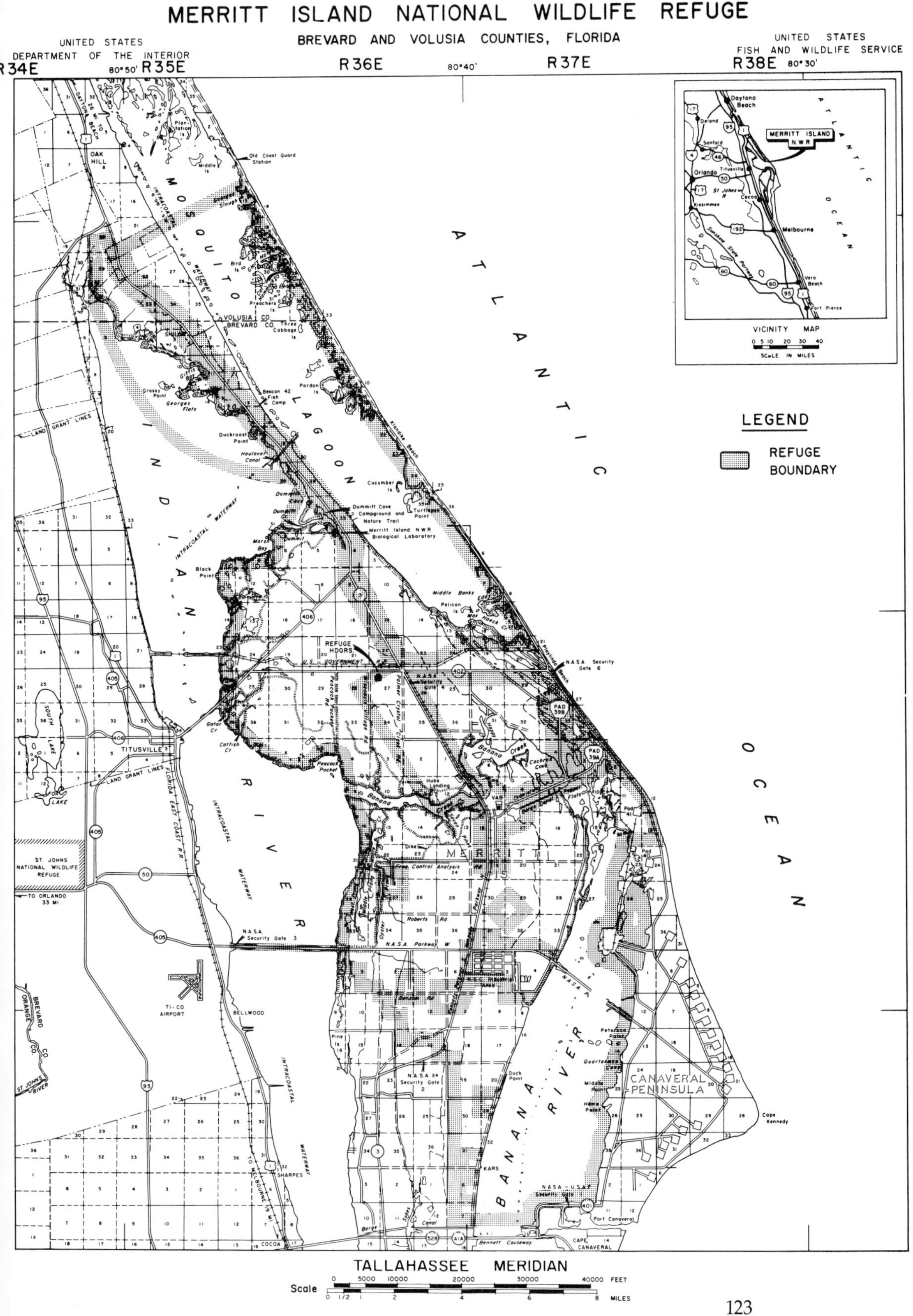

MERRITT ISLAND NATIONAL WILDLIFE REFUGE
BREVARD AND VOLUSIA COUNTIES, FLORIDA
UNITED STATES
DEPARTMENT OF THE INTERIOR
UNITED STATES
FISH AND WILDLIFE SERVICE
R34E
80°50' R35E
R36E
80°40'
R37E
R38E 80°30'
VICINITY MAP
SCALE IN MILES
MERRITT ISLAND N.W.R.
LEGEND
REFUGE BOUNDARY
ATLANTIC OCEAN
MOSQUITO LAGOON
INDIAN RIVER
BANANA RIVER
MERRITT
CANAVERAL PENINSULA
REFUGE HDQRS.
TITUSVILLE
OAK HILL
ST. JOHNS NATIONAL WILDLIFE REFUGE
TO ORLANDO 33 MI.
TI-CO AIRPORT
BELLWOOD
SHARPES
COCOA
CAPE CANAVERAL
Port Canaveral
Cape Kennedy
PAD 39B
PAD 39A
TALLAHASSEE MERIDIAN
Scale
FEET
MILES

ST. VINCENT NATIONAL WILDLIFE REFUGE

Waterfowl: Various species of ducks.
Wildlife: Mammals, birds, reptiles (including alligators), amphibians, and fish.
Habitats: Sand beaches, tidal marshes, freshwater ponds and marshes, saw palmetto cover, cabbage palm and magnolia hammocks, pine woodland, and scrub oak ridges.
Size: 12,358 acres.
Location: An island in the Gulf of Mexico offshore from the tip of the Indian Pass peninsula about 21 miles west of Apalachicola. All access to the island is by private boat or commercial guides. A permit is required from the refuge manager to explore the interior of the refuge, but use of the beaches and some ponds is unrestricted.
Literature Available: Information circular and map.
Address: Refuge Manager, St. Vincent National Wildlife Refuge, P.O. Box 447, Apalachicola, Florida 32320.

Mississippi

NOXUBEE NATIONAL WILDLIFE REFUGE

Waterfowl: Mallards, gadwalls, green-winged teal, American wigeon, wood ducks, and ring-necked ducks.
Wildlife: Mammals, birds (212 species), reptiles, amphibians, and fish.
Habitats: Pure bottomland hardwoods and cypress, two large lakes, streams, wooded areas, fields, and high ridges.
Size: 46,000 acres.
Location: Eastcentral Mississippi, about 25 miles northeast of Louisville.
Literature Available: Information circular and map, and bird checklist.
Address: Refuge Manager, Noxubee National Wildlife Refuge, Route 1, Brooksville, Mississippi 39739.

YAZOO NATIONAL WILDLIFE REFUGE

Waterfowl: Mallards, black ducks, gadwalls, pintails, green-winged teal, American wigeon, northern shovelers, wood ducks, and ring-necked ducks.
Wildlife: Mammals, birds (140 species), reptiles (including alligators), amphibians, and fish.
Habitats: Lakes, marshes, bayous, woodland, and fields.
Size: 12,000+ acres.
Location: In western Mississippi, in the bottomlands of the Mississippi River valley, about 30 miles south of Greenville.
Literature Available: Information sheet and map, and bird checklist.
Address: Refuge Manager, Yazoo National Wildlife Refuge, Route 1, Box 286, Hollandale, Mississippi 38748.

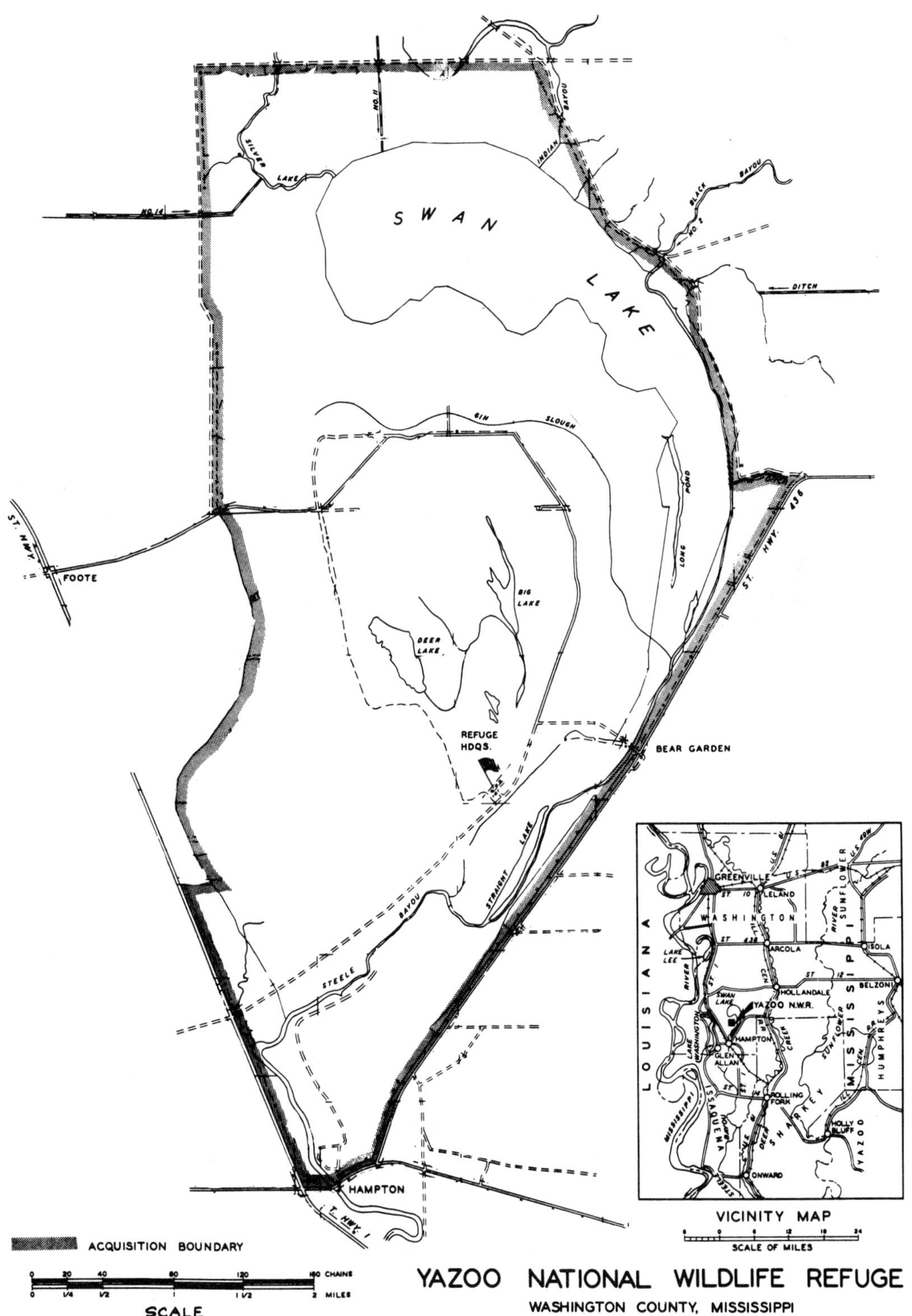

YAZOO NATIONAL WILDLIFE REFUGE

WASHINGTON COUNTY, MISSISSIPPI

A pair of wood ducks under green timber on the Yazoo National Wildlife Refuge, Mississippi. Photo by Earl R. Cunningham / U.S. Fish and Wildlife Service.

Arkansas

BIG LAKE NATIONAL WILDLIFE REFUGE

Waterfowl: Mallards, wood ducks, and hooded mergansers.
Wildlife: Mammals, birds (201 species), reptiles, amphibians, and fish.
Habitats: Open water, swamps, seasonally flooded hardwoods, and cropland.
Size: 9,900 acres.
Location: In northeastern Arkansas, 2½ miles northeast of Manila.
Literature Available: Information sheet and map, and bird checklist.
Address: Refuge Manager, Big Lake National Wildlife Refuge, P.O. Box 67, Manila, Arkansas 72442.

HOLLA BEND NATIONAL WILDLIFE REFUGE

Waterfowl: Canada geese, mallards, gadwalls, pintails, green-winged teal, and American wigeon.
Wildlife: Mammals, birds (203 species), reptiles, amphibians, and fish.
Habitats: Freshwater ponds, sloughs, lakes, pools, wooded areas, and cropland.
Size: 6,367 acres.
Location: In central Arkansas, 8 miles south of Dardanelle.
Literature Available: Information sheet and map, and bird checklist.
Address: Refuge Manager, Holla Bend National Wildlife Refuge, P.O. Box 1043, Russellville, Arkansas 72801.

WAPANOCCA NATIONAL WILDLIFE REFUGE

Waterfowl: Mallards, wood ducks, and hooded mergansers.
Wildlife: Mammals, birds (205 species), reptiles, amphibians, and fish.
Habitats: Freshwater impoundments, bottomlands with timber, and agricultural land.
Size: 5,485 acres.
Location: In eastcentral Arkansas, 4 miles west of the Mississippi River and just south of Turrell.
Literature Available: Information circular and map, and bird checklist.
Address: Refuge Manager, Wapanocca National Wildlife Refuge, P.O. Box 257, Turrell, Arkansas 72384.

WHITE RIVER NATIONAL WILDLIFE REFUGE

Waterfowl: Canada geese, mallards, black ducks, gadwalls, pintails, green-winged teal, American wigeon, northern shovelers, wood ducks, ring-necked ducks, and lesser scaup.
Wildlife: Mammals (30 species), birds (227 species), reptiles (38 species), amphibians (10 species), and fish.
Habitats: A 65-mile section of the White River, bayous, chutes, channels, lakes, forested areas, and fields.
Size: 116,302 acres.
Location: In southeastern Arkansas.
Literature Available: Information sheet and map, checklists for mammals, birds, reptiles, and amphibians.
Address: Refuge Manager, White River National Wildlife Refuge, P.O. Box 308, DeWitt, Arkansas 72042.

Louisiana

BRETON NATIONAL WILDLIFE REFUGE

Waterfowl: Redheads, scaup, black ducks, American wigeon, and buffleheads.
Wildlife: Mammals, birds, reptiles, and fish.
Habitats: Barrier islands, sandy beaches, inlets, ponds, saltwater marshes, and black mangroves.
Size: 4,507 acres.

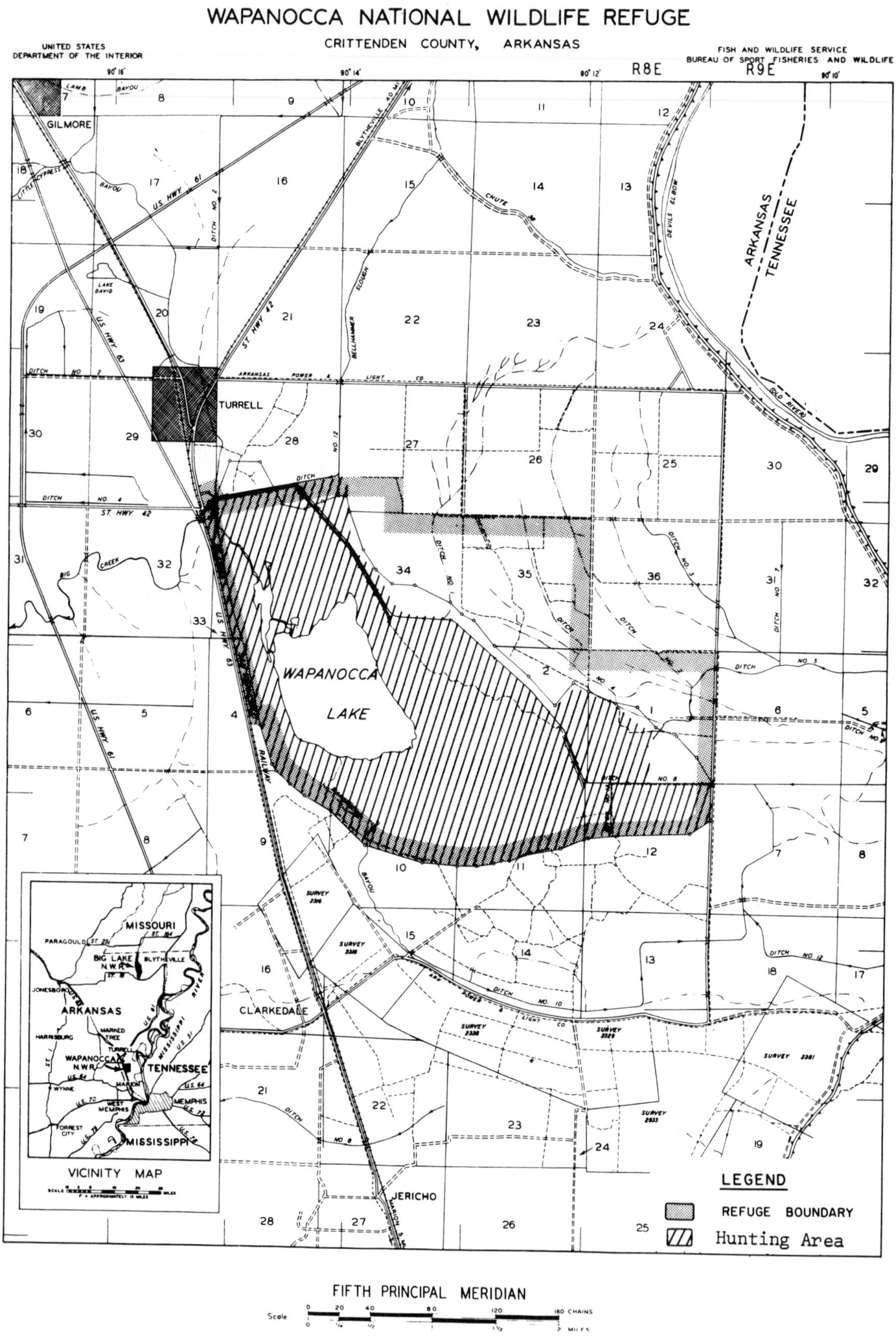

WAPANOCCA NATIONAL WILDLIFE REFUGE
CRITTENDEN COUNTY, ARKANSAS
UNITED STATES DEPARTMENT OF THE INTERIOR
FISH AND WILDLIFE SERVICE
BUREAU OF SPORT FISHERIES AND WILDLIFE
R8E
R9E
GILMORE
TURRELL
CLARKEDALE
JERICHO
WAPANOCCA LAKE
ARKANSAS
TENNESSEE
DEVILS ELBOW
OLD RIVER
US HWY 61
US HWY 63
ST HWY 42
BIG CREEK
BELLHAMMER SLOUGH
ARKANSAS POWER & LIGHT CO
VICINITY MAP
MISSOURI
PARAGOULD
BIG LAKE N.W.R.
BLYTHEVILLE
JONESBORO
HARRISBURG
MARKED TREE
WAPANOCCA N.W.R.
MARION
WYNNE
WEST MEMPHIS
MEMPHIS
FORREST CITY
MISSISSIPPI
MISSISSIPPI RIVER
LEGEND
REFUGE BOUNDARY
Hunting Area
FIFTH PRINCIPAL MERIDIAN
Scale
160 CHAINS
2 MILES

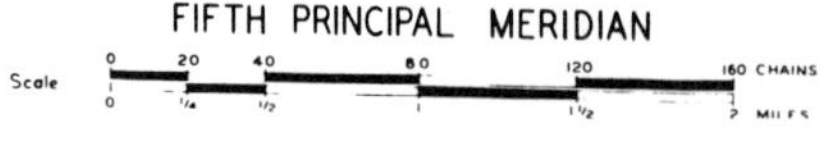

Location: Off the northeastern portion of the Mississippi River Delta. The refuge consists of Breton Island and the adjacent Chandeleur Islands—the latter a series of barrier islands extending crescent-shape for about 20 miles off the Mississippi coast. Access is only by private boat.
Literature Available: Information booklet and map.
Address: Refuge Manager, Delta-Breton Islands National Wildlife Refuge, Pilottown, Louisiana 70053.

DELTA NATIONAL WILDLIFE REFUGE

Waterfowl: Snow geese (blue phase), gadwalls, pintails, American widgeon, green-winged teal, and northern shovelers.
Wildlife: Mammals, birds, reptiles, amphibians, and fish.

Habitats: Marshes, ponds within marshes, canals, bayous, and passes.
Size: 48,800 acres.
Location: 7 miles south of Venice on the east bank of the Mississippi River. Access is by private boat only.
Literature Available: Information circular and map, and bird and fish checklists.
Address: Refuge Manager, Delta National Wildlife Refuge, Venice, Louisiana 70091.

LACASSINE NATIONAL WILDLIFE REFUGE

Waterfowl: Canada geese, white-fronted geese, snow geese, fulvous whistling ducks, mallards (including the mottled duck form), gadwalls, pintails, green-winged teal, blue-winged teal, American wigeon, northern shovelers, ring-necked ducks, lesser scaup, ruddy ducks, and hooded mergansers.
Wildlife: Mammals (34 species), birds (203 species), reptiles (55 species), amphibians (20 species), and fish (38 species).
Habitats: Marshes, natural ridges, levees, spoil banks, and farm areas.
Size: 31,776 acres.
Location: In southern Louisiana on State Route 3056, 11 miles southwest of Lake Arthur.
Literature Available: Information circular and map, and bird checklist.
Address: Refuge Manager, Lacassine National Wildlife Refuge, Route 1, Box 186, Lake Arthur, Louisiana 70549.

SABINE NATIONAL WILDLIFE REFUGE

Waterfowl: Snow geese, mallards (including the mottled duck form), black ducks, gadwalls, pintails, green-winged teal, blue-winged teal, northern shovelers, American wigeon, and lesser scaup.
Wildlife: Mammals, birds (250 species), reptiles, amphibians, and fish.
Habitats: Marsh, impoundments, bayous, ponds, lakes, wooded islands, and ridges.
Size: 142,000 acres.
Location: In extreme southwestern Louisiana, 6 miles southwest of Hackberry.
Literature Available: Bird checklist and young people's wildlife checklist.
Address: Refuge Manager, Sabine National Wildlife Refuge, MRH Box 107, Hackberry, Louisiana 70645.

Great Lakes States

Minnesota

AGASSIZ NATIONAL WILDLIFE REFUGE

Waterfowl: Whistling swans, Canada geese, mallards, and blue-winged teal.
Wildlife: Mammals (including moose and timber wolves), birds (245 species), reptiles, amphibians, and fish.
Habitats: Marsh, black spruce-tamarack bogs, open water, and wooded areas.
Size: 61,000 acres.
Location: In the northwestern corner of Minnesota, about 11 miles east of Holt on County Road 7.
Literature Available: Information circular and map, bird checklist, and auto tour route leaflet.
Address: Refuge Manager, Agassiz National Wildlife Refuge, Middle River, Minnesota 56737.

BIG STONE NATIONAL WILDLIFE REFUGE

Waterfowl: Canada geese, snow geese, mallards, gadwalls, pintails, green-winged teal, blue-winged teal, American wigeon, northern shovelers, wood ducks, redheads, ring-necked ducks, canvasbacks, lesser scaup, common goldeneyes, ruddy ducks, and common mergansers.
Wildlife: Mammals, birds (219 species), reptiles, amphibians, and fish.
Habitats: Minnesota River and marshes.
Size: 10,800 acres.
Location: In western Minnesota, 3 miles southeast of Ortonville.
Literature Available: Map and bird checklist.
Address: Refuge Manager, Big Stone National Wildlife Refuge, 25 N.W. Second Street, Ortonville, Minnesota 56278.

RICE LAKE NATIONAL WILDLIFE REFUGE

Waterfowl: Mallards, black ducks, wood ducks, American wigeon, blue-winged teal, ring-necked ducks, and scaup.
Wildlife: Mammals (42 species), birds (212 species), reptiles, amphibians, and fish.
Habitats: Rice Lake, Rice River, islands, fields, forests, and swamps.
Size: 18,056 acres.
Location: In northcentral Minnesota, 7 miles south of McGregor.
Literature Available: Information circular and map, bird and mammal checklists, and wild rice circular.
Address: Refuge Manager, Rice Lake National Wildlife Refuge, Route 2, McGregor, Minnesota 55760.

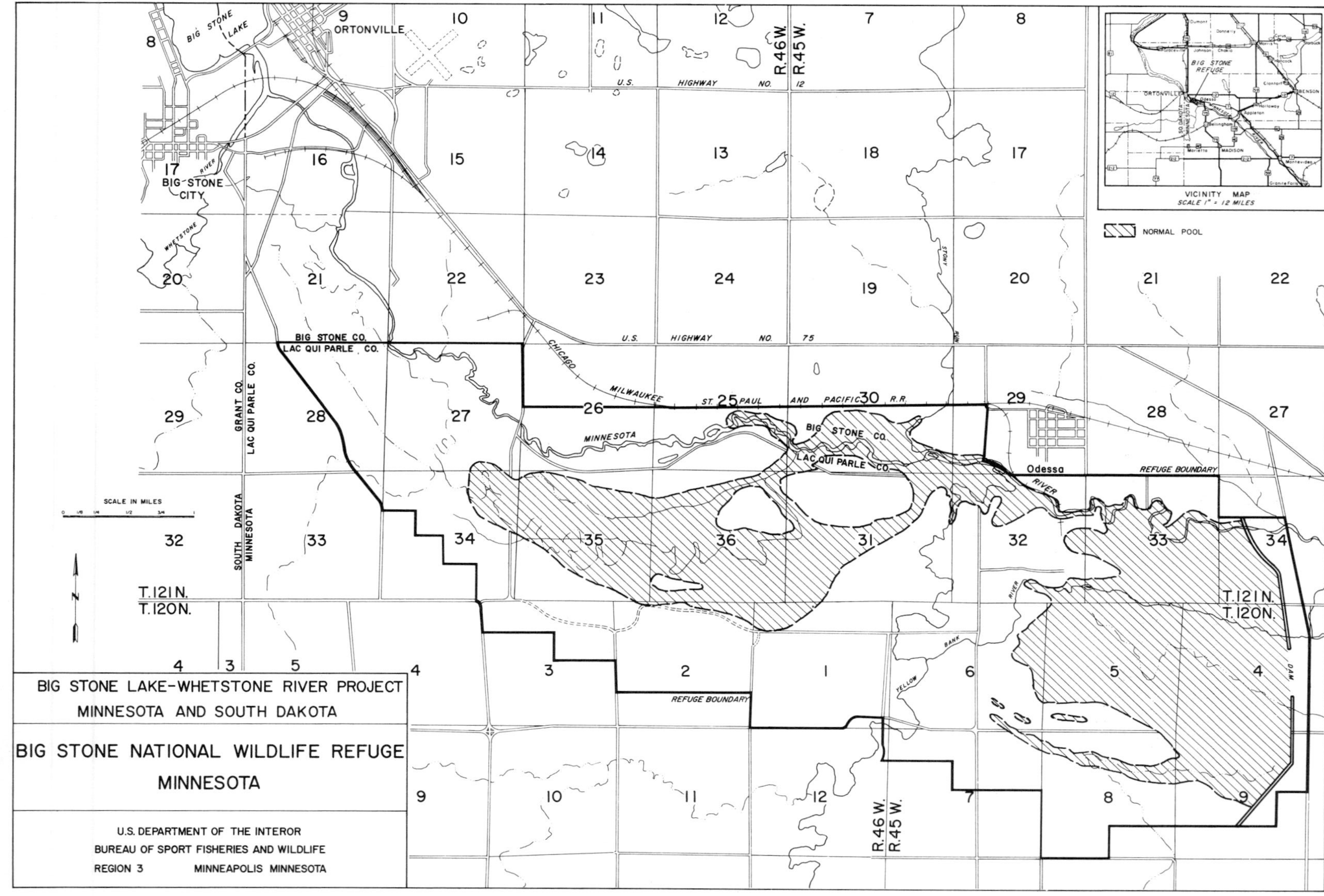
BIG STONE LAKE-WHETSTONE RIVER PROJECT
MINNESOTA AND SOUTH DAKOTA
BIG STONE NATIONAL WILDLIFE REFUGE
MINNESOTA
U.S. DEPARTMENT OF THE INTEROR
BUREAU OF SPORT FISHERIES AND WILDLIFE
REGION 3 MINNEAPOLIS MINNESOTA
SCALE IN MILES
N
T.121N.
T.120N.
SOUTH DAKOTA
MINNESOTA
GRANT CO.
LAC QUI PARLE CO.
BIG STONE CO.
LAC QUI PARLE CO.
BIG STONE LAKE
BIG STONE CITY
WHETSTONE RIVER
ORTONVILLE
U.S. HIGHWAY NO. 12
U.S. HIGHWAY NO. 75
CHICAGO MILWAUKEE ST. PAUL AND PACIFIC R.R.
MINNESOTA RIVER
STONY RUN
YELLOW BANK RIVER
REFUGE BOUNDARY
Odessa
DAM
R.46 W.
R.45 W.
NORMAL POOL
VICINITY MAP
SCALE 1" = 12 MILES
BIG STONE REFUGE
SO DAKOTA
MINNESOTA
ORTONVILLE
Odessa
MADISON
BENSON

Swans using a wetland area on Sherburne National Wildlife Refuge, Minnesota. Photo by U.S. Fish and Wildlife Service.

SHERBURNE NATIONAL WILDLIFE REFUGE

Waterfowl: Canada geese, mallards, pintails, blue-winged teal, American wigeon, wood ducks, and lesser scaup.
Wildlife: Mammals, birds (253 species), reptiles, amphibians, and fish.
Habitats: Lakes, marshes, forest, and cropland.
Size: 30,552 acres.
Location: In eastern Minnesota, about 45 miles north of the Twin Cities and 9 miles southwest of Princeton.
Literature Available: Information circular and map, and bird checklist.
Address: Refuge Manager, Sherburne National Wildlife Refuge, Route 2, Zimmerman, Minnesota 55398.

A typical river scene on the Upper Mississippi River Wild Life and Fish Refuge. Photo by U.S. Fish and Wildlife Service.

TAMARAC NATIONAL WILDLIFE REFUGE

Waterfowl: Canada geese, mallards, green-winged teal, blue-winged teal, wood ducks, ring-necked ducks, lesser scaup, and common goldeneyes.
Wildlife: Mammals, birds (221 species), reptiles, amphibians, and fish.
Habitats: Ottertail and Buffalo rivers, lakes, marshes, bogs, wooded potholes, and fields.
Size: 42,000 acres.
Location: In westcentral Minnesota, west of Ponsford.
Literature Available: Information booklet and bird checklist.
Address: Refuge Manager, Tamarac National Wildlife Refuge, Rochert, Minnesota 56578.

UPPER MISSISSIPPI RIVER WILD LIFE AND FISH REFUGE

Waterfowl: Whistling swans, Canada geese, mallards, gadwalls, American wigeon, teal, wood ducks, canvasbacks, and other diving ducks.
Wildlife: Mammals (57 species), birds (291 species), reptiles (23 species), amphibians (12 species), and fish (113 species).
Habitats: The Mississippi River, wooded islands, marshes, and bluffs.
Size: 194,000 acres.
Location: Extends for 284 miles along the Mississippi River through portions of Minnesota, Wisconsin, Iowa, and Illinois. The main headquarters is located in Winona, Minnesota.
Literature Available: Information circular and map and checklists for mammals, birds, reptiles, and amphibians; river maps for various navigation pools in the refuge are also available for a nominal fee.
Address: Refuge Manager, Upper Mississippi River Wild Life and Fish Refuge, P.O. Box 226, Winona, Minnesota 55987.

Wisconsin

HORICON NATIONAL WILDLIFE REFUGE

Waterfowl: Canada geese, mallards, blue-winged teal, and wood ducks.
Wildlife: Mammals, birds (239 species), reptiles, amphibians, and fish.
Habitats: Horicon Marsh including cattail marsh, open water, and fields.
Size: 21,000 acres.
Location: In eastcentral Wisconsin. The refuge headquarters is reached by driving east from Waupun on State Route 49 for 6.5 miles, then south for 3.7 miles on County Road Z to a sign pointing to the headquarters.
Literature Available: Information circular and map, and bird checklist.
Address: Refuge Manager, Horicon National Wildlife Refuge, Route 2, Mayville, Wisconsin 53050.

NECEDAH NATIONAL WILDLIFE REFUGE

Waterfowl: Canada geese, mallards, black ducks, wood ducks, teal, and hooded mergansers.
Wildlife: Mammals, birds (227 species), reptiles, amphibians, and fish.
Habitats: Marsh, open water, and upland areas.
Size: 40,000 acres.
Location: In central Wisconsin, about 4 miles west of Necedah off State Route 21, then 2 miles north on the entrance road.
Literature Available: Information circular and map, bird checklist, and regulation sheet.
Address: Refuge Manager, Necedah National Wildlife Refuge, Star Route, Necedah, Wisconsin 54646.

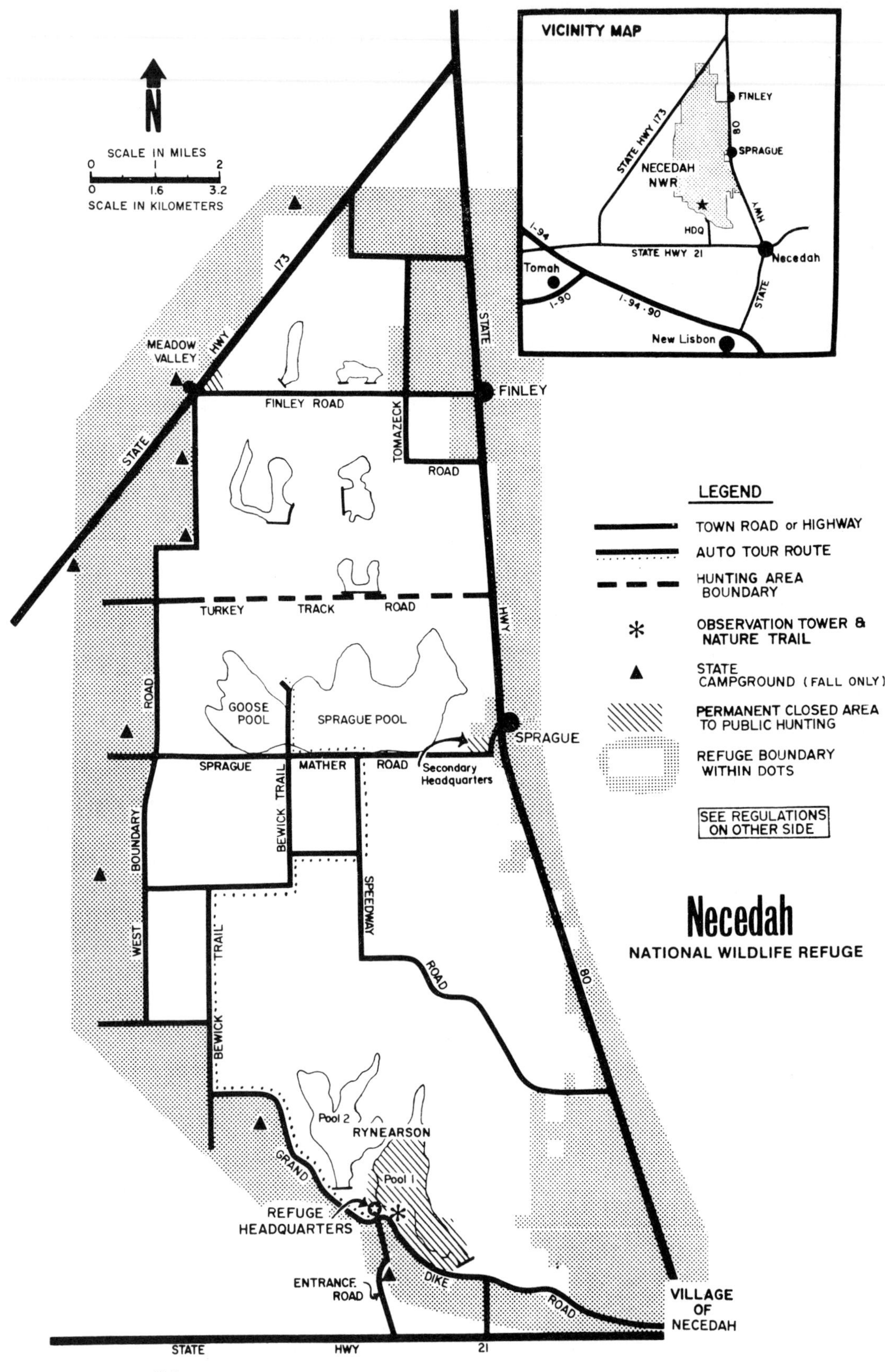

VICINITY MAP
FINLEY
SPRAGUE
NECEDAH NWR
STATE HWY 173
HDQ
HWY 80
I-94
STATE HWY 21
Necedah
Tomah
I-90
I-94-90
STATE
New Lisbon
N
SCALE IN MILES
0 1 2
0 1.6 3.2
SCALE IN KILOMETERS
MEADOW VALLEY
HWY 173
STATE
FINLEY ROAD
TOMAZECK ROAD
FINLEY
STATE HWY
TURKEY TRACK ROAD
GOOSE POOL
SPRAGUE POOL
SPRAGUE
SPRAGUE MATHER ROAD
Secondary Headquarters
WEST BOUNDARY ROAD
BEWICK TRAIL
SPEEDWAY ROAD
80
Pool 2
RYNEARSON
Pool 1
GRAND DIKE ROAD
REFUGE HEADQUARTERS
ENTRANCE ROAD
VILLAGE OF NECEDAH
STATE HWY 21
LEGEND
TOWN ROAD or HIGHWAY
AUTO TOUR ROUTE
HUNTING AREA BOUNDARY
OBSERVATION TOWER & NATURE TRAIL
STATE CAMPGROUND (FALL ONLY)
PERMANENT CLOSED AREA TO PUBLIC HUNTING
REFUGE BOUNDARY WITHIN DOTS
SEE REGULATIONS ON OTHER SIDE
Necedah
NATIONAL WILDLIFE REFUGE

The marshes and other wetlands of the Horicon National Wildlife Refuge form one of Wisconsin's major waterfowl areas. Photo by U.S. Fish and Wildlife Service.

Michigan

SENEY NATIONAL WILDLIFE REFUGE

Waterfowl: Canada geese, snow geese, mallards, black ducks, ring-necked ducks, common mergansers, and hooded mergansers.
Wildlife: Mammals, birds, reptiles, amphibians, and fish.
Habitats: Marshes, ponds, lakes, woodland, and farmland.
Size: 95,455 acres.
Location: The Upper Peninsula, just west of Germfask.
Literature Available: General information sheet and map.
Address: Refuge Manager, Seney National Wildlife Refuge, Seney, Michigan 49883.

SHIAWASSEE NATIONAL WILDLIFE REFUGE

Waterfowl: Whistling swans, Canada geese, mallards, black ducks, and blue-winged teal.
Wildlife: Mammals, birds, reptiles, amphibians, and fish.
Habitats: Rivers, flooded plains, and farmland.
Size: 8,860 acres.
Location: The central part of the Lower Peninsula, about 7 miles southwest of Saginaw.
Literature Available: General information sheet.
Address: Refuge Manager, Shiawassee National Wildlife Refuge, 6975 Mower Road, R.D. 1, Saginaw, Michigan 48601.

Illinois

CHAUTAUQUA NATIONAL WILDLIFE REFUGE

Waterfowl: Canada geese, snow geese, mallards, wood ducks, and various other duck species.
Wildlife: Mammals (28 species), birds (240 species), reptiles, amphibians, and fish.
Habitats: Lake Chautauqua, marshes, swamps, bottomland hardwood forests, a sandy bluff, springs, and fields.
Size: 4,477 acres.
Location: In central Illinois, about 9 miles north of Havana off Manito Blacktop Road.
Literature Available: Information sheet and map, and mammal and bird checklists.
Address: Refuge Manager, Chautauqua National Wildlife Refuge, Havana, Illinois 62644.

Seney National Wildlife Refuge is an important Michigan waterfowl area. Photo by U.S. Fish and Wildlife Service.

CHAUTAUQUA NATIONAL WILDLIFE REFUGE
MASON COUNTY, ILLINOIS

UNITED STATES DEPARTMENT OF THE INTERIOR

FISH AND WILDLIFE SERVICE BUREAU OF SPORT FISHERIES AND WILDLIFE

Open to waterfowl hunting only.
Blinds must be constructed by the hunter from existing dead vegetation & are available on a first-come basis daily.
Access to hunting area is by water only. Boats may be rented or launched at Boatyard No. 3 or at Liverpool.
Camping is not allowed on the refuge.

CRAB ORCHARD NATIONAL WILDLIFE REFUGE

Waterfowl: Canada geese, snow geese, mallards, black ducks, gadwalls, pintails, green-winged teal, blue-winged teal, American wigeon, northern shovelers, wood ducks, ring-necked ducks, lesser scaup, common goldeneyes, buffleheads, ruddy ducks, hooded mergansers, and common mergansers.
Wildlife: Mammals, birds (238 species), reptiles, amphibians, and fish.
Habitats: Lakes, ponds, wooded areas, and fields.
Size: 43,000 acres.
Location: In southern Illinois, just east of Carbondale.
Literature Available: Information circular and bird checklists.
Address: Refuge Manager, Crab Orchard National Wildlife Refuge, P.O. Box J, Carterville, Illinois 62918.

MARK TWAIN NATIONAL WILDLIFE REFUGE

Waterfowl: Canada geese, snow geese, mallards, black ducks, pintails, wood ducks, ring-necked ducks, and lesser scaup.
Wildlife: Mammals, birds (221 species), reptiles, amphibians, and fish.
Habitats: Mississippi River, islands, wooded bottomlands, marshes, sloughs, ponds, and fields.
Size: 21,000 acres.
Location: A 250-mile section of the Mississippi River in Iowa, Illinois, and Missouri. There are eight units along the Mississippi River, and four other units along the Illinois River. Each unit has its own regulations; full details are available from the refuge manager.
Literature Available: Information circular and map, bird and other checklists.
Address: Refuge Manager, Mark Twain National Wildlife Refuge, P.O. Box 225, Quincy, Illinois 62301.

Indiana

MUSCATATUCK NATIONAL WILDLIFE REFUGE

Waterfowl: Canada geese, snow geese, and wood ducks.
Wildlife: Mammals, birds, reptiles, amphibians, and fish.
Habitats: Ponds and lakes, marshes, woodland, and farmland.
Size: 7,702 acres.
Location: In southcentral Indiana, 3 miles east of Seymour.
Literature Available: General information circular and map.
Address: Refuge Manager, Muscatatuck National Wildlife Refuge, P.O. Box 631, Seymour, Indiana 47274.

Ohio

OTTAWA NATIONAL WILDLIFE REFUGE

Waterfowl: Whistling swans, geese, and ducks.
Wildlife: Mammals, birds (290 species), reptiles, amphibians, and fish.
Habitat: Freshwater marshes and adjacent areas.
Size: 4,800 acres.
Location: Northern Ohio, east of Toledo.
Literature Available: Information sheet and map.
Address: Refuge Manager, Ottawa National Wildlife Refuge, 14000 W. State, Route 2, Oak Harbor, Ohio 43449.

Northcentral States

Montana

BENTON LAKE NATIONAL WILDLIFE REFUGE

Waterfowl: Snow geese, mallards, gadwalls, pintails, green-winged teal, blue-winged teal, American wigeon, and northern shovelers.
Wildlife: Mammals, birds (142 species), reptiles, amphibians, and fish.
Habitats: Prairie marsh and lake.
Size: 12,383 acres.
Location: In northcentral Montana, 12 miles north of Great Falls.
Literature Available: Information circular and map and bird checklist.
Address: Refuge Manager, Benton Lake National Wildlife Refuge, P.O. Box 450, Black Eagle, Montana 59414.

BOWDOIN NATIONAL WILDLIFE REFUGE

Waterfowl: Canada geese, mallards, gadwalls, pintails, blue-winged teal, American wigeon, northern shovelers, and ruddy ducks.
Wildlife: Mammals, birds (213 species), reptiles, amphibians, and fish.
Habitats: Milk River, lakes, ponds, marsh, and fields.
Size: 15,500 acres.
Location: In northeastern Montana, 7 miles east of Malta.
Literature Available: Information circular, map, bird checklist, and self-guiding tour route circular.
Address: Refuge Manager, Bowdoin National Wildlife Refuge, P.O. Box J, Malta, Montana 59538.

CHARLES M. RUSSELL NATIONAL WILDLIFE RANGE

Waterfowl: Canada geese, mallards, pintails, and blue-winged teal.
Wildlife: Mammals, birds (218 species), reptiles, amphibians, and fish.
Habitats: Prairie, forested coulees, badlands, river bottoms, and reservoirs.
Size: 1,000,000 acres.
Location: In northcentral Montana, extending 125 miles along the Missouri River from the Fort Peck Dam.
Literature Available: Information circular and map, bird checklist, wildlife tour route leaflet, and special regulations.
Address: Refuge Manager, Charles M. Russell National Wildlife Range, Box 110, Airport Road, Lewistown, Montana 59457; or Assistant Refuge Manager, Charles M. Russell National Wildlife Range, Slippery Ann Wildlife Station, Roy, Montana 59471; or Assistant Refuge Manager, Charles M. Russell National Wildlife Range, P.O. Box 166, Fort Peck, Montana 59223.

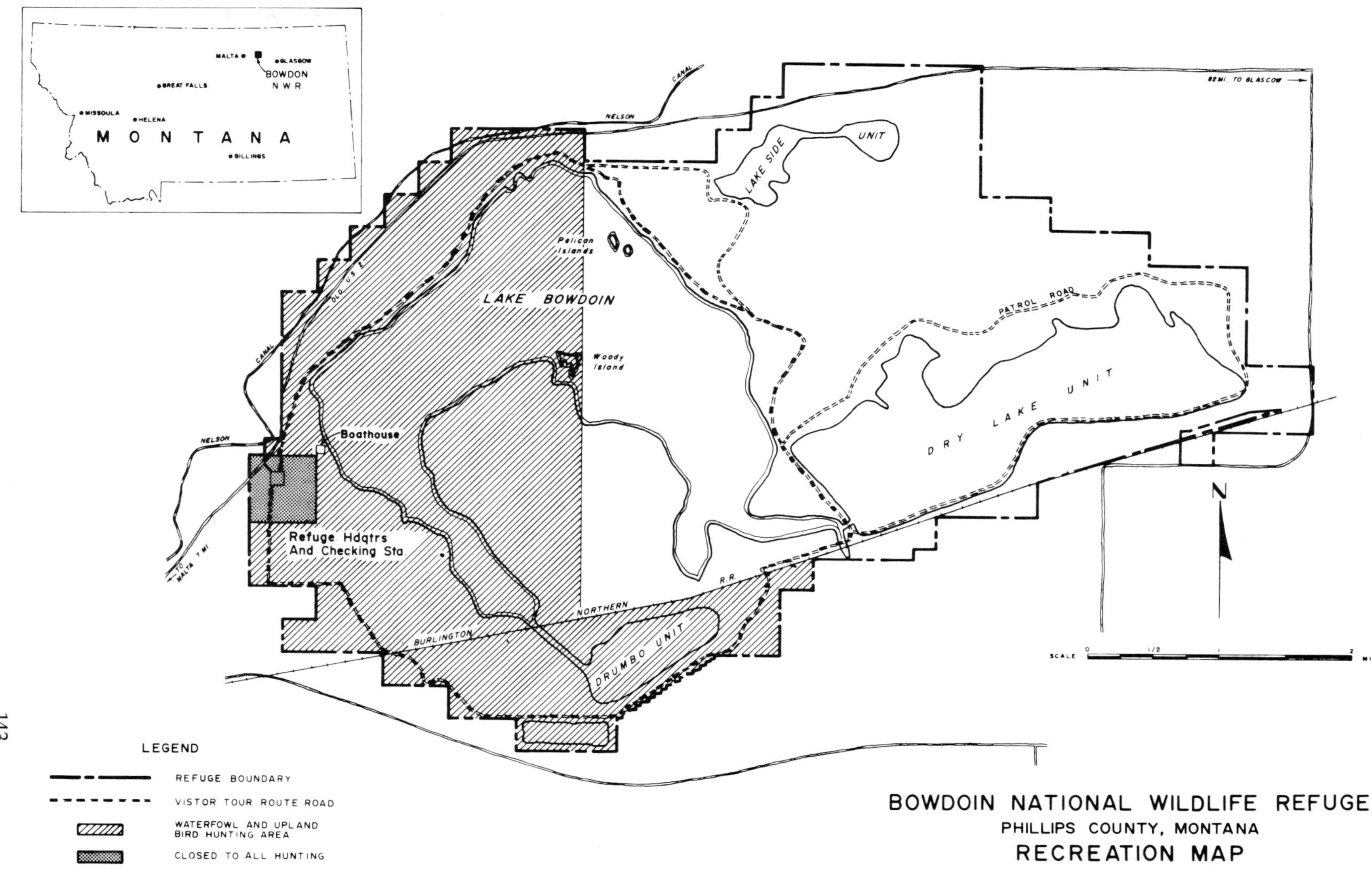
MONTANA
MALTA
GLASGOW
BOWDON N.W.R.
GREAT FALLS
MISSOULA
HELENA
BILLINGS
NELSON
CANAL
22 MI. TO GLASCOW
LAKE SIDE UNIT
Pelican Islands
LAKE BOWDOIN
OLD U.S. 2
CANAL
PATROL ROAD
Woody Island
DRY LAKE UNIT
NELSON
Boathouse
Refuge Hdqtrs And Checking Sta.
TO MALTA 7 MI.
R.R.
NORTHERN
BURLINGTON
DRUMBO UNIT
SCALE 0 1/2 1 2 MILES
LEGEND
REFUGE BOUNDARY
VISTOR TOUR ROUTE ROAD
WATERFOWL AND UPLAND BIRD HUNTING AREA
CLOSED TO ALL HUNTING
BOWDOIN NATIONAL WILDLIFE REFUGE
PHILLIPS COUNTY, MONTANA
RECREATION MAP

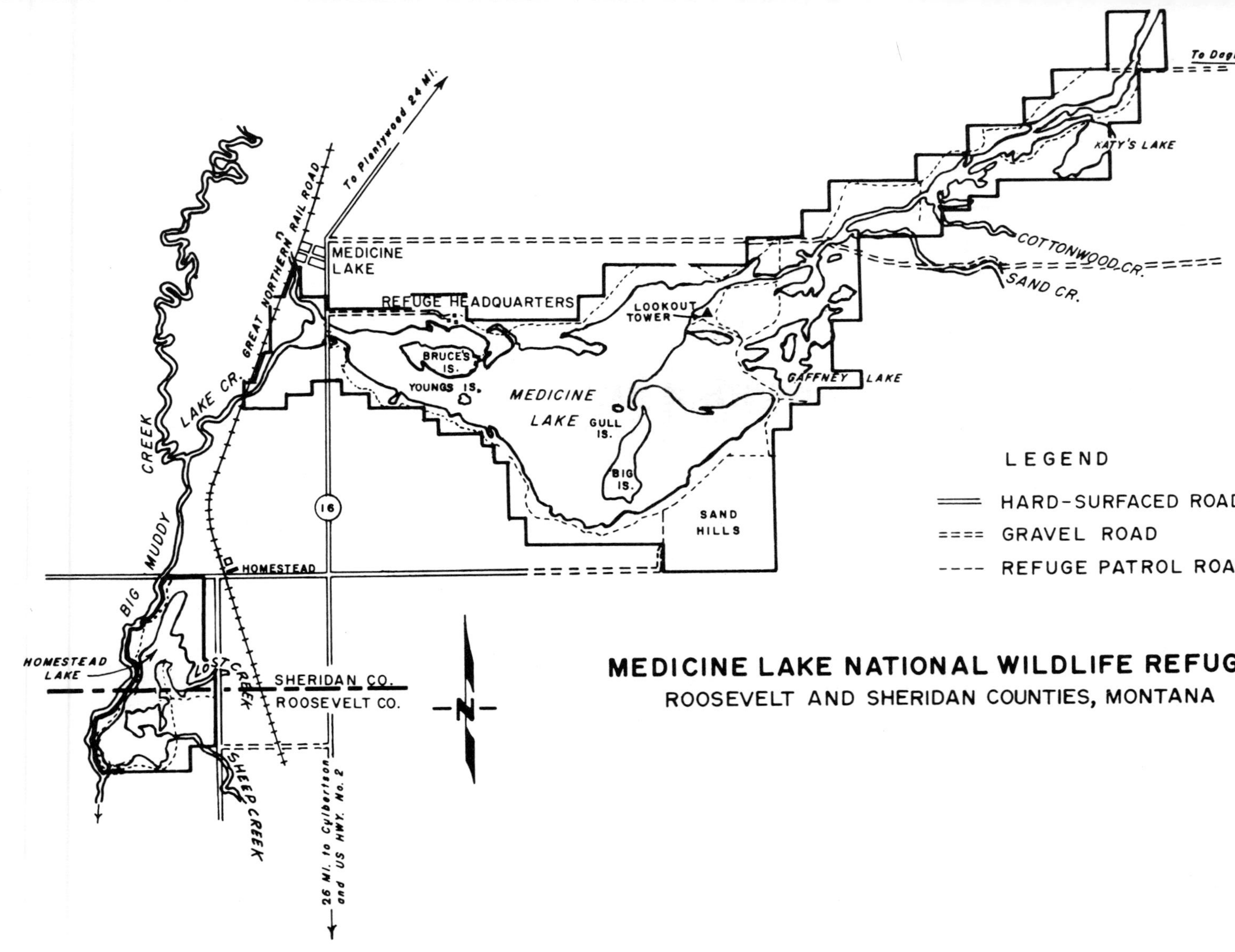

MEDICINE LAKE NATIONAL WILDLIFE REFUGE
ROOSEVELT AND SHERIDAN COUNTIES, MONTANA

MEDICINE LAKE NATIONAL WILDLIFE REFUGE

Waterfowl: Canada geese, mallards, gadwalls, pintails, American wigeon, blue-winged teal, northern shovelers, redheads, canvasbacks, and ruddy ducks.
Wildlife: Mammals, birds (204 species), reptiles, amphibians, and fish.
Habitats: Lakes, ponds, pasture, meadowland, and farming plots.
Size: 31,457 acres.
Location: Northeastern Montana, just south of Medicine Lake.
Literature Available: Information sheet and map, bird checklist, and auto tour guide.
Address: Refuge Manager, Medicine Lake National Wildlife Refuge, Medicine Lake, Montana 59247.

RAVALLI NATIONAL WILDLIFE REFUGE

Waterfowl: Mallards, wood ducks, teal, and hooded mergansers.
Wildlife: Mammals, birds (163 species), reptiles, amphibians, and fish.
Habitats: Marshes, wet meadows, cottonwood, ponderosa pine stands, upland areas, and fields.
Size: 2,800 acres.
Location: In western Montana, a few miles north of Stevensville.
Literature Available: Map and bird checklist.
Address: Refuge Manager, Ravalli National Wildlife Refuge, Box 257, Stevensville, Montana 59870.

RED ROCK LAKES NATIONAL WILDLIFE REFUGE

Waterfowl: Whistling swans, trumpeter swans, Canada geese, mallards, gadwalls, pintails, cinnamon teal, American wigeon, canvasbacks, and lesser scaup.
Wildlife: Mammals (44 species), birds (215 species), reptiles, amphibians, and fish.
Habitats: Mountains, lakes, ponds, creeks, and marshes.
Size: 40,000 acres.
Location: In southwestern Montana, about 28 miles east of Monida.
Literature Available: Information circular, maps, mammal and bird checklists, Trumpeter Swan report, and other information.
Address: Refuge Manager, Red Rock Lakes National Wildlife Refuge, Monida Star Route, Box 15, Lima, Montana 59739.

This aerial view of the Red Rock Lakes National Wildlife Refuge, Montana, is looking east with the Red Rock River and marsh in the foreground and Upper Red Rock Lake in the background. Photo by Ray Glahn / U.S. Fish and Wildlife Service.

North Dakota

ARROWWOOD NATIONAL WILDLIFE REFUGE

Waterfowl: Canada geese, mallards, gadwalls, pintails, blue-winged teal, American wigeon, northern shovelers, and wood ducks.
Wildlife: Mammals, birds, reptiles, amphibians, and fish.
Habitats: Arrowwood Lake, ponds, marshes, grassland, and cultivated fields.
Size: 15,934 acres.
Location: In eastern North Dakota, 6 miles east of Edmunds.
Literature Available: Map, bird checklist, and trail guide.
Address: Refuge Manager, Arrowwood National Wildlife Refuge, Rural Route 1, Pingree, North Dakota 58476.

AUDUBON NATIONAL WILDLIFE REFUGE

Waterfowl: Canada geese, white-fronted geese, snow geese, mallards, gadwalls, pintails, green-winged teal, blue-winged teal, American wigeon, northern shovelers, redheads, lesser scaup, buffleheads, ruddy ducks, and common mergansers.
Wildlife: Mammals, birds (186 species), reptiles, amphibians, and fish.
Habitats: Lake Audubon, marshy bays, shoreline, prairie potholes, short grass prairie, and planted shelter belts.
Size: 14,735 acres.
Location: In westcentral North Dakota, behind Garrison Dam, north of Coleharbor.
Literature Available: Information circular and map, and bird checklists.
Address: Refuge Manager, Audubon National Wildlife Refuge, R.R. 1, Coleharbor, North Dakota 58531.

DES LACS NATIONAL WILDLIFE REFUGE

Waterfowl: Canada geese, white-fronted geese, snow geese, mallards, gadwalls, pintails, and blue-winged teal.
Wildlife: Mammals, birds, reptiles, amphibians, and fish.
Habitats: Lakes, marshes, shallow bays, short-grass prairie, lowland meadows, and wooded coulees.
Size: 18,841 acres.
Location: In northwestern North Dakota, just west of Kenmare.
Literature Available: Information sheet and map, bird checklist, and tour route guide.
Address: Refuge Manager, Des Lacs National Wildlife Refuge, Kenmare, North Dakota 58746.

J. CLARK SALYER NATIONAL WILDLIFE REFUGE

Waterfowl: Canada geese, white-fronted geese, snow geese, mallards, gadwalls, pintails, blue-winged teal, American wigeon, northern shovel-

An aerial view of the Souris River on the J. Clark Salyer National Wildlife Refuge, North Dakota. Photo by U.S. Fish and Wildlife Service.

ers, wood ducks, redheads, canvasbacks, lesser scaup, and ruddy ducks.
Wildlife: Mammals, birds, reptiles, amphibians, and fish.
Habitats: Souris River, pools, marshes, and nesting islands.
Size: 58,700 acres.
Location: In northcentral North Dakota, headquarters being located 3 miles north of Upham.
Literature Available: Information circular and map, bird checklist, and canoe trail guide.
Address: Refuge Manager, J. Clark Salyer National Wildlife Refuge, Upham, North Dakota 58789.

LAKE ILO NATIONAL WILDLIFE REFUGE

Waterfowl: Mallards, pintails, blue-winged teal, northern shovelers, and gadwalls.
Wildlife: Mammals, birds, reptiles, amphibians, and fish.
Habitats: Lake Ilo and wildlife plantings around the lake.
Size: 3,963 acres.

Location: In western North Dakota, 1 mile west of Dunn Center.
Literature Available: Information sheet and map.
Address: Refuge Manager, Lake Ilo National Wildlife Refuge, Dunn Center, North Dakota 58626.

LONG LAKE NATIONAL WILDLIFE REFUGE

Waterfowl: Canada geese, white-fronted geese, mallards, gadwalls, pintails, and blue-winged teal.
Wildlife: Mammals, birds (193 species), reptiles, amphibians, and fish.
Habitats: Long Lake, marshes, prairie grasslands, ravines, tree and shrub plantings, and cultivated fields.
Size: 22,310 acres.
Location: In southcentral North Dakota, 4 miles southeast of Moffit.
Literature Available: Information sheet and map, and bird checklist.
Address: Refuge Manager, Long Lake National Wildlife Refuge, Moffit, North Dakota 58560.

LOSTWOOD NATIONAL WILDLIFE REFUGE

Waterfowl: Mallards, pintails, scaup, teal, gadwalls, northern shovelers, American wigeon, redheads, and canvasbacks.
Wildlife: Mammals, birds, reptiles, amphibians, and fish.
Habitats: Lakes, sloughs, potholes, and rolling prairie.
Size: 26,747 acres.
Location: In northwestern North Dakota, 18 miles west of Kenmare.
Literature Available: Information sheet and map, and mammal and bird checklists.
Address: Refuge Manager, Lostwood National Wildlife Refuge, Rural Route 2, Kenmare, North Dakota 58746.

SLADE NATIONAL WILDLIFE REFUGE

Waterfowl: Mallards, gadwalls, pintails, blue-winged teal, and northern shovelers.
Wildlife: Mammals, birds (197 species), reptiles, amphibians, and fish.
Habitats: Potholes, lakes, and marshes.
Size: 3,000 acres.
Location: Southcentral North Dakota near Dawson.
Literature Available: Bird checklist.
Address: Refuge Manager, Slade National Wildlife Refuge, Route 1, Cayuga, North Dakota 58013.

TEWAUKON NATIONAL WILDLIFE REFUGE

Waterfowl: Snow geese, mallards, pintails, scaup, and various other species of ducks.
Wildlife: Mammals, birds (235 species), reptiles, amphibians, and fish.
Habitats: Wild Rice River, Lake Tewaukon, Cutler Marsh, White Lake, Clouds Lake, and prairie potholes.
Size: 7,869 acres.

Potholes such as this on the Lostwood National Wildlife Refuge, North Dakota, are important waterfowl production areas. Photo by M. C. Hammond / U.S. Fish and Wildlife Service.

Location: The southeastern corner of North Dakota on State Route 11, 4 miles south of Cayuga.
Literature Available: Information sheet and map, bird checklist, and tour route leaflet.
Address: Refuge Manager, Tewaukon National Wildlife Refuge, Cayuga, North Dakota 58013.

UPPER SOURIS NATIONAL WILDLIFE REFUGE

Waterfowl: Canada geese, white-fronted geese, snow geese, mallards, gadwalls, pintails, and blue-winged teal.
Wildlife: Mammals, birds, reptiles, amphibians, and fish.
Habitats: Lake Darling, marshes, cropland, and pastures.
Size: 32,000 acres.

Location: In northwestern North Dakota, 25 miles northwest of Minot.
Literature Available: Information sheet and map, bird checklist, and regulations.
Address: Refuge Manager, Upper Souris National Wildlife Refuge, Foxholm, North Dakota 58738.

South Dakota

LACREEK NATIONAL WILDLIFE REFUGE

Waterfowl: Trumpeter swans, Canada geese, mallards, gadwalls, blue-winged teal, northern shovelers, and ruddy ducks.
Wildlife: Mammals, birds (235 species), reptiles, amphibians, and fish.
Habitats: Open water, marsh and prairie uplands.
Size: 16,147 acres.
Location: In southwestern South Dakota, a few miles southeast of Martin.
Literature Available: Map and bird checklist.
Address: Refuge Manager, Lacreek National Wildlife Refuge, South Rural Route, Martin, South Dakota 57551.

LAKE ANDES NATIONAL WILDLIFE REFUGE

Waterfowl: Canada geese, mallards, gadwalls, pintails, green-winged teal, blue-winged teal, American wigeon, and lesser scaup.
Wildlife: Mammals, birds (200 species), reptiles, amphibians, and fish.
Habitats: Lake Andes, marsh, and upland.
Size: 5,450 acres.
Location: Southeastern South Dakota, just east of Lake Andes.
Literature Available: Map and bird checklist.
Address: Refuge Manager, Lake Andes National Wildlife Refuge, P.O. Box 279, Lake Andes, South Dakota 57356.

SAND LAKE NATIONAL WILDLIFE REFUGE

Waterfowl: Canada geese, snow geese, mallards, pintails, gadwalls, American wigeon, green-winged teal, blue-winged teal, northern shovelers, redheads, canvasbacks, and lesser scaup.
Wildlife: Mammals, birds (226 species), reptiles, amphibians, and fish.
Habitats: James River, marshes, open water, fields, and plains.
Size: 21,451 acres.
Location: In northeastern South Dakota, near Columbia.
Literature Available: Information circular, map, and bird checklists.
Address: Refuge Manager, Sand Lake National Wildlife Refuge, Columbia, South Dakota 57433.

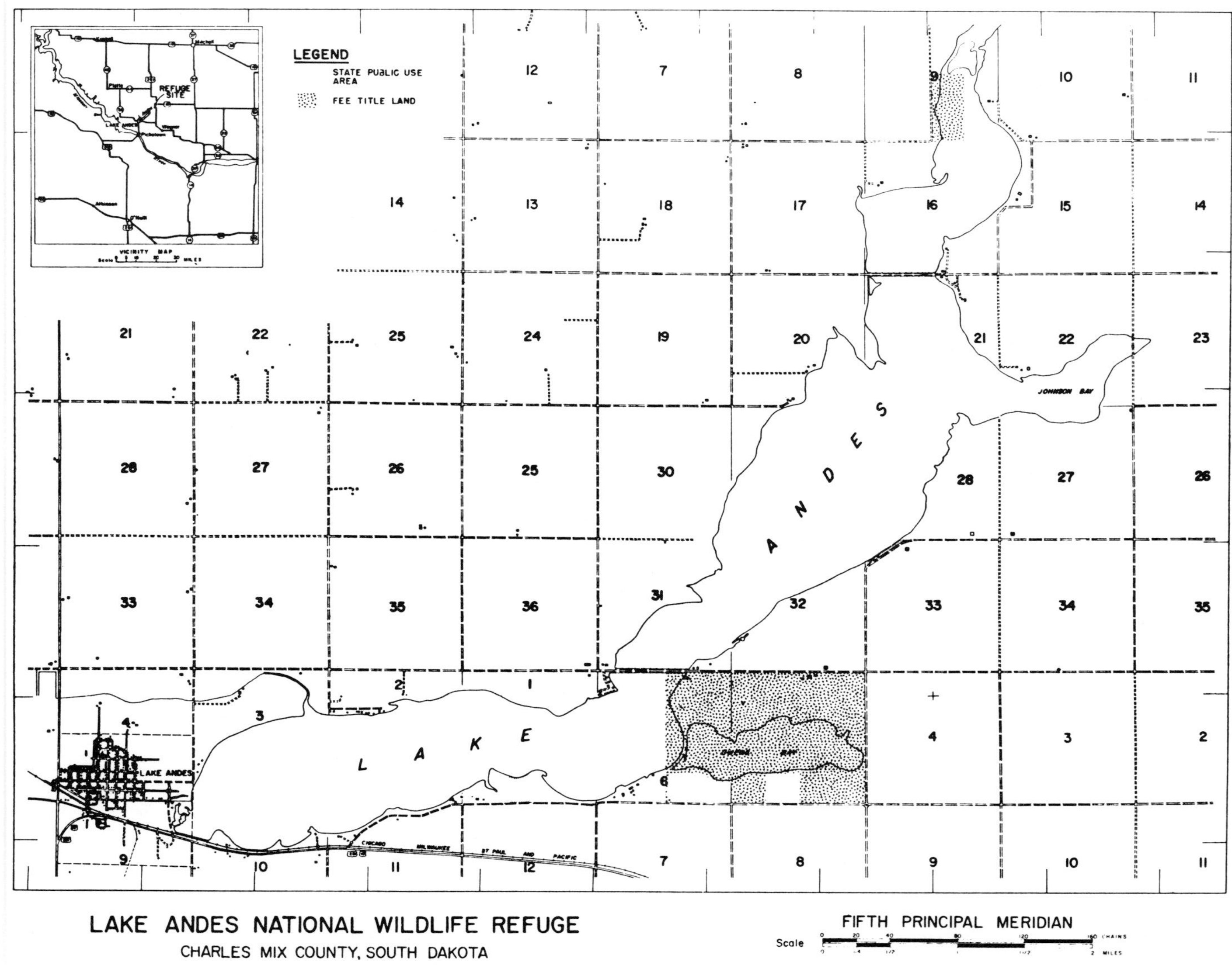

LAKE ANDES NATIONAL WILDLIFE REFUGE
CHARLES MIX COUNTY, SOUTH DAKOTA

WAUBAY NATIONAL WILDLIFE REFUGE

Waterfowl: Canada geese, mallards, gadwalls, blue-winged teal, and lesser scaup.
Wildlife: Mammals, birds (232 species), reptiles, amphibians, and fish.
Habitats: Rolling prairie hills, potholes, marshes, lakes, ponds, oak timber, and grassland.
Size: 4,650 acres.
Location: In northeastern South Dakota, about 8 miles north of Waubay on Spring Lake.
Literature Available: Information sheet and map, and bird checklist.
Address: Refuge Manager, Waubay National Wildlife Refuge, R.R. 1, Waubay, South Dakota 57273.

Wyoming

HUTTON LAKE NATIONAL WILDLIFE REFUGE

Waterfowl: Canada geese, mallards, gadwalls, pintails, green-winged teal, blue-winged teal, American wigeon, northern shovelers, redheads, canvasbacks, lesser scaup, buffleheads, ruddy ducks, and common mergansers.
Wildlife: Mammals, birds (176 species), reptiles, amphibians, and fish.
Habitats: Lakes, creeks, and marsh.
Size: 2,000 acres.
Location: In Albany County, 12 miles southwest of Laramie.
Literature Available: Map and bird checklist.
Address: Refuge Manager, Arapaho National Wildlife Refuge, P.O. Box 457, Walden, Colorado 80480.

SEEDSKADEE NATIONAL WILDLIFE REFUGE

Waterfowl: Canada geese, mallards, gadwalls, pintails, green-winged teal, blue-winged teal, American wigeon, northern shovelers, common goldeneyes, and common mergansers.
Wildlife: Mammals, birds (174 species), reptiles, amphibians, and fish.
Habitats: Green River, 35 miles of river bottomland, and meadows.
Size: 14,285 acres.
Location: On the Green River in southwestern Wyoming, southwest of Farson. The headquarters is in the Sweetwater County Courthouse in Green River.
Literature Available: Map and bird checklist.
Address: Refuge Manager, Seedskadee National Wildlife Refuge, Box 67, Green River, Wyoming 82935.

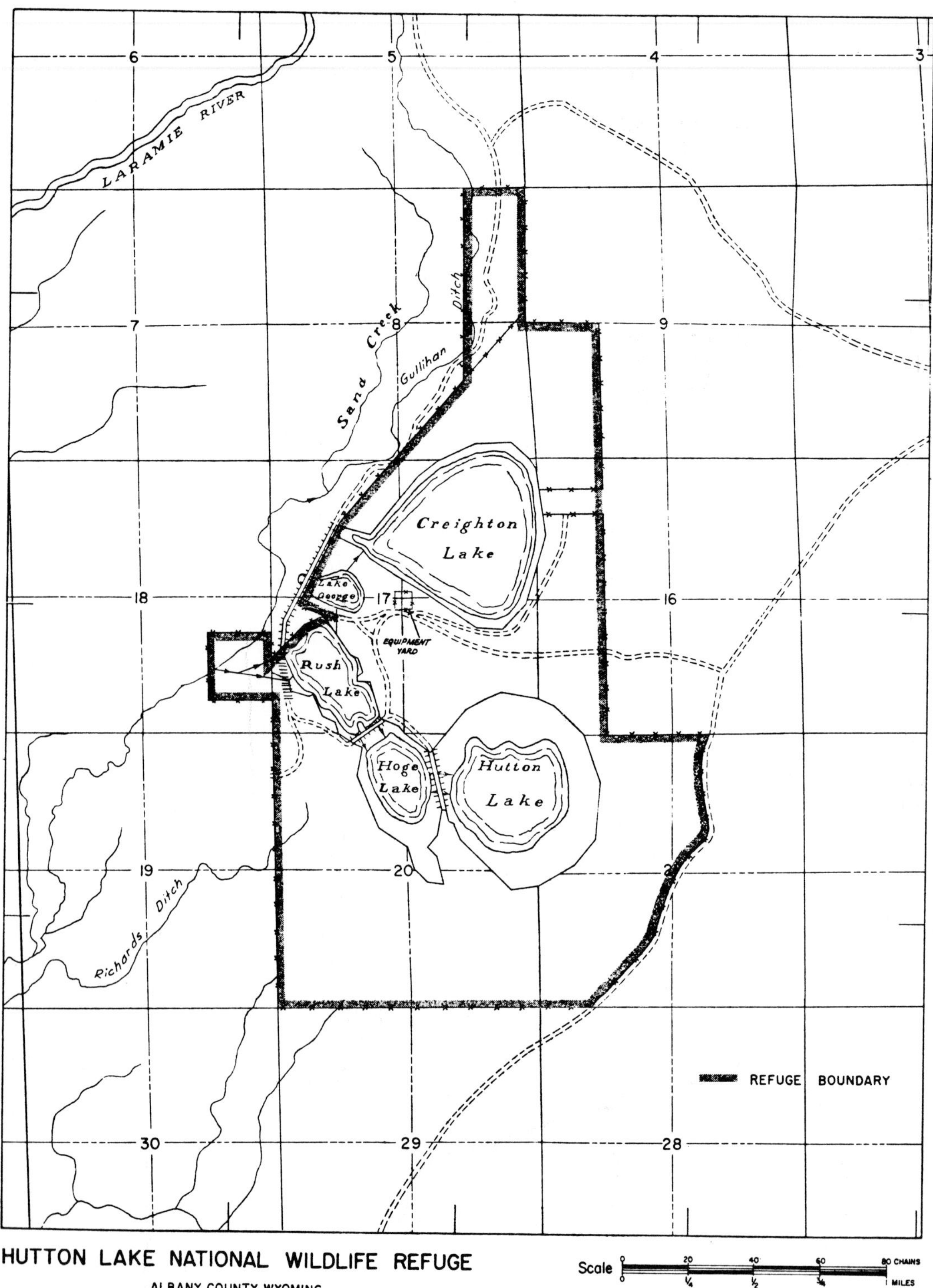

HUTTON LAKE NATIONAL WILDLIFE REFUGE

ALBANY COUNTY, WYOMING

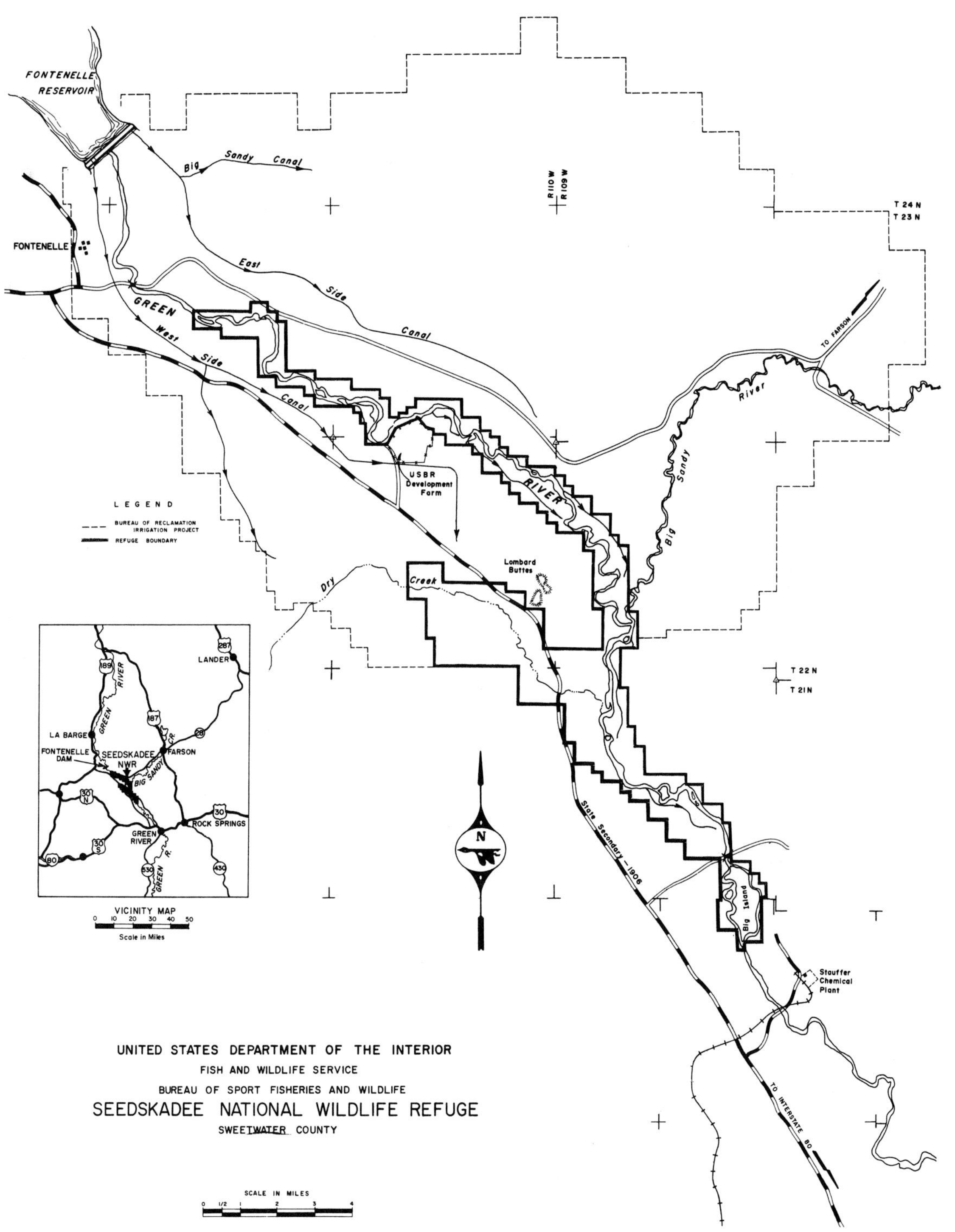
FONTENELLE RESERVOIR
Big Sandy Canal
R 110 W
R 109 W
T 24 N
T 23 N
FONTENELLE
East Side Canal
GREEN
West Side Canal
TO FARSON
Big Sandy River
USBR Development Farm
RIVER
LEGEND
BUREAU OF RECLAMATION IRRIGATION PROJECT
REFUGE BOUNDARY
Lombard Buttes
Dry Creek
T 22 N
T 21 N
LANDER
GREEN RIVER
LA BARGE
FONTENELLE DAM
SEEDSKADEE NWR
FARSON
BIG SANDY CR.
ROCK SPRINGS
GREEN RIVER
GREEN R.
N
State Secondary - 1906
Big Island
VICINITY MAP
0 10 20 30 40 50
Scale in Miles
Stauffer Chemical Plant
UNITED STATES DEPARTMENT OF THE INTERIOR
FISH AND WILDLIFE SERVICE
BUREAU OF SPORT FISHERIES AND WILDLIFE
SEEDSKADEE NATIONAL WILDLIFE REFUGE
SWEETWATER COUNTY
TO INTERSTATE 80
SCALE IN MILES
0 1/2 1 2 3 4

Nebraska

CRESCENT LAKE NATIONAL WILDLIFE REFUGE

Waterfowl: Canada geese, mallards, gadwalls, pintails, green-winged teal, blue-winged teal, American wigeon, northern shovelers, and ruddy ducks.
Wildlife: Mammals, birds (218 species), reptiles, amphibians, and fish.
Habitats: Prairie, sandhills, and lakes.
Size: 46,000 acres.
Location: In the Panhandle region of western Nebraska, 28 miles north of Oshkosh.
Literature Available: Information circular and map, bird checklist, and native sandhills grasses booklet.
Address: Refuge Manager, Crescent Lake National Wildlife Refuge, Star Route, Ellsworth, Nebraska 69340.

FORT NIOBRARA NATIONAL WILDLIFE REFUGE

Waterfowl: Canada geese, mallards, gadwalls, pintails, green-winged teal, blue-winged teal, American wigeon, northern shovelers, redheads, ring-necked ducks, lesser scaup, and common mergansers.
Wildlife: Mammals, birds (201 species), reptiles, amphibians, and fish.
Habitats: Niobrara River, ponds, sandhills prairie, and mixed hardwoods.
Size: 19,123 acres.
Location: In northcentral Nebraska, 3 miles east of Valentine.
Literature Available: Information circular and map, and bird checklist.
Address: Refuge Manager, Fort Niobrara National Wildlife Refuge, Hidden Timber Road, Valentine, Nebraska 69201.

VALENTINE NATIONAL WILDLIFE REFUGE

Waterfowl: Mallards, gadwalls, pintails, green-winged teal, blue-winged teal, American wigeon, northern shovelers, redheads, canvasbacks, lesser scaup, buffleheads, ruddy ducks, and common mergansers.
Wildlife: Mammals, birds (221 species), reptiles, amphibians, and fish.
Habitats: Marshes, lakes, meadows, and grassy hills.
Size: 71,516 acres.
Location: In northcentral Nebraska, southwest of Valentine.
Literature Available: Information sheet and map, bird checklist, regulations, and fishing information.
Address: Refuge Manager, Valentine National Wildlife Refuge, Valentine, Nebraska 69201.

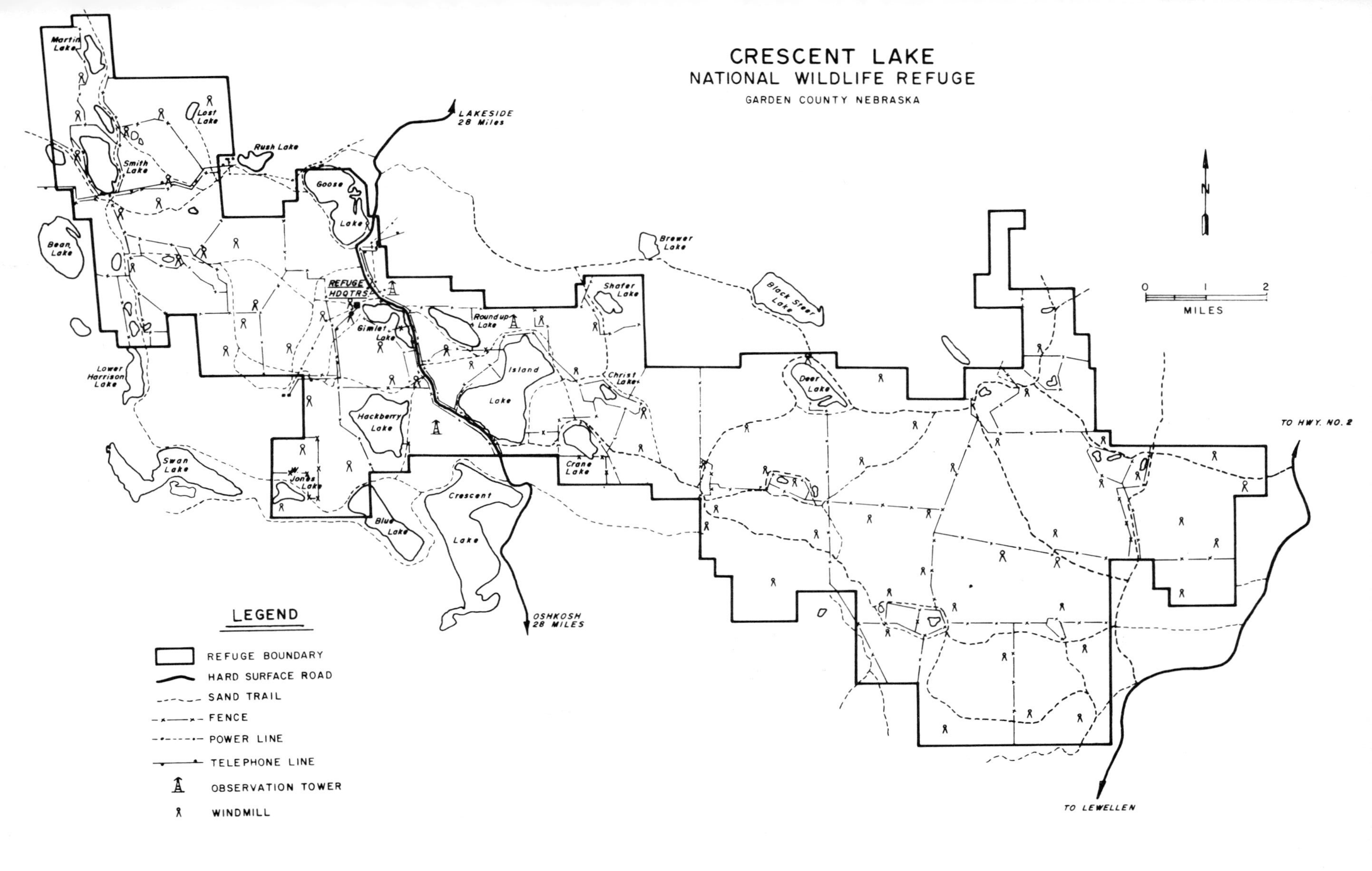
CRESCENT LAKE
NATIONAL WILDLIFE REFUGE
GARDEN COUNTY NEBRASKA
LAKESIDE 28 Miles
Martin Lake
Lost Lake
Rush Lake
Smith Lake
Goose Lake
Bean Lake
Lower Harrison Lake
Swan Lake
Jones Lake
REFUGE HDQTRS.
Gimlet Lake
Hackberry Lake
Roundup Lake
Island Lake
Blue Lake
Crescent Lake
Crane Lake
Christ Lake
Shafer Lake
Brewer Lake
Black Steer Lake
Deer Lake
OSHKOSH 28 MILES
TO HWY. NO. 2
TO LEWELLEN
N
0
1
2
MILES
LEGEND
REFUGE BOUNDARY
HARD SURFACE ROAD
SAND TRAIL
FENCE
POWER LINE
TELEPHONE LINE
OBSERVATION TOWER
WINDMILL

Iowa

DeSOTO NATIONAL WILDLIFE REFUGE

Waterfowl: Canada geese, white-fronted geese, snow geese, mallards, black ducks, gadwalls, pintails, green-winged teal, blue-winged teal, American wigeon, northern shovelers, wood ducks, ring-necked ducks, lesser scaup, buffleheads, and common mergansers.
Wildlife: Mammals, birds (195 species), reptiles, amphibians, and fish.
Habitats: Missouri River, DeSoto Lake, long sandbars, steep banks, and fields.
Size: 7,800 acres.
Location: In western Iowa, 6 miles west of Missouri Valley on U.S. Route 30.
Literature Available: Information circular and map, bird checklists, and steamboat Bertrand circular.
Address: Refuge Manager, DeSoto National Wildlife Refuge, Route 1-B, Missouri Valley, Iowa 51555.

UNION SLOUGH NATIONAL WILDLIFE REFUGE

Waterfowl: Canada geese, snow geese, mallards, black ducks, gadwalls, pintails, green-winged teal, blue-winged teal, American wigeon, northern shovelers, wood ducks, redheads, ring-necked ducks, canvasbacks, and ruddy ducks.
Wildlife: Mammals, birds (219 species), reptiles, amphibians, and fish.
Habitats: Union Slough, marshes, upland areas, and agricultural lands.
Size: 2,155 acres.
Location: On the eastern edge of the northern Great Plains in northcentral Iowa, 6 miles west of Titonka.
Literature Available: Information circular and map, bird checklists, and calendar of events.
Address: Refuge Manager, Union Slough National Wildlife Refuge, P.O. Box AF, Titonka, Iowa 50480.

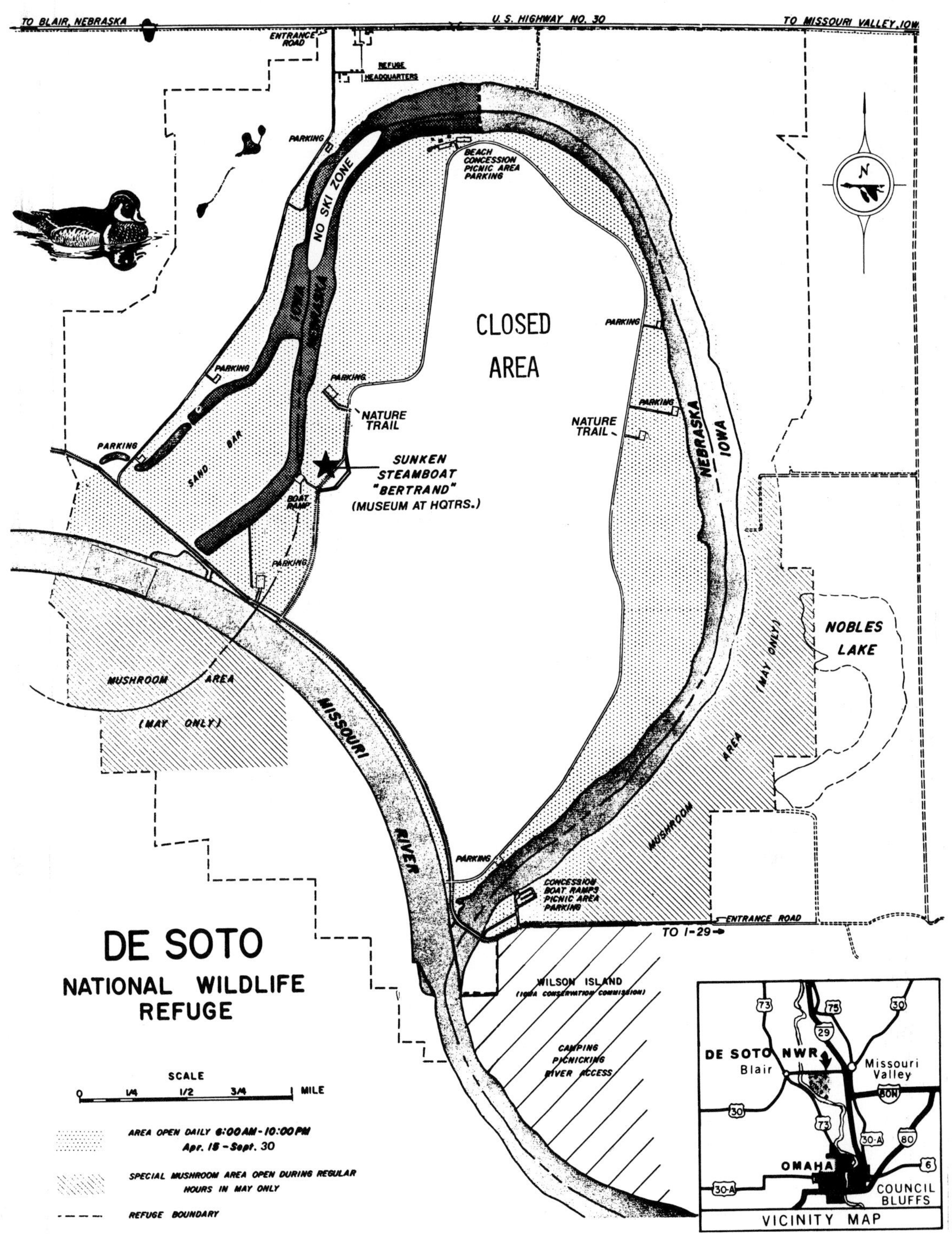

TO BLAIR, NEBRASKA
U.S. HIGHWAY NO. 30
TO MISSOURI VALLEY, IOW
ENTRANCE ROAD
REFUGE HEADQUARTERS
PARKING
BEACH CONCESSION PICNIC AREA PARKING
NO SKI ZONE
N
CLOSED AREA
PARKING
PARKING
PARKING
NATURE TRAIL
PARKING
NATURE TRAIL
PARKING
SAND BAR
SUNKEN STEAMBOAT "BERTRAND" (MUSEUM AT HQTRS.)
BOAT RAMP
PARKING
NEBRASKA
IOWA
MUSHROOM AREA
(MAY ONLY)
MISSOURI
RIVER
(MAY ONLY)
MUSHROOM AREA
NOBLES LAKE
PARKING
CONCESSION BOAT RAMPS PICNIC AREA PARKING
ENTRANCE ROAD
TO I-29
DE SOTO
NATIONAL WILDLIFE REFUGE
WILSON ISLAND
(IOWA CONSERVATION COMMISSION)
CAMPING
PICNICKING
RIVER ACCESS
SCALE
0 1/4 1/2 3/4 1 MILE
AREA OPEN DAILY 6:00 AM - 10:00 PM Apr. 15 - Sept. 30
SPECIAL MUSHROOM AREA OPEN DURING REGULAR HOURS IN MAY ONLY
REFUGE BOUNDARY
73
75
30
29
DE SOTO NWR
Blair
Missouri Valley
80N
30
73
30-A
80
6
OMAHA
30-A
COUNCIL BLUFFS
VICINITY MAP

The Bear River Migratory Bird Refuge in northern Utah is one of the outstanding waterfowl production areas in the United States. Photo by U.S. Fish and Wildlife Service.

Utah

BEAR RIVER MIGRATORY BIRD REFUGE

Waterfowl: Whistling swans, Canada geese, mallards, gadwalls, pintails, green-winged teal, northern shovelers, redheads, canvasbacks, and ruddy ducks.
Wildlife: Mammals (29 species), birds (222 species), reptiles, amphibians, and fish.
Habitats: Impoundments, marshes, open water, and mud flats.
Size: 64,895 acres.
Location: In northern Utah on the Bear River delta, 15 miles west of Brigham City.

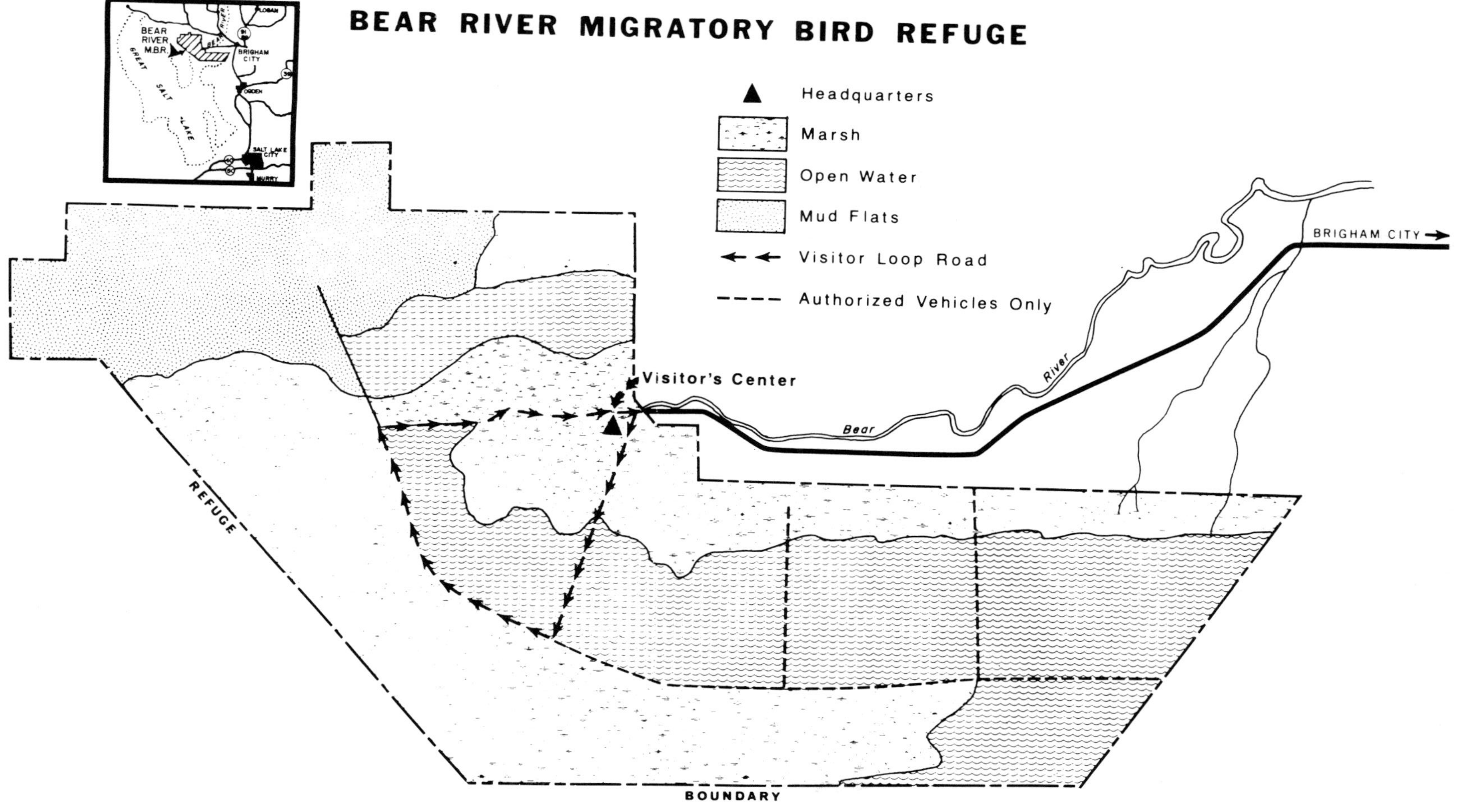

BEAR RIVER MIGRATORY BIRD REFUGE
Headquarters
Marsh
Open Water
Mud Flats
Visitor Loop Road
Authorized Vehicles Only
Visitor's Center
Bear
River
BRIGHAM CITY
REFUGE
BOUNDARY
BEAR RIVER M.B.R.
BRIGHAM CITY
GREAT SALT LAKE

Literature Available: Information circular and map, checklists for mammals and birds, children's birdlist, and seasonal abundance of birds circular.
Address: Refuge Manager, Bear River Migratory Bird Refuge, P.O. Box 459, Brigham City, Utah 84302.

OURAY NATIONAL WILDLIFE REFUGE

Waterfowl: Canada geese, mallards, gadwalls, pintails, green-winged teal, blue-winged teal, cinnamon teal, and ruddy ducks.
Wildlife: Mammals, birds (132 species), reptiles, amphibians, and fish.
Habitats: Green River, vegetated islands, marshland, bottomlands, wooded areas, and clay-gravel ridges.
Size: 13,000 acres.
Location: In northeastern Utah, 30 miles southwest of Vernal.
Literature Available: Information circular and map, and bird checklist.
Address: Refuge Manager, Ouray National Wildlife Refuge, 447 E. Main Street, Suite 4, Vernal, Utah 84078.

Colorado

ALAMOSA NATIONAL WILDLIFE REFUGE

Waterfowl: Mallards, gadwalls, pintails, green-winged teal, blue-winged teal, cinnamon teal, northern shovelers, and common mergansers.
Wildlife: Mammals, birds (131 species), reptiles, amphibians, and fish.
Habitats: Marshes, river, and sandy bluff.
Size: 9,186 acres.
Location: In the San Luis Valley of southcentral Colorado, 3 miles southeast of Alamosa.
Literature Available: Information booklet, map, and bird checklist.
Address: Refuge Manager, Alamosa National Wildlife Refuge, P.O. Box 1148, Alamosa, Colorado 81101.

ARAPAHO NATIONAL WILDLIFE REFUGE

Waterfowl: Mallards, gadwalls, green-winged teal, blue-winged teal, American wigeon, and lesser scaup.
Wildlife: Mammals, birds (119 species), reptiles, amphibians, and fish.
Habitats: Bottomland along the Illinois River, ponds, and irrigated meadows.
Size: 29,520 acres.
Location: Northern Colorado, just south of Walden.
Literature Available: Information circular, map, and bird checklists.
Address: Refuge Manager, Arapaho National Wildlife Refuge, P.O. Box 457, Walden, Colorado 80480.

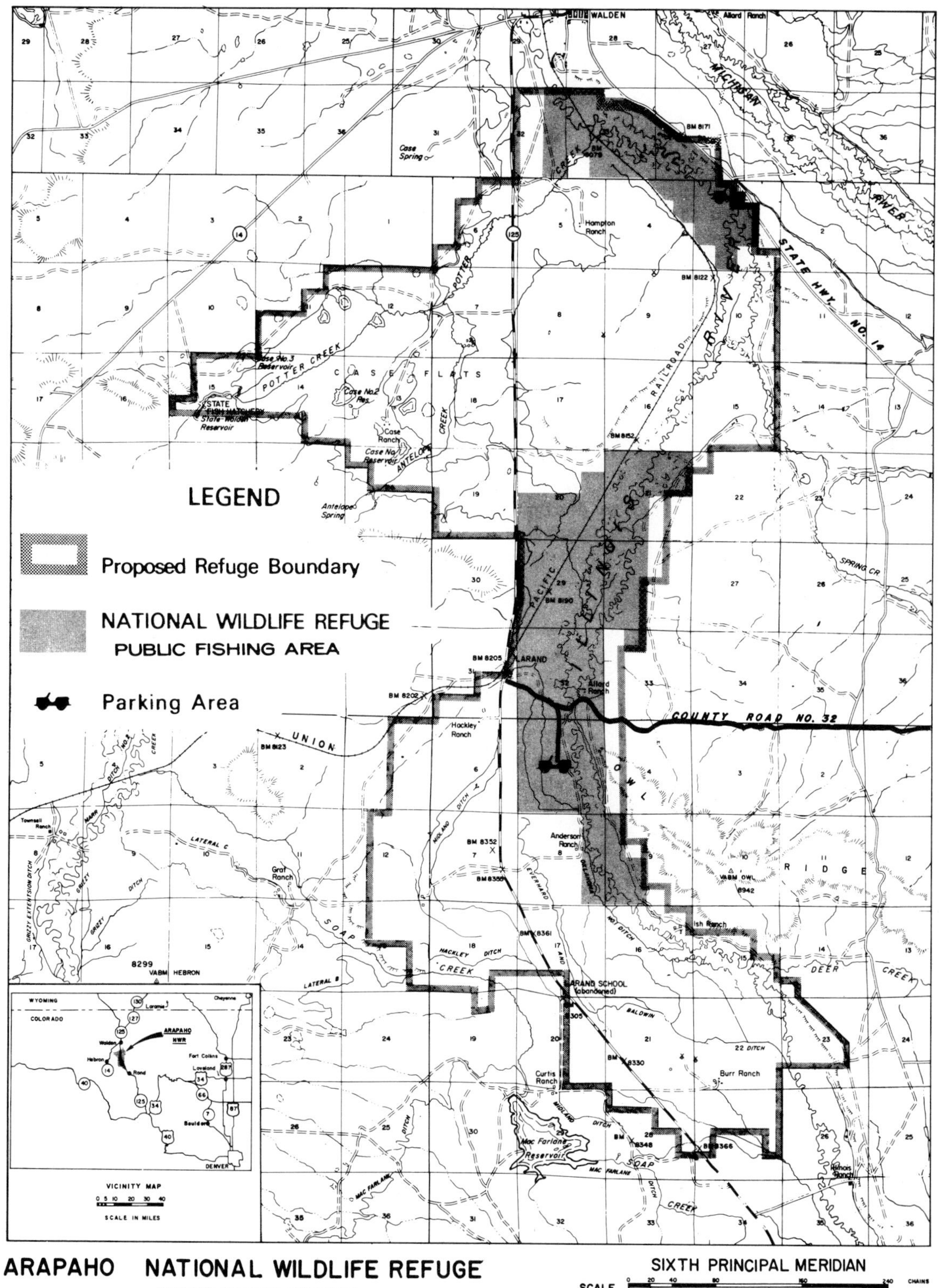
LEGEND
Proposed Refuge Boundary
NATIONAL WILDLIFE REFUGE
PUBLIC FISHING AREA
Parking Area
WALDEN
Allard Ranch
MICHIGAN
RIVER
STATE HWY. NO. 14
Case Spring
Hampton Ranch
POTTER CREEK
CASE FLATS
Case No.3 Reservoir
Case No.2 Res.
STATE FISH HATCHERY
State-Walden Reservoir
Case Ranch
Case No.1 Reservoir
ANTELOPE CREEK
Antelope Spring
RAILROAD
PACIFIC
UNION
SPRING CR
LARAND
Allard Ranch
COUNTY ROAD NO. 32
Hackley Ranch
Anderson Ranch
Townsell Ranch
Graf Ranch
LATERAL C
GRIZZY EXTENSION DITCH
SOAP
HACKLEY DITCH
CREEK
RIDGE
VABM OWL 8942
Ish Ranch
DEER CREEK
8299 VABM HEBRON
LARAND SCHOOL (abandoned)
BALDWIN
22 DITCH
Burr Ranch
Curtis Ranch
MIDLAND DITCH
Mac Farlane Reservoir
MAC FARLANE
SOAP CREEK
Illinois Ranch
WYOMING
COLORADO
Laramie
Cheyenne
ARAPAHO NWR
Walden
Hebron
Rand
Fort Collins
Loveland
Boulder
DENVER
VICINITY MAP
SCALE IN MILES
ARAPAHO NATIONAL WILDLIFE REFUGE
JACKSON COUNTY, COLORADO
SIXTH PRINCIPAL MERIDIAN
SCALE
CHAINS
MILES

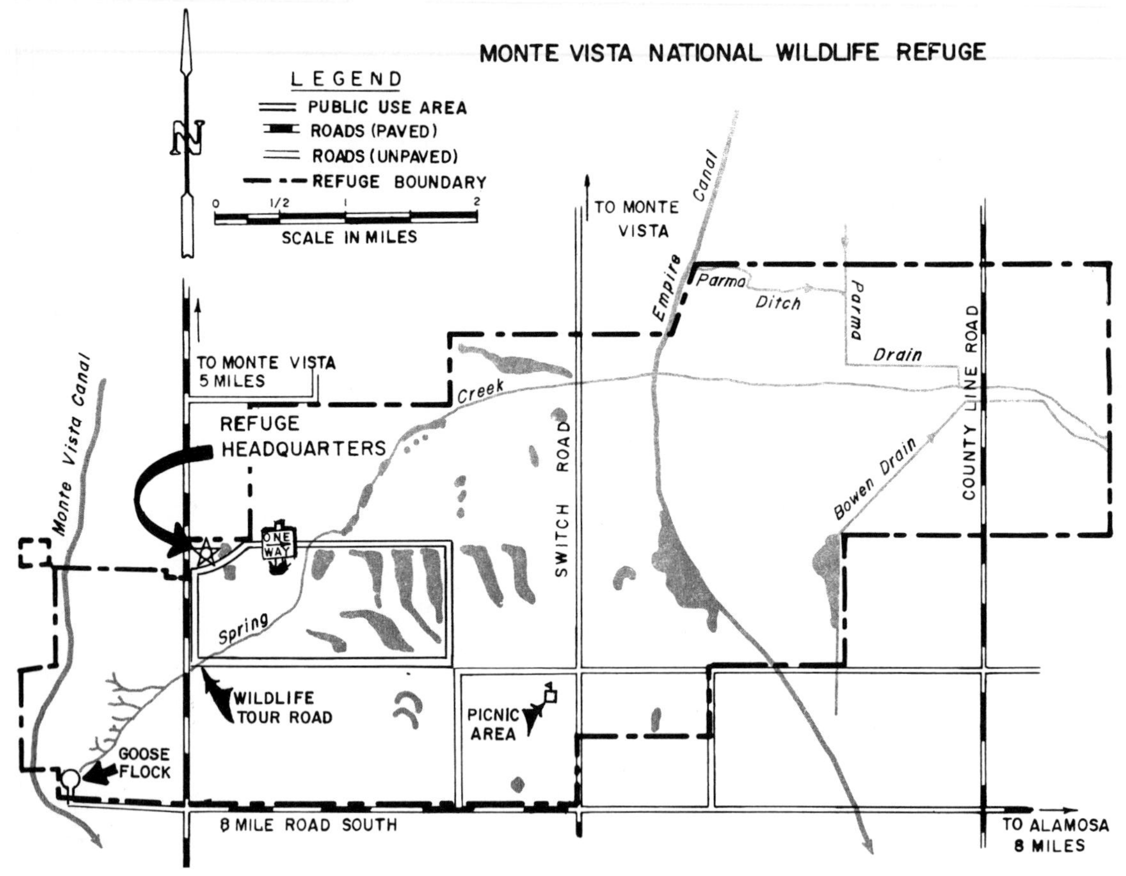

BROWNS PARK NATIONAL WILDLIFE REFUGE

Waterfowl: Canada geese and redheads.
Wildlife: Mammals, birds, reptiles, amphibians, and fish.
Habitats: Green River bottomlands, benchlands, and red sandstone canyon walls.
Size: 14,500 acres.
Location: In northwestern Colorado, near Greystone.
Literature Available: Information sheet and map.
Address: Refuge Manager, Browns Park National Wildlife Refuge, Greystone, Colorado 81636.

MONTE VISTA NATIONAL WILDLIFE REFUGE

Waterfowl: Canada geese, mallards, gadwalls, pintails, green-winged teal, blue-winged teal, cinnamon teal, northern shovelers, redheads, and common mergansers.
Wildlife: Mammals, birds (172 species), reptiles, amphibians, and fish.
Habitats: Lakes, ponds, wet meadows, grazing lands, and farmlands.
Size: 13,836 acres.

Location: In southcentral Colorado, 6 miles south of Monte Vista.
Literature Available: Information sheet and map, and bird checklists.
Address: Refuge Manager, Monte Vista National Wildlife Refuge, Box 511, Monte Vista, Colorado 81144.

Kansas

FLINT HILLS NATIONAL WILDLIFE REFUGE

Waterfowl: Canada geese, white-fronted geese, snow geese, mallards, gadwalls, pintails, green-winged teal, blue-winged teal, northern shovelers, American wigeon, wood ducks, redheads, ring-necked ducks, canvasbacks, lesser scaup, and common mergansers.
Wildlife: Mammals, birds (189 species), reptiles, amphibians, and fish.
Habitats: Portions of the John Redmond Reservoir, flooded sloughs, shallow marshes, hardwood timber, and agricultural land.
Size: 18,500 acres.
Location: In eastern Kansas, north of Burlington.
Literature Available: Information sheet and map, and bird checklists.
Address: Refuge Manager, Flint Hills National Wildlife Refuge, P.O. Box 213, Burlington, Kansas 66839.

KIRWIN NATIONAL WILDLIFE REFUGE

Waterfowl: Canada geese, white-fronted geese, mallards, pintails, and green-winged teal.
Wildlife: Mammals (34 species), birds (186 species), reptiles, amphibians, and fish.
Habitats: Reservoir, grassland, and cultivated fields.
Size: 10,778 acres.
Location: In northcentral Kansas, 5 miles southwest of Kirwin.
Literature Available: Information circular and map, and bird and mammal checklists.
Address: Refuge Manager, Kirwin National Wildlife Refuge, Box 125, Kirwin, Kansas 67644.

QUIVIRA NATIONAL WILDLIFE REFUGE

Waterfowl: Canada geese, white-fronted geese, mallards, pintails, green-winged teal, blue-winged teal, American wigeon, and northern shovelers.
Wildlife: Mammals, birds (245 species), reptiles, amphibians, and fish.
Habitats: Marshes, lakes, rangeland, farmland, and low sandhills.
Size: 21,820 acres.
Location: In central Kansas, 12 miles north of Stafford.
Literature Available: Information circular and map, and bird checklist.
Address: Refuge Manager, Quivira National Wildlife Refuge, P.O. Box G, Stafford, Kansas 67578.

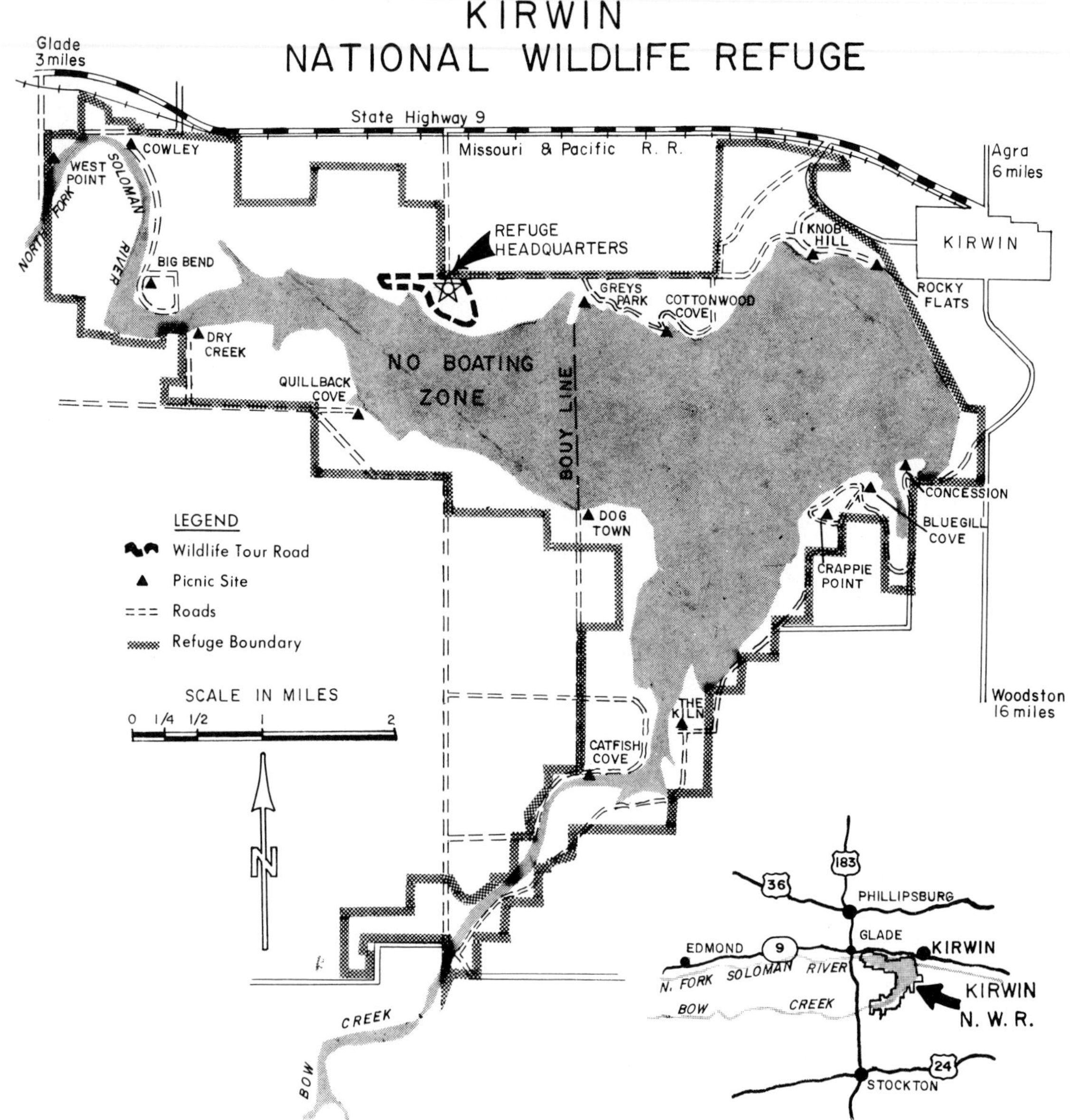
KIRWIN
NATIONAL WILDLIFE REFUGE
Glade 3 miles
State Highway 9
Missouri & Pacific R. R.
Agra 6 miles
KIRWIN
COWLEY
WEST POINT
NORTH FORK
SOLOMAN RIVER
BIG BEND
DRY CREEK
REFUGE HEADQUARTERS
KNOB HILL
ROCKY FLATS
GREYS PARK
COTTONWOOD COVE
NO BOATING ZONE
QUILLBACK COVE
BOUY LINE
CONCESSION
BLUEGILL COVE
CRAPPIE POINT
DOG TOWN
THE KILN
CATFISH COVE
Woodston 16 miles
LEGEND
Wildlife Tour Road
Picnic Site
Roads
Refuge Boundary
SCALE IN MILES
0 1/4 1/2 1 2
N
BOW CREEK
36
183
PHILLIPSBURG
GLADE
EDMOND
9
KIRWIN
N. FORK SOLOMAN RIVER
BOW CREEK
KIRWIN N. W. R.
24
STOCKTON

Missouri

MINGO NATIONAL WILDLIFE REFUGE

Waterfowl: Canada geese, mallards, gadwalls, pintails, and northern shovelers.
Wildlife: Mammals (38 species), birds (207 species), reptiles (36 species), amphibians (23 species), and fish.
Habitats: Hardwood swamps and upland areas.
Size: 21,670 acres.
Location: In southeastern Missouri, a few miles northwest of Puxico.
Literature Available: Information circular and map, checklists for mammals, birds, reptiles, amphibians, trees, shrubs, and vines, boardwalk nature trail guide, and observation blind trail guide.
Address: Refuge Manager, Mingo National Wildlife Refuge, R.R. 1, Box 9A, Puxico, Missouri 63960.

SQUAW CREEK NATIONAL WILDLIFE REFUGE

Waterfowl: Canada geese, snow geese, mallards, and pintails.
Wildlife: Mammals (33 species), birds (263 species), reptiles, amphibians, and fish.
Habitats: Lowland cordgrass prairie, woodland, marshes, and prairie hills.
Size: 6,886 acres.
Location: In northwestern Missouri, near Mound City.
Literature Available: Information sheet, bird and mammal checklists, and calendar of events.
Address: Refuge Manager, Squaw Creek National Wildlife Refuge, Box 101, Mound City, Missouri 64470.

SWAN LAKE NATIONAL WILDLIFE REFUGE

Waterfowl: Canada geese, snow geese, and various ducks.
Wildlife: Mammals, birds (210 species), reptiles, amphibians, and fish.
Habitats: Marshes, open water, and fields.
Size: 11,000 acres.
Location: In northcentral Missouri, a mile south of Sumner.
Literature Available: Information sheet and map.
Address: Refuge Manager, Swan Lake National Wildlife Refuge, Sumner, Missouri 64681.

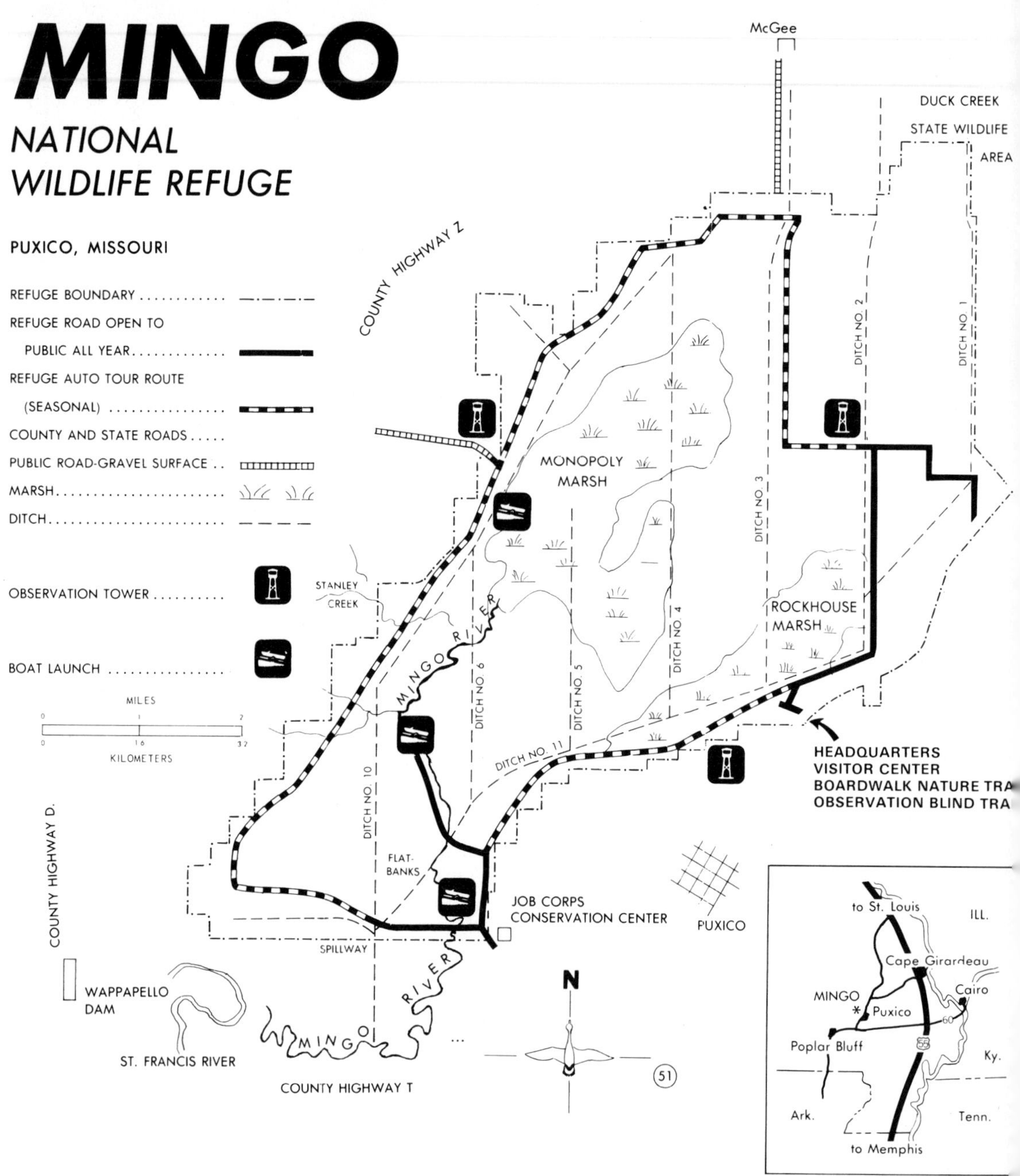
MINGO
NATIONAL WILDLIFE REFUGE
PUXICO, MISSOURI
REFUGE BOUNDARY
REFUGE ROAD OPEN TO PUBLIC ALL YEAR
REFUGE AUTO TOUR ROUTE (SEASONAL)
COUNTY AND STATE ROADS
PUBLIC ROAD-GRAVEL SURFACE
MARSH
DITCH
OBSERVATION TOWER
BOAT LAUNCH
MILES
KILOMETERS
McGee
DUCK CREEK STATE WILDLIFE AREA
COUNTY HIGHWAY Z
DITCH NO. 1
DITCH NO. 2
DITCH NO. 3
DITCH NO. 4
DITCH NO. 5
DITCH NO. 6
DITCH NO. 10
DITCH NO. 11
MONOPOLY MARSH
ROCKHOUSE MARSH
STANLEY CREEK
MINGO RIVER
HEADQUARTERS
VISITOR CENTER
BOARDWALK NATURE TRA
OBSERVATION BLIND TRA
COUNTY HIGHWAY D.
FLAT-BANKS
JOB CORPS CONSERVATION CENTER
PUXICO
SPILLWAY
WAPPAPELLO DAM
ST. FRANCIS RIVER
COUNTY HIGHWAY T
N
51
to St. Louis
ILL.
Cape Girardeau
Cairo
MINGO
Puxico
60
Poplar Bluff
55
Ky.
Ark.
Tenn.
to Memphis

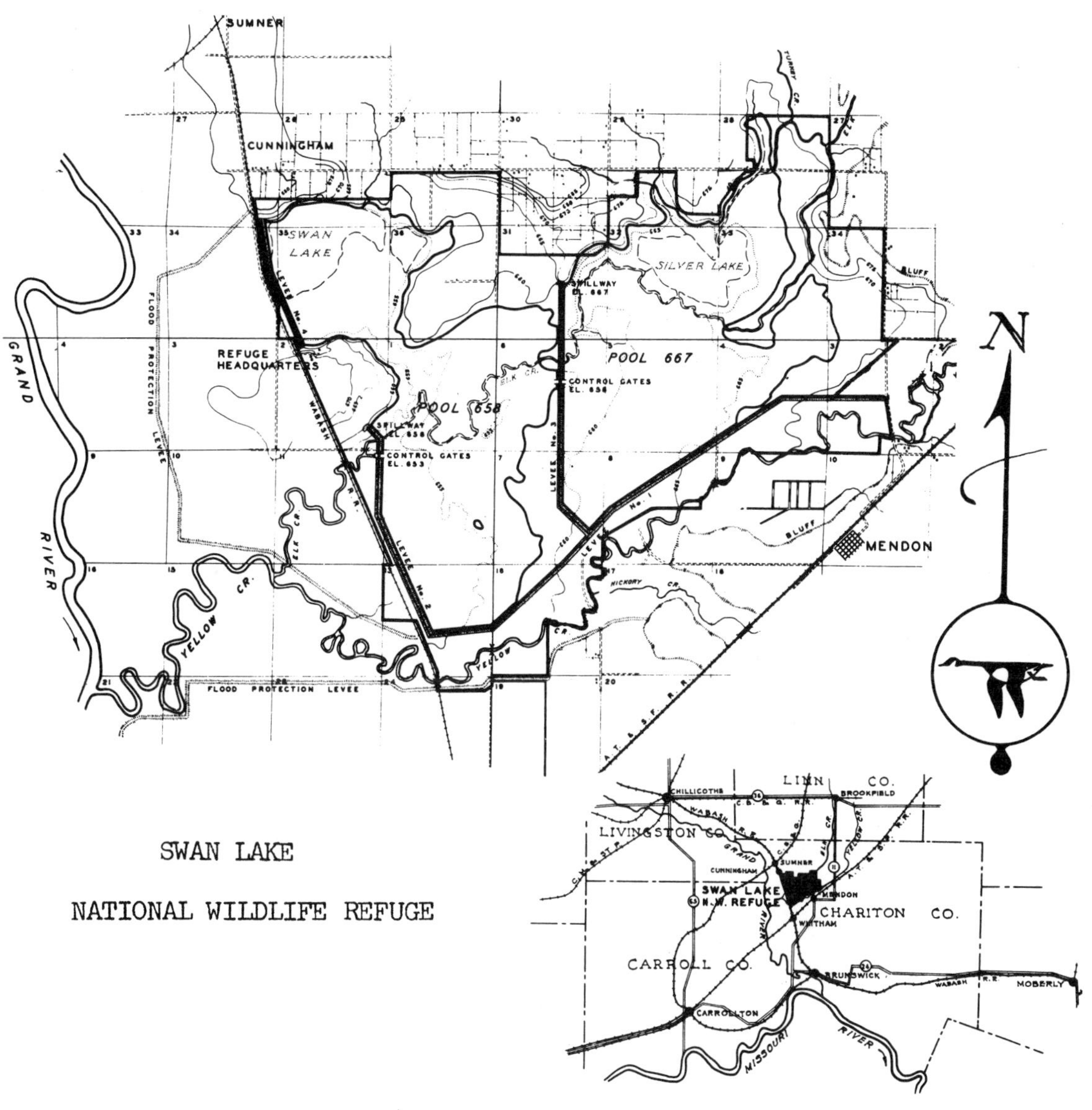

SWAN LAKE

NATIONAL WILDLIFE REFUGE

Southwestern States

Arizona

CIBOLA NATIONAL WILDLIFE REFUGE

Waterfowl: Canada geese, mallards, and pintails.
Wildlife: Mammals, birds (202 species), reptiles (27 species), amphibians (5 species), and fish.
Habitats: Riverbottom land, desert ridges and washes, river channel, marshes, and agricultural land.
Size: 16,627 acres.
Location: The Lower Colorado River in Cibola Valley, Arizona, and the Palo Verde Valley, California, 20 miles south of Blythe, California.
Literature Available: Information circular and map, and checklists for birds, reptiles, and amphibians.
Address: Refuge Manager, Cibola National Wildlife Refuge, P.O. Box AP, Blythe, California 92225.

HAVASU NATIONAL WILDLIFE REFUGE

Waterfowl: Canada geese, snow geese, mallards, gadwalls, pintails, green-winged teal, cinnamon teal, American wigeon, northern shovelers, redheads, and ruddy ducks.
Wildlife: Mammals (42 species), birds (276 species), reptiles, amphibians, and fish.
Habitats: River, marshes, ponds, gorge, mud delta, and upland desert.
Size: 41,500 acres.
Location: In western Arizona and southeastern California. The Topock Marsh Unit is just north of Topock, Arizona; the Topock Gorge Unit extends south from Topock to Lake Havasu; and the Bill Williams Delta Unit is located near Parker Dam.
Literature Available: Information circulars and maps, and bird and mammal checklists.
Address: Refuge Manager, Havasu National Wildlife Refuge, P.O. Box A, Needles, California 92363.

IMPERIAL NATIONAL WILDLIFE REFUGE

Waterfowl: Canada geese, pintails, and green-winged teal.
Wildlife: Mammals (39 species), birds (205 species), reptiles, amphibians, and fish.
Habitats: Colorado River, desert mountains, sloughs, lakes, and mesquite.
Size: 25,765 acres.
Location: Arizona and California sides of the Colorado River from 24 miles north of Yuma, Arizona, northward for 30 miles along the river.

Literature Available: Refuge regulations and map, and bird and mammal checklists.
Address: Refuge Manager, Imperial National Wildlife Refuge, P.O. Box 2217, Martinez Lake, Arizona 85364.

New Mexico

BITTER LAKE NATIONAL WILDLIFE REFUGE

Waterfowl: Canada geese, snow geese, mallards, gadwalls, pintails, American wigeon, northern shovelers, and ruddy ducks.
Wildlife: Mammals, birds (290 species), reptiles, amphibians, and fish.
Habitats: Lakes, marshes, Pecos River, and bluffs.
Size: 23,310 acres.
Location: The southeastern portion of New Mexico, 11 miles northeast of Roswell.
Literature Available: Information circular and map, bird and wildlife checklists, and self-guiding tour leaflet.
Address: Refuge Manager, Bitter Lake National Wildlife Refuge, P.O. Box 7, Roswell, New Mexico 88201.

BOSQUE DEL APACHE NATIONAL WILDLIFE REFUGE

Waterfowl: Canada geese, snow geese, mallards (including the Mexican duck form), gadwalls, pintails, green-winged teal, American wigeon, and northern shovelers.
Wildlife: Mammals, birds (281 species), reptiles, amphibians, and fish.
Habitats: Bottomlands, marshes, ponds, foothills, and mesas.
Size: 57,191 acres.
Location: Along the Rio Grande River, 20 miles south of Socorro.
Literature Available: Information circular and map, bird and wildlife checklists, and regulations.
Address: Refuge Manager, Bosque del Apache National Wildlife Refuge, P.O. Box 278, San Antonio, New Mexico 87832.

LAS VEGAS NATIONAL WILDLIFE REFUGE

Waterfowl: Canada geese, mallards, gadwalls, pintails, green-winged teal, blue-winged teal, cinnamon teal, American wigeon, northern shovelers, redheads, ring-necked ducks, canvasbacks, lesser scaup, common goldeneyes, buffleheads, ruddy ducks, and common mergansers.
Wildlife: Mammals, birds (164 species), reptiles, amphibians, and fish.
Habitats: Marshes, open water, streams, native grassland, timbered canyons, and cropland.
Size: 9,450 acres.
Location: In northeastern New Mexico, just southeast of Las Vegas.
Literature Available: Information circular and map, and bird checklist.
Address: Refuge Manager, Las Vegas National Wildlife Refuge, P.O. Box 1070, Las Vegas, New Mexico 87701.

A shallow waterfowl production marsh on the Bosque del Apache National Wildlife Refuge, New Mexico. Photo by U.S. Fish and Wildlife Service.

MAXWELL NATIONAL WILDLIFE REFUGE

Waterfowl: Canada geese, mallards, gadwalls, pintails, green-winged teal, blue-winged teal, cinnamon teal, American wigeon, northern shovelers, redheads, lesser scaup, buffleheads, ruddy ducks, and common mergansers.
Wildlife: Mammals, birds (153 species), reptiles, amphibians, and fish.
Habitats: Lakes, ponds, marshes, and cropland.
Size: 3,300 acres.
Location: In northeastern New Mexico, 4 miles northwest of Maxwell.
Literature Available: Information leaflet and map, and bird checklist.
Address: Refuge Manager, Maxwell National Wildlife Refuge, P.O. Box 1070, Las Vegas, New Mexico 87701.

Oklahoma

SALT PLAINS NATIONAL WILDLIFE REFUGE

Waterfowl: Canada geese, white-fronted geese, snow geese, mallards, pintails, and green-winged teal.
Wildlife: Mammals (30 species), birds (256 species), reptiles, amphibians, and fish.
Habitats: Great Salt Plains Reservoir, ponds, marshes, beaches, and salt flats.
Size: 32,000 acres.
Location: In northern Oklahoma, north of Jet.
Literature Available: Information sheet and map, bird and mammal checklists, children's wildlife checklist, and nature trail guides.
Address: Refuge Manager, Salt Plains National Wildlife Refuge, Jet, Oklahoma 73749.

SEQUOYAH NATIONAL WILDLIFE REFUGE

Waterfowl: Mallards, gadwalls, pintails, American wigeon, blue-winged teal, green-winged teal, redheads, canvasbacks, and scaup.
Wildlife: Mammals, birds (245 species), reptiles, amphibians, and fish.
Habitats: Robert S. Kerr Reservoir, steep shoreline, ponds, sloughs, marshes, steep ridges, meadows, and woodlands.
Size: 20,800 acres.
Location: In eastcentral Oklahoma, 3 miles south of Vian.
Literature Available: Information sheet and map, bird checklists, and refuge regulations.
Address: Refuge Manager, Sequoyah National Wildlife Refuge, P.O. Box 398, Sallisaw, Oklahoma 74955.

TISHOMINGO NATIONAL WILDLIFE REFUGE

Waterfowl: Canada geese, white-fronted geese, mallards, gadwalls, pintails, green-winged teal, American wigeon, northern shovelers, wood ducks, lesser scaup, and common mergansers.
Wildlife: Mammals, birds (252 species), reptiles, amphibians, and fish.
Habitats: Lakes, rivers, creeks, upland areas, and fields.
Size: 16,600 acres.
Location: In southeastern Oklahoma, south of Tishomingo.
Literature Available: Information circular and map, and bird checklists.
Address: Refuge Manager, Tishomingo National Wildlife Refuge, P.O. Box 248, Tishomingo, Oklahoma 73460.

WASHITA NATIONAL WILDLIFE REFUGE

Waterfowl: Canada geese, white-fronted geese, mallards, pintails, and American wigeon.
Wildlife: Mammals, birds (183 species), reptiles, amphibians, and fish.

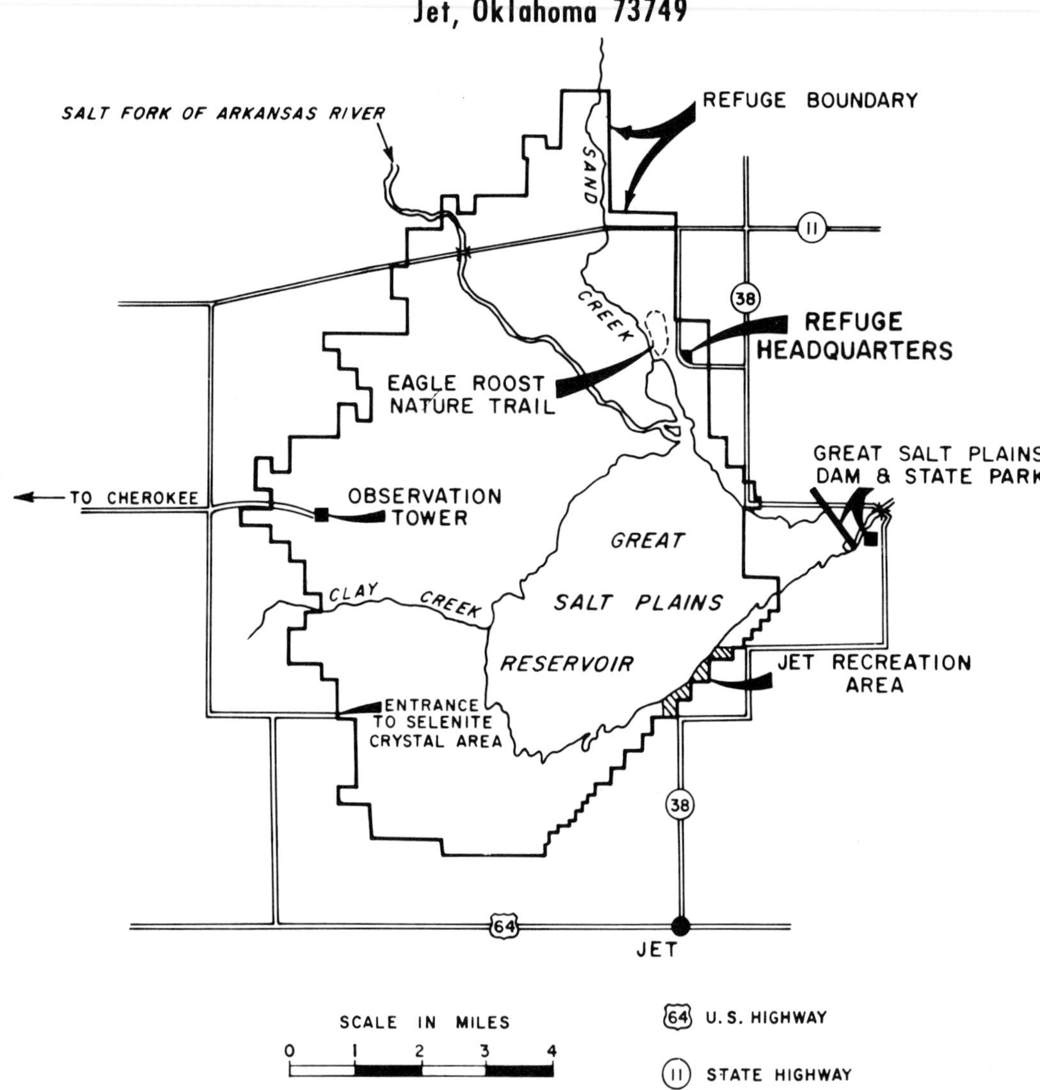

Habitats: Foss Reservoir, Washita River, short-grass plains, rolling bottomlands, creeks, and uplands.
Size: 8,084 acres.
Location: In western Oklahoma, several miles west of Butler.
Literature Available: Information sheet and map, bird checklist, and refuge regulations.
Address: Refuge Manager, Washita National Wildlife Refuge, R.R. 1, Box 68, Butler, Oklahoma 73625.

WICHITA MOUNTAINS WILDLIFE REFUGE

Waterfowl: Mallards, gadwalls, American wigeon, redheads, and ring-necked ducks.
Wildlife: Mammals (50 species including bison and Texas longhorn cattle), birds (241 species), reptiles (50 species), amphibians (14 species), and fish (36 species).
Habitats: Prairie grasslands, rocky outcrops, stony rocklands, woodlands, lakes, and streams.
Size: 59,020 acres.
Location: In southwestern Oklahoma, near Medicine Park and Cache.
Literature Available: Information circular and map, checklists for mammals, birds, reptiles, amphibians, and fish, trail guides, regulations, longhorn cattle circular, and bison circular.
Address: Refuge Manager, Wichita Mountains Wildlife Refuge, P.O. Box 448, Cache, Oklahoma 73527.

Texas

ANAHUAC NATIONAL WILDLIFE REFUGE

Waterfowl: Canada geese, white-fronted geese, snow geese, pintails, American wigeon, and teal.
Wildlife: Mammals (including red wolves), birds (253 species), reptiles (including alligators), amphibians, and fish.
Habitats: Open salt water, coastal marsh, wet prairie, ponds, and sloughs.
Size: 9,836 acres.
Location: In southeastern Texas, along East Bay on the Gulf of Mexico, a few miles southeast of Anahuac.
Literature Available: Information circular and map, bird checklists, children's wildlife checklist, and regulations.
Address: Refuge Manager, Anahuac National Wildlife Refuge, P.O. Box 278, Anahuac, Texas 77514.

ARANSAS NATIONAL WILDLIFE REFUGE

Waterfowl: Canada geese, gadwalls, pintails, blue-winged teal, American wigeon, northern shovelers, and lesser scaup.
Wildlife: Mammals, birds (350 species), reptiles, amphibians, and fish. The critically endangered whooping crane winters only on the Aransas National Wildlife Refuge. The birds begin arriving in mid-October and leave in late March and early April.
Habitats: Tidal marshes, ponds, wooded dunes, oak thickets, and meadows.
Size: 54,829 acres.
Location: On the Gulf of Mexico, 7 miles southeast of Austwell.

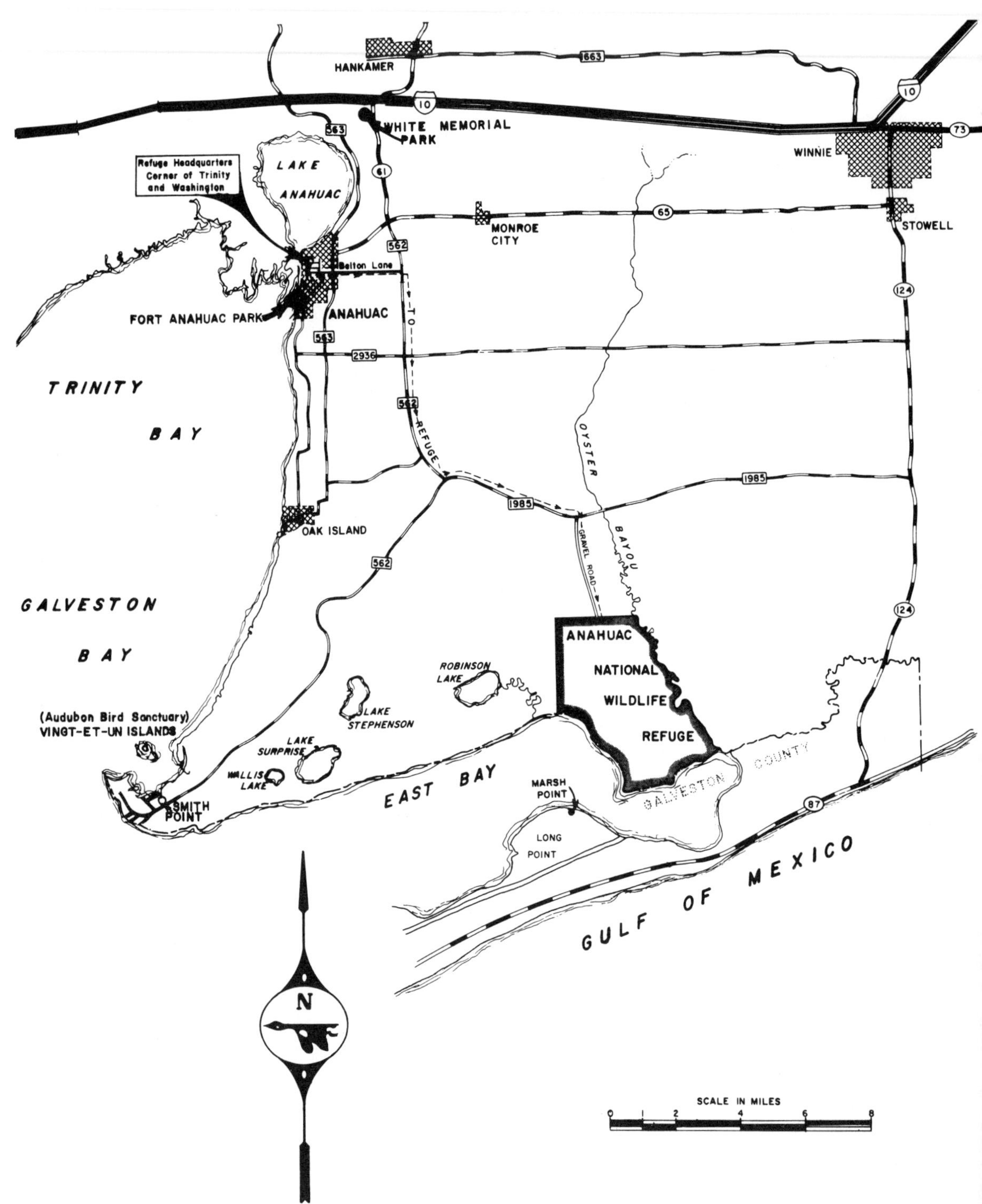
HANKAMER
663
10
WHITE MEMORIAL PARK
563
Refuge Headquarters Corner of Trinity and Washington
LAKE ANAHUAC
61
WINNIE
73
MONROE CITY
65
STOWELL
562
Belton Lane
TO
FORT ANAHUAC PARK
ANAHUAC
124
2936
TRINITY
BAY
REFUGE
OYSTER
1985
OAK ISLAND
GRAVEL ROAD
BAYOU
GALVESTON
BAY
ANAHUAC NATIONAL WILDLIFE REFUGE
ROBINSON LAKE
LAKE STEPHENSON
(Audubon Bird Sanctuary) VINGT-ET-UN ISLANDS
LAKE SURPRISE
WALLIS LAKE
EAST BAY
MARSH POINT
GALVESTON COUNTY
SMITH POINT
LONG POINT
87
GULF OF MEXICO
N
SCALE IN MILES
0 1 2 4 6 8

Literature Available: Information circular and map, bird and wildlife checklists, trail guides, birding guides, and whooping crane booklet.
Address: Refuge Manager, Aransas National Wildlife Refuge, P.O. Box 68, Austwell, Texas 77950.

BRAZORIA NATIONAL WILDLIFE REFUGE

Waterfowl: Canada geese, snow geese, gadwalls, pintails, green-winged teal, and northern shovelers.
Wildlife: Mammals, birds (242 species), reptiles, amphibians, and fish.
Habitats: Bays, lakes, bayous, and ridges.
Size: 9,978 acres.
Location: Along the Gulf of Mexico, near Angleton.
Literature Available: Map and bird checklist.
Address: Refuge Manager, Brazoria National Wildlife Refuge, P.O. Box 1088, Angleton, Texas 77515.

BUFFALO LAKE NATIONAL WILDLIFE REFUGE

Waterfowl: Canada geese, snow geese, mallards, gadwalls, pintails, green-winged teal, blue-winged teal, American wigeon, and nothern shovelers.
Wildlife: Mammals, birds (275 species), reptiles, amphibians, and fish.
Habitats: Buffalo Lake and fields.
Size: 7,677 acres.
Location: In northwestern Texas, 1½ miles south of Umbarger.
Literature Available: Information circular and map, and bird checklists.
Address: Refuge Manager, Buffalo Lake National Wildlife Refuge, Box 228, Umbarger, Texas 79091.

HAGERMAN NATIONAL WILDLIFE REFUGE

Waterfowl: Canada geese, white-fronted geese, snow geese, mallards, American wigeon, green-winged teal, redheads, canvasbacks, ring-necked ducks, and scaup.
Wildlife: Mammals, birds (282 species), reptiles, amphibians, and fish.
Habitats: Open water, marshes, streams, meadows, wooded areas, and farmland.
Size: 11,319 acres.
Location: In northeastern Texas, west of Denison and Sherman.
Literature Available: Information circular and map, bird checklists, and regulations.
Address: Refuge Manager, Hagerman National Wildlife Refuge, Route 3, Box 123, Sherman, Texas 75090.

LAGUNA ATASCOSA NATIONAL WILDLIFE REFUGE

Waterfowl: Canada geese, snow geese, pintails, northern shovelers, redheads, and ruddy ducks.
Wildlife: Mammals (31 species including ocelots), birds (313 species), reptiles, amphibians, and fish.

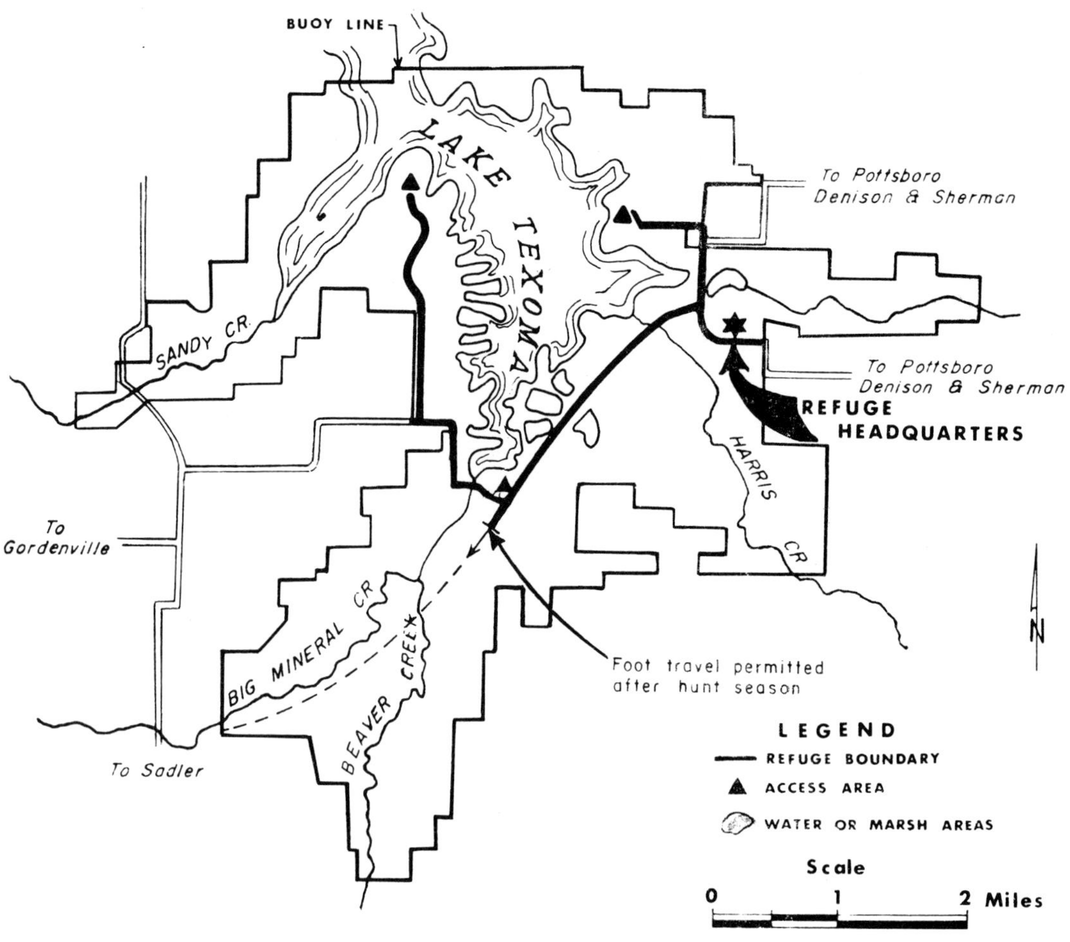

Habitats: Lake, marshes, coastal prairies, salt flats, and low vegetated ridges.
Size: 45,190 acres.
Location: In extreme southern Texas, 25 miles east of Harlingen.
Literature Available: Information leaflet and map, and bird and mammal checklists.
Address: Refuge Manager, Laguna Atascosa National Wildlife Refuge, 306 E. Jackson Street, P.O. Box 2683, Harlingen, Texas 78550.

MULESHOE NATIONAL WILDLIFE REFUGE

Waterfowl: Canada geese, snow geese, mallards, gadwalls, pintails, green-winged teal, blue-winged teal, cinnamon teal, American wigeon, northern shovelers, redheads, ring-necked ducks, canvasbacks, lesser scaup, buffleheads, and ruddy ducks.

MULESHOE NATIONAL WILDLIFE REFUGE

BAILEY COUNTY, TEXAS

UNITED STATES
DEPARTMENT OF THE INTERIOR

UNITED STATES
FISH AND WILDLIFE SERVICE

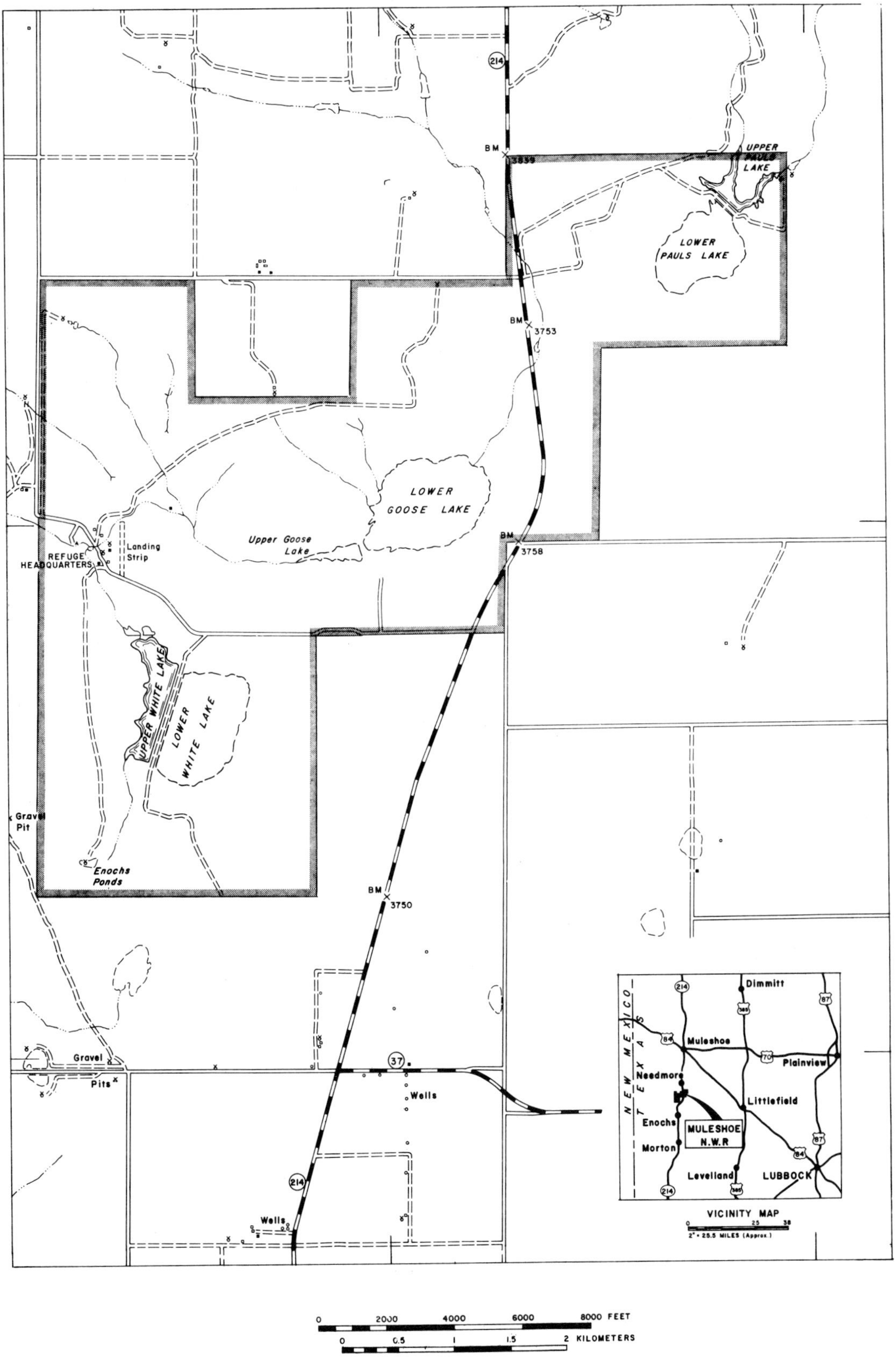

UPPER PAULS LAKE
LOWER PAULS LAKE
BM 3839
BM 3753
BM 3758
BM 3750
LOWER GOOSE LAKE
Upper Goose Lake
REFUGE HEADQUARTERS
Landing Strip
UPPER WHITE LAKE
LOWER WHITE LAKE
Gravel Pit
Enochs Ponds
Gravel Pits
Wells
214
37

VICINITY MAP
Dimmitt
Muleshoe
Plainview
Needmore
Littlefield
Enochs
Morton
Levelland
LUBBOCK
MULESHOE N.W.R
NEW MEXICO
TEXAS
2" = 25.5 MILES (Approx.)

0 2000 4000 6000 8000 FEET
0 0.5 1 1.5 2 KILOMETERS

Wildlife: Mammals, birds (263 species), reptiles, amphibians, and fish.
Habitats: Lakes, short-grass rangelands, and rocky outcroppings.
Size: 5,800 acres.
Location: In the Texas Panhandle, 20 miles south of Muleshoe.
Literature Available: Information sheet, map, and bird checklist.
Address: Refuge Manager, Muleshoe National Wildlife Refuge, P.O. Box 549, Muleshoe, Texas 79347.

SAN BERNARD NATIONAL WILDLIFE REFUGE

Waterfowl: Canada geese, white-fronted geese, snow geese, mallards (including the mottled duck form), green-winged teal, blue-winged teal, American wigeon, and northern shovelers.
Wildlife: Mammals, birds (245 species), reptiles, amphibians, and fish.
Habitats: Salt marsh, mud flats, brackish lakes, ponds, and salty prairies.
Size: 19,382 acres.
Location: Along the Gulf of Mexico, 10 miles southwest of Freeport.
Literature Available: Map and bird checklists.
Address: Refuge Manager, San Bernard National Wildlife Refuge, P.O. Drawer 1088, Angleton, Texas 77515.

SANTA ANA NATIONAL WILDLIFE REFUGE

Waterfowl: Black-bellied whistling ducks, gadwalls, pintails, blue-winged teal, cinnamon teal, American wigeon, northern shovelers, and masked ducks (rare).
Wildlife: Mammals (29 species), birds (320 species), reptiles, amphibians, fish, and plants (450 species). Santa Ana National Wildlife Refuge is both unique and famous for the number of Mexican bird species that extend their distribution northward just to the refuge.
Habitats: Subtropical forest, the Rio Grande River, lakes, and marshes.
Size: 1,980 acres.
Location: Extreme southern Texas, on the Mexican border, about 7½ miles south of Alamo.
Literature Available: Information circular and map, and bird checklists.
Address: Refuge Manager, Santa Ana National Wildlife Refuge, 306 E. Jackson Street, P.O. Box 2683, Harlingen, Texas 78550.

A wetland scene on the Santa Ana National Wildlife Refuge, Texas. Photo by U.S. Fish and Wildlife Service.

Pacific States

Washington

COLUMBIA NATIONAL WILDLIFE REFUGE

Waterfowl: Canada geese, mallards, pintails, green-winged teal, blue-winged teal, cinnamon teal, American wigeon, ring-necked ducks, lesser scaup, common goldeneyes, buffleheads, and ruddy ducks.
Wildlife: Mammals, birds (197 species), reptiles, amphibians, and fish.
Habitats: Lakes, sloughs, streams, wet meadows, and marshes.
Size: 28,800 acres.
Location: In southeastern Washington, 7 miles north of Othello.
Literature Available: Information circular, map, bird checklist, and self-guiding tour leaflet.
Address: Refuge Manager, Columbia National Wildlife Refuge, 44 South 8th Avenue, Othello, Washington 99344.

COLUMBIAN WHITE-TAILED DEER NATIONAL WILDLIFE REFUGE

Waterfowl: Whistling swans, Canada geese, mallards, pintails, and American wigeon.
Wildlife: Mammals (including Columbian white-tailed deer), birds, reptiles, amphibians, and fish.
Habitats: River bottomland, sloughs, channels, pastures, brushy thickets, and blocks of trees.
Size: 5,200 acres.
Location: In southwestern Washington, near Cathlamet.
Literature Available: Information leaflet and map.
Address: Refuge Manager, Columbia White-Tailed Deer National Wildlife Refuge, Route 1, Box 376C, Cathlamet, Washington 98612.

McNARY NATIONAL WILDLIFE REFUGE

Waterfowl: Whistling swans, Canada geese, mallards, gadwalls, pintails, green-winged teal, blue-winged teal, cinnamon teal, American wigeon, northern shovelers, redheads, ring-necked ducks, canvasbacks, lesser scaup, common goldeneyes, barrow's goldeneyes, buffleheads, ruddy ducks, and common mergansers.
Wildlife: Mammals, birds (159 species), reptiles, amphibians, and fish.
Habitats: River, islands, marsh, and cultivated crops.
Size: 3,631 acres.
Location: In southeastern Washington, 6 miles south of Pasco and 20 miles upstream from McNary Dam.
Literature Available: Information leaflet and map, and bird checklist.
Address: Refuge Manager, McNary National Wildlife Refuge, Box 308, Burbank, Washington 99323.

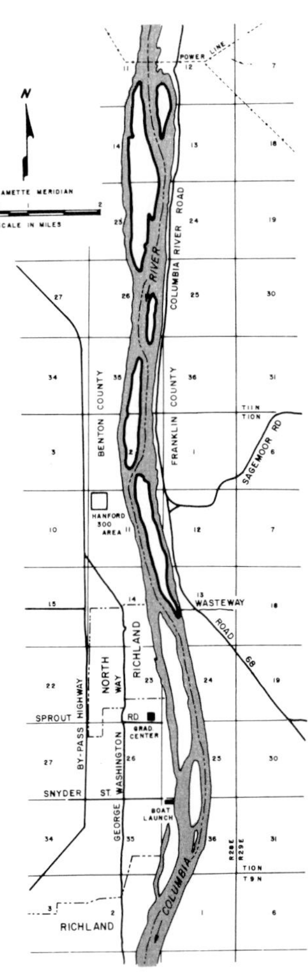

NARY NATIONAL WILDLIFE REFUGE
HANFORD ISLANDS DIVISION

BENTON AND FRANKLIN COUNTIES
WASHINGTON

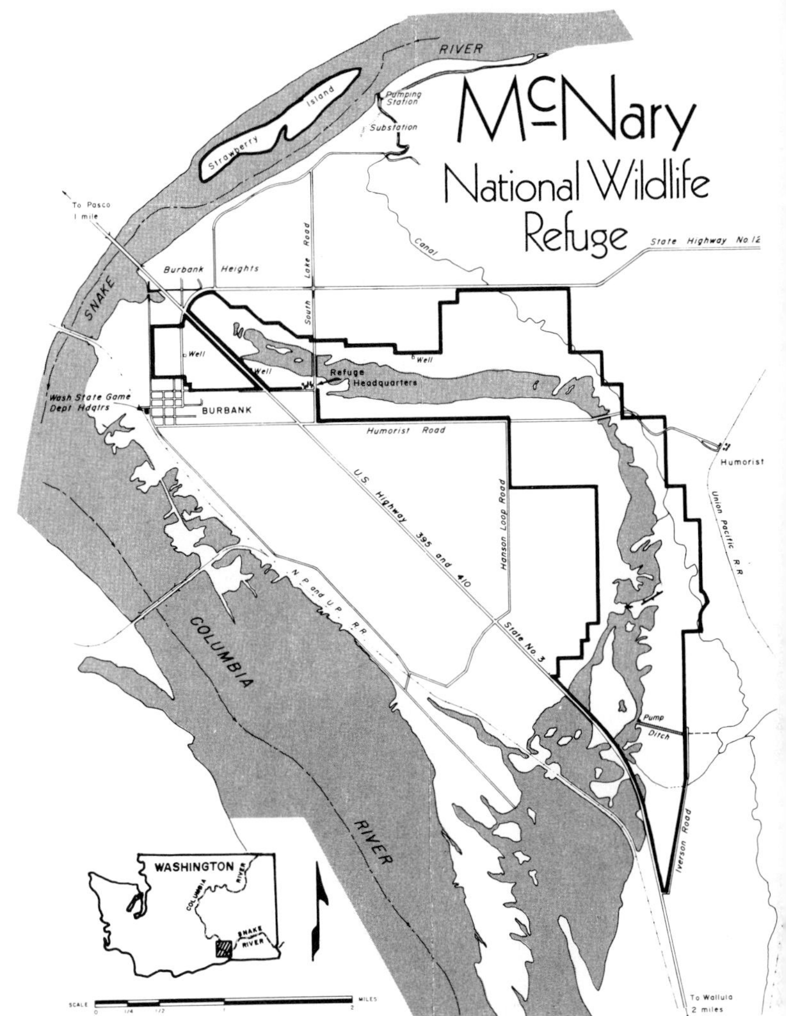

RIDGEFIELD NATIONAL WILDLIFE REFUGE

Waterfowl: Whistling swans, Canada geese, mallards, pintails, green-winged teal, cinnamon teal, American wigeon, and northern shovelers.
Wildlife: Mammals, birds, reptiles, amphibians, and fish.
Habitats: Marsh, ponds, pasture, and Douglas fir stands.
Size: 3,000 acres.
Location: In northwestern Washington, near Ridgefield, at the confluence of the Lake and Lewis rivers.
Literature Available: Information sheet and map, bird checklists, trail guide, and pictorial wildlife guide.
Address: Refuge Manager, Ridgefield National Wildlife Refuge, P.O. Box 467, Ridgefield, Washington 98642.

TOPPENISH NATIONAL WILDLIFE REFUGE

Waterfowl: Canada geese, mallards, pintails, green-winged teal, cinnamon teal, American wigeon, northern shovelers, and wood ducks.
Wildlife: Mammals, birds, reptiles, amphibians, and fish.
Habitats: Toppenish Creek, Yakima River, brushy creek bottomlands, wet meadows, sagebrush uplands, and croplands.
Size: 1,764 acres.
Location: In southcentral Washington, 5 miles south of Toppenish. There are three refuge units.
Literature Available: Information sheet and map, and bird checklists.
Address: Refuge Manager, Toppenish National Wildlife Refuge, Route 1, Box 1300, Toppenish, Washington 98948.

TURNBULL NATIONAL WILDLIFE REFUGE

Waterfowl: Whistling swans, trumpeter swans (introduced), Canada geese, mallards, gadwalls, pintails, green-winged teal, blue-winged teal, cinnamon teal, American wigeon, northern shovelers, redheads, lesser scaup, common goldeneyes, buffleheads, and ruddy ducks.
Wildlife: Mammals, birds, reptiles, amphibians, and fish.
Habitats: Lakes, display pool, marshes, and pine uplands.
Size: 15,565 acres.
Location: In eastern Washington, 6 miles south of Cheney.
Literature Available: Information circular and map, and bird checklists.
Address: Refuge Manager, Turnbull National Wildlife Refuge, Route 3, Box 385, Cheney, Washington 99004.

WILLAPA NATIONAL WILDLIFE REFUGE

Waterfowl: Whistling swans, trumpeter swans, Canada geese, brant, mallards, gadwalls, pintails, green-winged teal, American wigeon, wood ducks, canvasbacks, greater scaup, buffleheads, white-winged scoters, and surf scoters.
Wildlife: Mammals, birds (256 species), reptiles, amphibians, and fish.
Habitats: Willapa Bay, estuary, marshes, rivers, coastal rain forest, virgin western red cedars (on Long Island), and pastureland.

RIDGEFIELD NATIONAL WILDLIFE REFUGE

CLARK COUNTY, WASHINGTON

RECREATION MAP

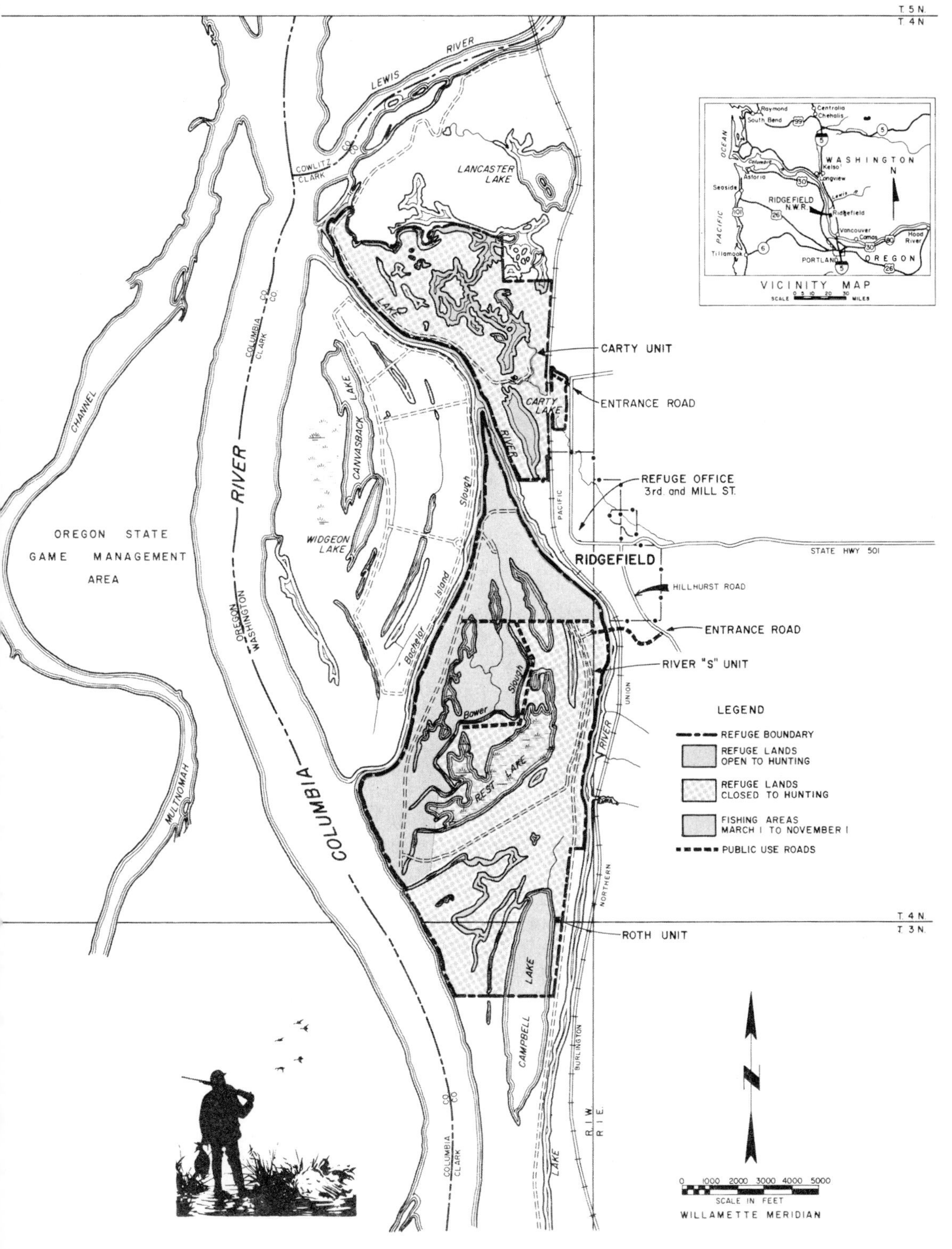

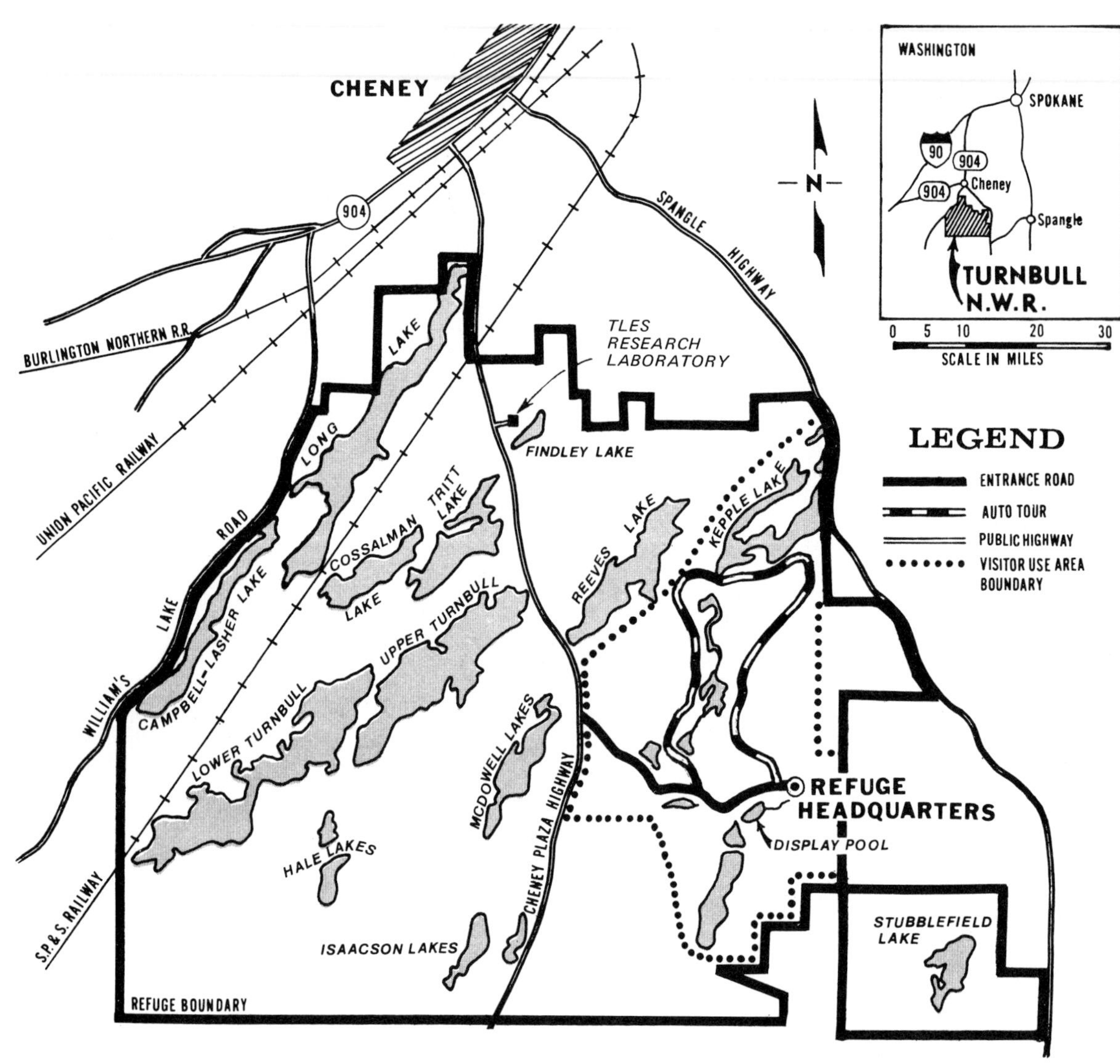

Size: 11,500 acres plus 11,900 acres of state tidelands and waters in Willapa Bay.
Location: In southwestern Washington on Willapa Bay near Ilwaco.
Literature Available: Information circular and map, bird checklists, and other circulars.
Address: Refuge Manager, Willapa National Wildlife Refuge, Ilwaco, Washington 98624.

Findley Lake with a cattail border and a background of Ponderosa Pine on the Turnbull National Wildlife Refuge, Washington. Photo by David B. Marshall / U.S. Fish and Wildlife Service.

Oregon

ANKENY NATIONAL WILDLIFE REFUGE

Waterfowl: Whistling swans, Canada geese, mallards, pintails, green-winged teal, American wigeon, northern shovelers, and wood ducks.
Wildlife: Mammals (52 species), birds (193 species), reptiles, amphibians, and fish.
Habitats: Ponds, creeks, woods, fields, and hedgerows.
Size: 2,796 acres.
Location: In northwestern Oregon's Willamette Valley just east of the confluence of the Santiam and Willamette rivers and south of Salem.
Literature Available: Information leaflet and map, and bird and mammal checklists.
Address: Refuge Manager, Ankeny National Wildlife Refuge, Route 1, Box 198, Jefferson, Oregon 97352.

BASKETT SLOUGH NATIONAL WILDLIFE REFUGE

Waterfowl: Whistling swans, Canada geese, mallards, pintails, green-winged teal, American wigeon, northern shovelers, and wood ducks.
Wildlife: Mammals (52 species), birds (193 species), reptiles, amphibians, and fish.
Habitats: Lakes, ponds, slough, and fields.
Size: 2,492 acres.
Location: In northwestern Oregon's Willamette Valley just west of Rickreall.
Literature Available: Information leaflet, and bird and mammal checklists.
Address: Refuge Manager, Baskett Slough National Wildlife Refuge, Route 1, Box 709, Dallas, Oregon 97338.

HART MOUNTAIN NATIONAL ANTELOPE REFUGE

Waterfowl: Whistling swans, Canada geese, mallards, gadwalls, pintails, green-winged teal, cinnamon teal, American wigeon, northern shovelers, redheads, canvasbacks, buffleheads, ruddy ducks, and common mergansers.
Wildlife: Mammals (including antelope, mule deer, California bighorn sheep), birds (213 species), reptiles, amphibians, and fish.
Habitats: Hart Mountain, lakes, ponds, creeks, desert, and cliffs.
Size: 275,000 acres.
Location: In southcentral Oregon, 65 miles northeast of Lakeview.
Literature Available: Information circular and map, bird checklists, native plant leaflet, and Indian leaflet.
Address: Refuge Manager, Hart Mountain National Antelope Refuge, P.O. Box 111, Lakeview, Oregon 97630.

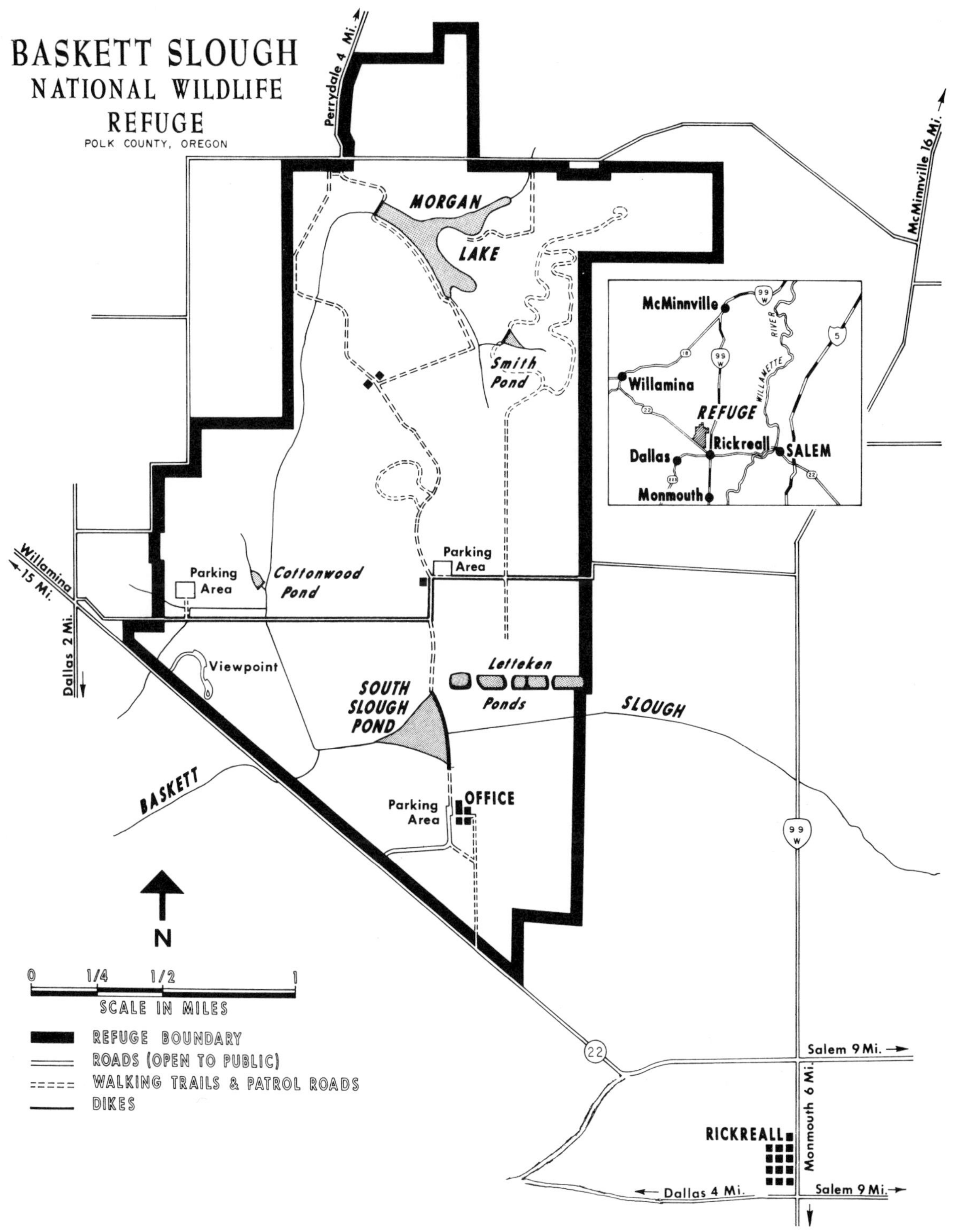
BASKETT SLOUGH
NATIONAL WILDLIFE
REFUGE
POLK COUNTY, OREGON
Perrydale 4 Mi.
McMinnville 16 Mi.
MORGAN
LAKE
Smith
Pond
McMinnville
Willamina
REFUGE
Rickreall
SALEM
Dallas
Monmouth
WILLAMETTE
RIVER
Willamina 15 Mi.
Dallas 2 Mi.
Parking
Area
Cottonwood
Pond
Parking
Area
Viewpoint
Letteken
Ponds
SOUTH
SLOUGH
POND
SLOUGH
BASKETT
Parking
Area
OFFICE
N
0
1/4
1/2
1
SCALE IN MILES
REFUGE BOUNDARY
ROADS (OPEN TO PUBLIC)
WALKING TRAILS & PATROL ROADS
DIKES
22
Salem 9 Mi.
Monmouth 6 Mi.
RICKREALL
Dallas 4 Mi.
Salem 9 Mi.

KLAMATH FOREST NATIONAL WILDLIFE REFUGE

Waterfowl: Whistling swans, Canada geese, white-fronted geese, snow geese, mallards, pintails, green-winged teal, cinnamon teal, American wigeon, northern shovelers, redheads, lesser scaup, ruddy ducks, and common mergansers.
Wildlife: Mammals, birds, reptiles, amphibians, and fish.
Habitat: A large natural marsh.
Size: 15,400 acres.
Location: In southern Oregon, 25 miles north of Chiloquin.
Literature Available: Information circular, map, and bird checklists.
Address: Refuge Manager, Klamath Basin National Wildlife Refuges, Route 1, Box 74, Tulelake, California 96134.

LEWIS AND CLARK NATIONAL WILDLIFE REFUGE

Waterfowl: Whistling swans, Canada geese, mallards, pintails, American wigeon, and green-winged teal.
Wildlife: Mammals, birds, reptiles, amphibians, and fish.
Habitats: Columbia River mouth and estuary, islands, mud flats, and tidal marshes.
Size: 35,000 acres.
Location: Extreme northwestern Oregon near Cathlamet, Washington.
Literature Available: Information circular and map, and bird checklist.
Address: Refuge Manager, Lewis and Clark National Wildlife Refuge, Route 1, Box 376C, Cathlamet, Washington 98612.

MALHEUR NATIONAL WILDLIFE REFUGE

Waterfowl: Whistling swans, Canada geese, snow geese, mallards, gadwalls, pintails, green-winged teal, cinnamon teal, American wigeon, northern shovelers, redheads, canvasbacks, lesser scaup, common goldeneyes, buffleheads, ruddy ducks, and common mergansers.
Wildlife: Mammals (57 species), birds (226 species), reptiles, amphibians, and fish.
Habitats: Shallow marshes, ponds, lakes, irrigated meadows, grassland, and sagebrush upland.
Size: 181,000 acres.
Location: In the high desert country of southeastern Oregon, 32 miles southeast of Burns.
Literature Available: Information circular and map, bird and mammal checklists, and historical notes.
Address: Refuge Manager, Malheur National Wildlife Refuge, P.O. Box 113, Burns, Oregon 97720.

UMATILLA NATIONAL WILDLIFE REFUGE

Waterfowl: Whistling swans, Canada geese, mallards, pintails, green-winged teal, American wigeon, common goldeneyes, and buffleheads.
Wildlife: Mammals, birds (172 species), reptiles, amphibians, and fish.
Habitats: Open water, marshes, cropland, and cheatgrass-sagebrush desert.
Size: 22,216 acres.

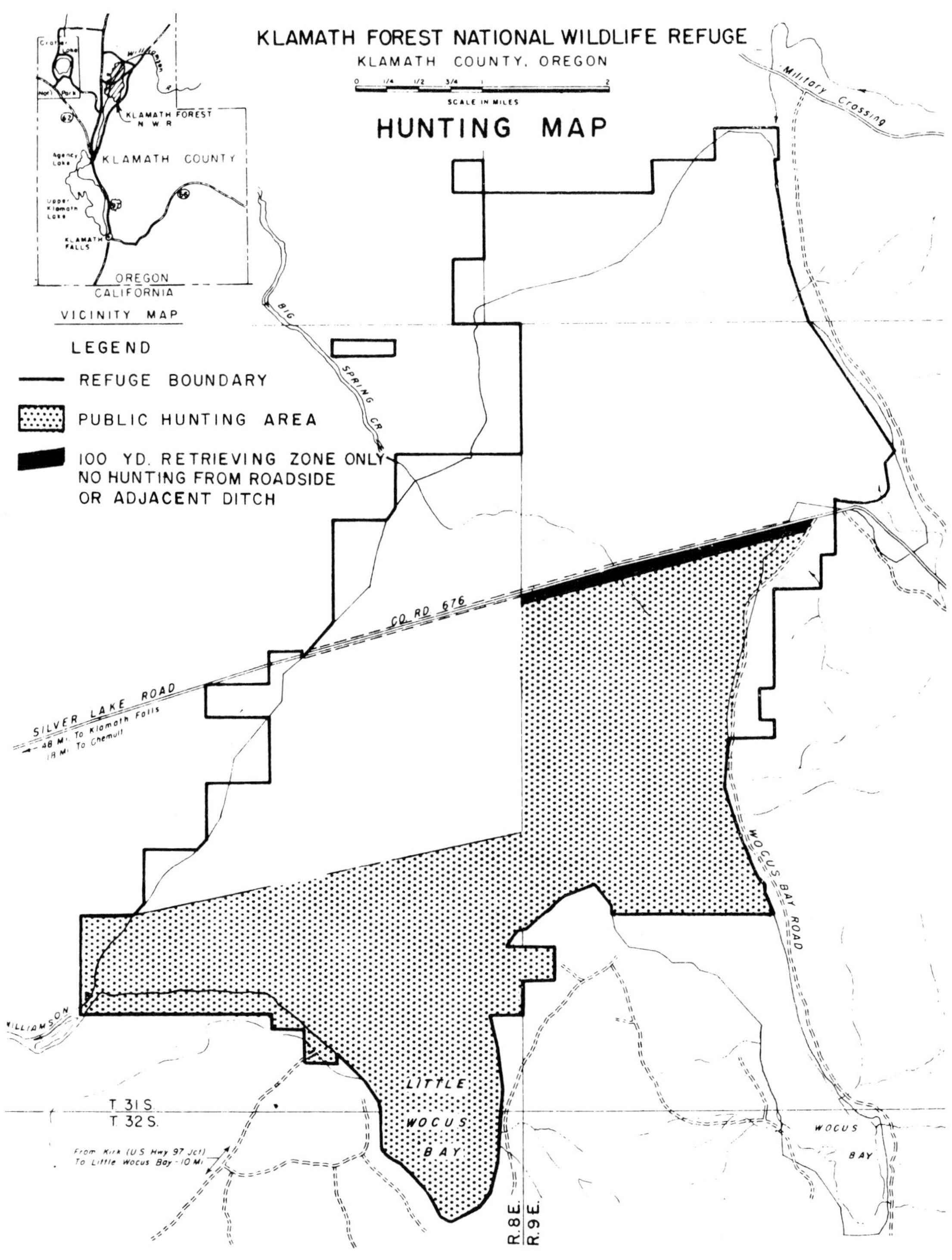
KLAMATH FOREST NATIONAL WILDLIFE REFUGE
KLAMATH COUNTY, OREGON
SCALE IN MILES
HUNTING MAP
KLAMATH FOREST N.W.R.
KLAMATH COUNTY
OREGON
CALIFORNIA
VICINITY MAP
LEGEND
REFUGE BOUNDARY
PUBLIC HUNTING AREA
100 YD. RETRIEVING ZONE ONLY
NO HUNTING FROM ROADSIDE
OR ADJACENT DITCH
Military Crossing
BIG SPRING CR
CO RD 676
SILVER LAKE ROAD
48 Mi To Klamath Falls
18 Mi To Chemult
WOCUS BAY ROAD
WILLIAMSON
LITTLE WOCUS BAY
WOCUS BAY
T. 31 S.
T. 32 S.
From Kirk (U.S. Hwy 97 Jct) To Little Wocus Bay - 10 Mi
R.8 E.
R.9 E.

A typical waterfowl production pond on the Malheur National Wildlife Refuge, Oregon. Photo by David B. Marshall / U.S. Fish and Wildlife Service.

Location: In northcentral Oregon, along 18 miles of the Columbia River between Boardman and Irrigon.
Literature Available: Information circular and map, and bird checklist.
Address: Refuge Manager, Umatilla National Wildlife Refuge, Box 239, Umatilla, Oregon 97882.

UPPER KLAMATH NATIONAL WILDLIFE REFUGE

Waterfowl: Whistling swans, Canada geese, white-fronted geese, snow geese, mallards, pintails, green-winged teal, cinnamon teal, American wigeon, northern shovelers, redheads, lesser scaup, ruddy ducks, and common mergansers.
Wildlife: Mammals, birds, reptiles, amphibians, and fish.
Habitats: The northern end of Upper Klamath Lake and marshes.
Size: 14,900 acres.

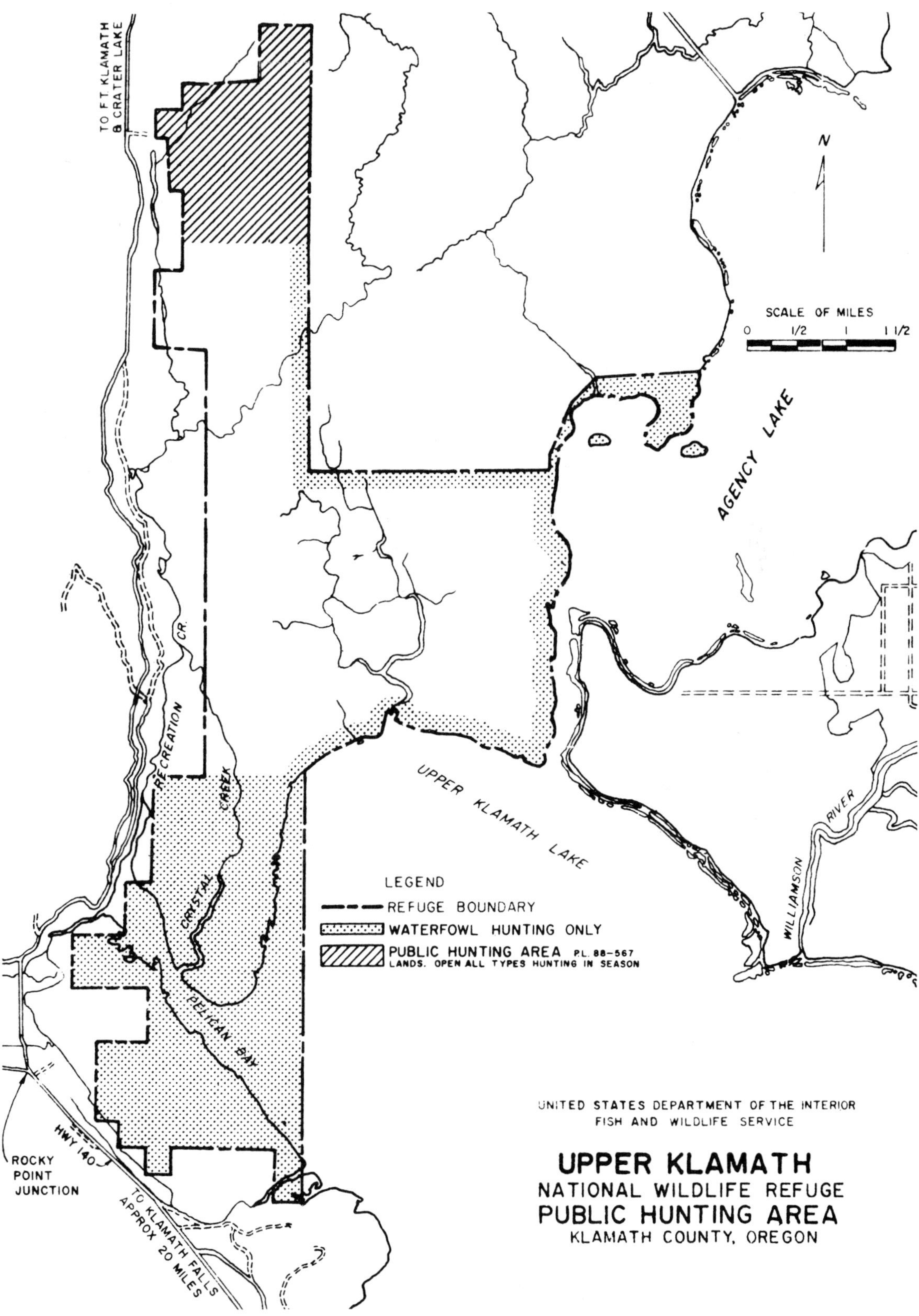
TO FT KLAMATH & CRATER LAKE
N
SCALE OF MILES
0 1/2 1 1 1/2
AGENCY LAKE
RECREATION CR.
CRYSTAL CREEK
UPPER KLAMATH LAKE
WILLIAMSON RIVER
PELICAN BAY
LEGEND
REFUGE BOUNDARY
WATERFOWL HUNTING ONLY
PUBLIC HUNTING AREA P.L. 88-567 LANDS. OPEN ALL TYPES HUNTING IN SEASON
ROCKY POINT JUNCTION
HWY 140
TO KLAMATH FALLS APPROX 20 MILES
UNITED STATES DEPARTMENT OF THE INTERIOR
FISH AND WILDLIFE SERVICE
UPPER KLAMATH
NATIONAL WILDLIFE REFUGE
PUBLIC HUNTING AREA
KLAMATH COUNTY, OREGON

Lichen-coated trees along Muddy Creek on the William L. Finley National Wildlife Refuge, Oregon. Photo by David B. Marshall / U.S. Fish and Wildlife Service.

Location: In southern Oregon, 35 miles northwest of Klamath Falls. Access is by boat only.
Literature Available: Information circular and map, and bird checklist.
Address: Refuge Manager, Klamath Basin National Wildlife Refuges, Route 1, Box 74, Tulelake, California 96134.

WILLIAM L. FINLEY NATIONAL WILDLIFE REFUGE

Waterfowl: Whistling swans, Canada geese, mallards, pintails, green-winged teal, American wigeon, northern shovelers, and wood ducks.
Wildlife: Mammals (52 species), birds (193 species), reptiles, amphibians, and fish.
Habitats: Woodlands, brushy hedgerows, marshes, creeks, meadows, fields, and pastures.
Size: 5,325 acres.

Location: In northwestern Oregon, 12 miles south of Corvallis off State Route 99W.
Literature Available: Information circular and map, and bird and mammal checklists.
Address: Refuge Manager, William L. Finley National Wildlife Refuge, Route 2, Box 208, Corvallis, Oregon 97330.

Idaho

BEAR LAKE NATIONAL WILDLIFE REFUGE

Waterfowl: Canada geese, mallards, gadwalls, pintails, green-winged teal, blue-winged teal, cinnamon teal, American wigeon, northern shovelers, and redheads.
Wildlife: Mammals, birds (130 species), reptiles, amphibians, and fish.
Habitats: Mud Lake, marsh, and grasslands.
Size: 17,600 acres.
Location: In southeastern Idaho, about 6 miles south of Montpelier.
Literature Available: Information booklet, circular and map, and bird checklist.
Address: Refuge Manager, Bear Lake National Wildlife Refuge, 802 Washington, Montpelier, Idaho 83254.

CAMAS NATIONAL WILDLIFE REFUGE

Waterfowl: Whistling swans, Canada geese, mallards, gadwalls, pintails, green-winged teal, blue-winged teal, cinnamon teal, American wigeon, northern shovelers, redheads, canvasbacks, lesser scaup, common goldeneyes, buffleheads, and ruddy ducks.
Wildlife: Mammals, birds (166 species), reptiles, amphibians, and fish.
Habitats: Marshes, hay meadows, flat land, and sandhills.
Size: 10,656 acres.
Location: In eastern Idaho, 38 miles north of Idaho Falls.
Literature Available: Information booklet and map, and bird checklist.
Address: Refuge Manager, Camas National Wildlife Refuge, Hamer, Idaho 83425.

DEER FLAT NATIONAL WILDLIFE REFUGE

Waterfowl: Canada geese, mallards, pintails, green-winged teal, cinnamon teal, American wigeon, wood ducks, common goldeneyes, and common mergansers.
Wildlife: Mammals, birds (172 species), reptiles, amphibians, and fish.
Habitats: Lake Lowell and 100 islands in a 110-mile section of the Snake River between Walter's Ferry Bridge, Idaho, and Farewell Bend, Oregon.
Size: 11,585 acres.

Location: In the Boise Valley of southwestern Idaho southwest of Nampa.
Literature Available: Information circular and map, and bird checklist.
Address: Refuge Manager, Deer Flat National Wildlife Refuge, Route 1, Box 335, Nampa, Idaho 83651.

GRAYS LAKE NATIONAL WILDLIFE REFUGE

Waterfowl: Canada geese, mallards, gadwalls, pintails, green-winged teal, blue-winged teal, cinnamon teal, American wigeon, northern shovelers, redheads, buffleheads, and ruddy ducks.
Wildlife: Mammals, birds (163 species), reptiles, amphibians, and fish.
Habitats: Bullrush marsh, ponds, island, and wet meadows.
Size: 32,600 acres.
Location: In southeastern Idaho, 30 miles north of Soda Springs.
Literature Available: Bird checklist, and whooping crane project leaflet.
Address: Refuge Manager, Grays Lake National Wildlife Refuge, P.O. Box 837, Soda Springs, Idaho 83276.

KOOTENAI NATIONAL WILDLIFE REFUGE

Waterfowl: Whistling swans, Canada geese, mallards, pintails, green-winged teal, blue-winged teal, wood ducks, and common goldeneyes.
Wildlife: Mammals, birds (215 species), reptiles, amphibians, and fish.
Habitats: Ponds, creeks, river, meadows, brush rows, fields, and wooded areas.
Size: 2,762 acres.
Location: In the northern tip of Idaho, 5 miles west of Bonners Ferry.
Literature Available: Information circular and map, and bird checklists.
Address: Refuge Manager, Kootenai National Wildlife Refuge, Route 1, Box 88, Bonners Ferry, Idaho 83805.

MINIDOKA NATIONAL WILDLIFE REFUGE

Waterfowl: Whistling swans, Canada geese, mallards, gadwalls, pintails, green-winged teal, American wigeon, redheads, ring-necked ducks, canvasbacks, lesser scaup, common goldeneyes, ruddy ducks, and common mergansers.
Wildlife: Mammals, birds (204 species), reptiles, amphibians, and fish.
Habitats: Snake River, Lake Walcott, bays, inlets, marshes, islands, sagebrush, grassland, and sand dunes.
Size: 25,630 acres.
Location: In southcentral Idaho, along 25 miles of the Snake River, 12 miles northeast of Rupert.
Literature Available: Information circular and map, and bird checklists.
Address: Refuge Manager, Minidoka National Wildlife Refuge, Route 4, Rupert, Idaho 83350.

Nevada

PAHRANAGAT NATIONAL WILDLIFE REFUGE

Waterfowl: Mallards, gadwalls, pintails, green-winged teal, and canvasbacks.
Wildlife: Mammals, birds (193 species), reptiles, amphibians, and fish.
Habitats: Water impoundments, marshes, ditches, desert, and cultivated fields.
Size: 5,380 acres.
Location: In southern Nevada, in the Pahranagat Valley, 6 miles south of Alamo.
Literature Available: Information booklet and map, and bird checklist.
Address: Refuge Manager, Pahranagat National Wildlife Refuge, 1500 North Decatur Boulevard, Las Vegas, Nevada 89108.

RUBY LAKE NATIONAL WILDLIFE REFUGE

Waterfowl: Whistling swans, Canada geese, mallards, gadwalls, pintails, green-winged teal, cinnamon teal, American wigeon, northern shovelers, redheads, ring-necked ducks, canvasbacks, lesser scaup, common goldeneyes, buffleheads, and ruddy ducks.
Wildlife: Mammals, birds (195 species), reptiles, amphibians, and fish.
Habitats: Ruby Lake, ponds, islands, wet meadows, and uplands.
Size: 37,630 acres.
Location: In northeastern Nevada, south of Ruby Valley.
Literature Available: Information circular and map, and bird checklist.
Address: Refuge Manager, Ruby Lake National Wildlife Refuge, Ruby Valley, Nevada 89833.

STILLWATER NATIONAL WILDLIFE REFUGE AND MANAGEMENT AREA

Waterfowl: Whistling swans, Canada geese, snow geese, mallards, gadwalls, pintails, green-winged teal, cinnamon teal, American wigeon, northern shovelers, redheads, canvasbacks, ruddy ducks, and common mergansers.
Wildlife: Mammals, birds (155 species), reptiles, amphibians, and fish.
Habitats: Lakes, marshes, desert, and sand dunes.
Size: 143,866 acres.
Location: In western Nevada, northeast of Fallon.
Literature Available: Information circular and map, and bird checklist.
Address: Refuge Manager, Stillwater Wildlife Management Area, Box 592, Fallon, Nevada 89406.

California

CLEAR LAKE NATIONAL WILDLIFE REFUGE

Waterfowl: Whistling swans, Canada geese, white-fronted geese, snow geese, mallards, pintails, green-winged teal, cinnamon teal, American wigeon, northern shovelers, redheads, lesser scaup, ruddy ducks, and common mergansers.
Wildlife: Mammals, birds, reptiles, amphibians, and fish.
Habitats: Clear Lake, marshes, creek, and springs.
Size: 33,400 acres.
Location: In the Klamath Basin of northern California, about 15 miles southeast of Tulelake.
Literature Available: Information circular, map, and bird checklist.
Address: Refuge Manager, Klamath Basin National Wildlife Refuges, Route 1, Box 74, Tulelake, California 96134.

KERN NATIONAL WILDLIFE REFUGE

Waterfowl: Canada geese, white-fronted geese, mallards, gadwalls, pintails, green-winged teal, cinnamon teal, American wigeon, northern shovelers, and ruddy ducks.
Wildlife: Mammals, birds (160 species), reptiles, amphibians, and fish.
Habitats: Ponds, marshes, canals, and fields.
Size: 10,618 acres.
Location: In southern California, at the southern end of the San Joaquin Valley, west of Delano.
Literature Available: Information sheet and map, and bird checklist.
Address: Refuge Manager, Kern-Pixley National Wildlife Refuges, P.O. Box 219, Delano, California 93215.

LOWER KLAMATH NATIONAL WILDLIFE REFUGE

Waterfowl: Whistling swans, Canada geese, white-fronted geese, snow geese, mallards, pintails, green-winged teal, cinnamon teal, American wigeon, northern shovelers, redheads, lesser scaup, ruddy ducks, and common mergansers.
Wildlife: Mammals, birds, reptiles, amphibians, and fish.
Habitats: Marshes, lakes, creeks, and fields.
Size: 47,500 acres.
Location: Northern California, on the Oregon border in the Klamath Basin.
Literature Available: Information circular, map, and bird checklist.
Address: Refuge Manager, Klamath Basin National Wildlife Refuges, Route 1, Box 74, Tulelake, California 96134.

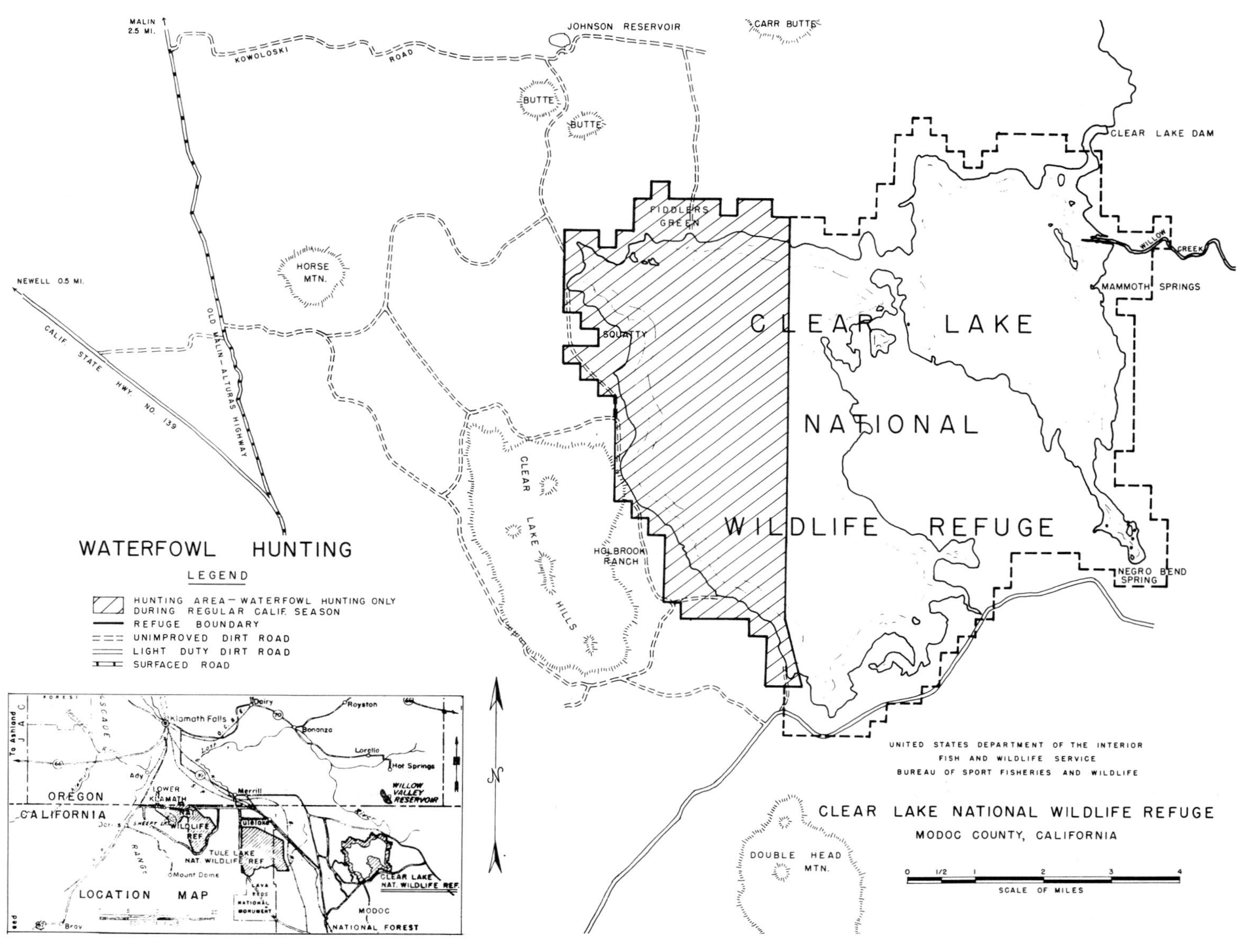

WATERFOWL HUNTING
LEGEND
HUNTING AREA—WATERFOWL HUNTING ONLY DURING REGULAR CALIF. SEASON
REFUGE BOUNDARY
UNIMPROVED DIRT ROAD
LIGHT DUTY DIRT ROAD
SURFACED ROAD
CLEAR LAKE NATIONAL WILDLIFE REFUGE
MALIN 2.5 MI.
KOWOLOSKI ROAD
JOHNSON RESERVOIR
CARR BUTTE
BUTTE
BUTTE
CLEAR LAKE DAM
WILLOW CREEK
MAMMOTH SPRINGS
FIDDLERS GREEN
HORSE MTN.
NEWELL 0.5 MI.
CALIF. STATE HWY. NO. 139
OLD MALIN—ALTURAS HIGHWAY
SQUATTY
CLEAR LAKE HILLS
HOLBROOK RANCH
NEGRO BEND SPRING
UNITED STATES DEPARTMENT OF THE INTERIOR
FISH AND WILDLIFE SERVICE
BUREAU OF SPORT FISHERIES AND WILDLIFE
CLEAR LAKE NATIONAL WILDLIFE REFUGE
MODOC COUNTY, CALIFORNIA
DOUBLE HEAD MTN.
0 1/2 1 2 3 4
SCALE OF MILES
LOCATION MAP
OREGON
CALIFORNIA
To Ashland
Klamath Falls
Dairy
Royston
Bonanza
Lorella
Hot Springs
WILLOW VALLEY RESERVOIR
Ady
LOWER KLAMATH
Merrill
WILDLIFE REF.
TULE LAKE NAT. WILDLIFE REF.
Mount Dome
CLEAR LAKE NAT. WILDLIFE REF.
LAVA BEDS NATIONAL MONUMENT
MODOC NATIONAL FOREST

Waterfowl concentrations on the Lower Klamath National Wildlife Refuge, California. Photo by Charles Gibbons / U.S. Fish and Wildlife Service.

MERCED NATIONAL WILDLIFE REFUGE

Waterfowl: Whistling swans, Canada geese, white-fronted geese, snow geese, Ross' geese, mallards, pintails, green-winged teal, American wigeon, and northern shovelers. Most of the world population of Ross' geese winter on this refuge.
Wildlife: Mammals, birds (177 species), reptiles, amphibians, and fish.
Habitats: Marshes, creeks, pastures, and cultivated fields.
Size: 2,561 acres.
Location: In the San Joaquin Valley of central California, 14 miles southwest of Merced.
Literature Available: Map and bird checklist.
Address: Refuge Manager, Merced National Wildlife Refuge, P.O. Box 2176, Los Banos, California 93625.

MODOC NATIONAL WILDLIFE REFUGE

Waterfowl: Whistling swans, Canada geese, white-fronted geese, snow geese, mallards, gadwalls, pintails, green-winged teal, cinnamon teal, American wigeon, northern shovelers, lesser scaup, common goldeneyes, buffleheads, ruddy ducks, and common mergansers.
Wildlife: Mammals, birds (187 species), reptiles, amphibians, and fish.
Habitats: Reservoir, river, ponds, and fields.
Size: 6,283 acres.
Location: In northeastern California, 3 miles south of Alturas.
Literature Available: Information sheet and map, and bird checklist.
Address: Refuge Manager, Modoc National Wildlife Refuge, P.O. Box 111, Lakeview, Oregon 97630.

PIXLEY NATIONAL WILDLIFE REFUGE

Waterfowl: Canada geese, white-fronted geese, mallards, gadwalls, pintails, green-winged teal, cinnamon teal, American wigeon, northern shovelers, and ruddy ducks.
Wildlife: Mammals, birds, reptiles, amphibians, and fish.
Habitats: Fields and flooded grasslands.
Size: 4,171 acres.
Location: In southern California, near the southern end of the San Joaquin Valley, northwest of Earlimart.
Literature Available: Information sheet and map.
Address: Refuge Manager, Kern-Pixley National Wildlife Refuges, P.O. Box 219, Delano, California 93215.

SACRAMENTO NATIONAL WILDLIFE REFUGE

Waterfowl: Whistling swans, Canada geese, white-fronted geese, snow geese, Ross' geese, mallards, pintails, green-winged teal, American wigeon, northern shovelers, and ruddy ducks.
Wildlife: Mammals (26 species), birds (174 species), reptiles, amphibians, and fish.
Habitats: Rice fields, millet ponds, and marshes.
Size: 10,776 acres.
Location: In the Sacramento Valley of northern California, 7 miles south of Willows on U.S. Route 99-W.
Literature Available: Information sheet and map, bird and mammal checklists, young people's bird list, tour route guide, and recreation guide.
Address: Refuge Manager, Sacramento National Wildlife Refuge, Route 1, Box 311, Willows, California 95988.

SALTON SEA NATIONAL WILDLIFE REFUGE

Waterfowl: Canada geese, snow geese, pintails, green-winged teal, cinnamon teal, American wigeon, northern shovelers, lesser scaup, and ruddy ducks.
Wildlife: Mammals, birds (258 species), reptiles, and fish.
Habitats: Salton Sea, marshes, cropland, and desert.
Size: 36,527 acres.

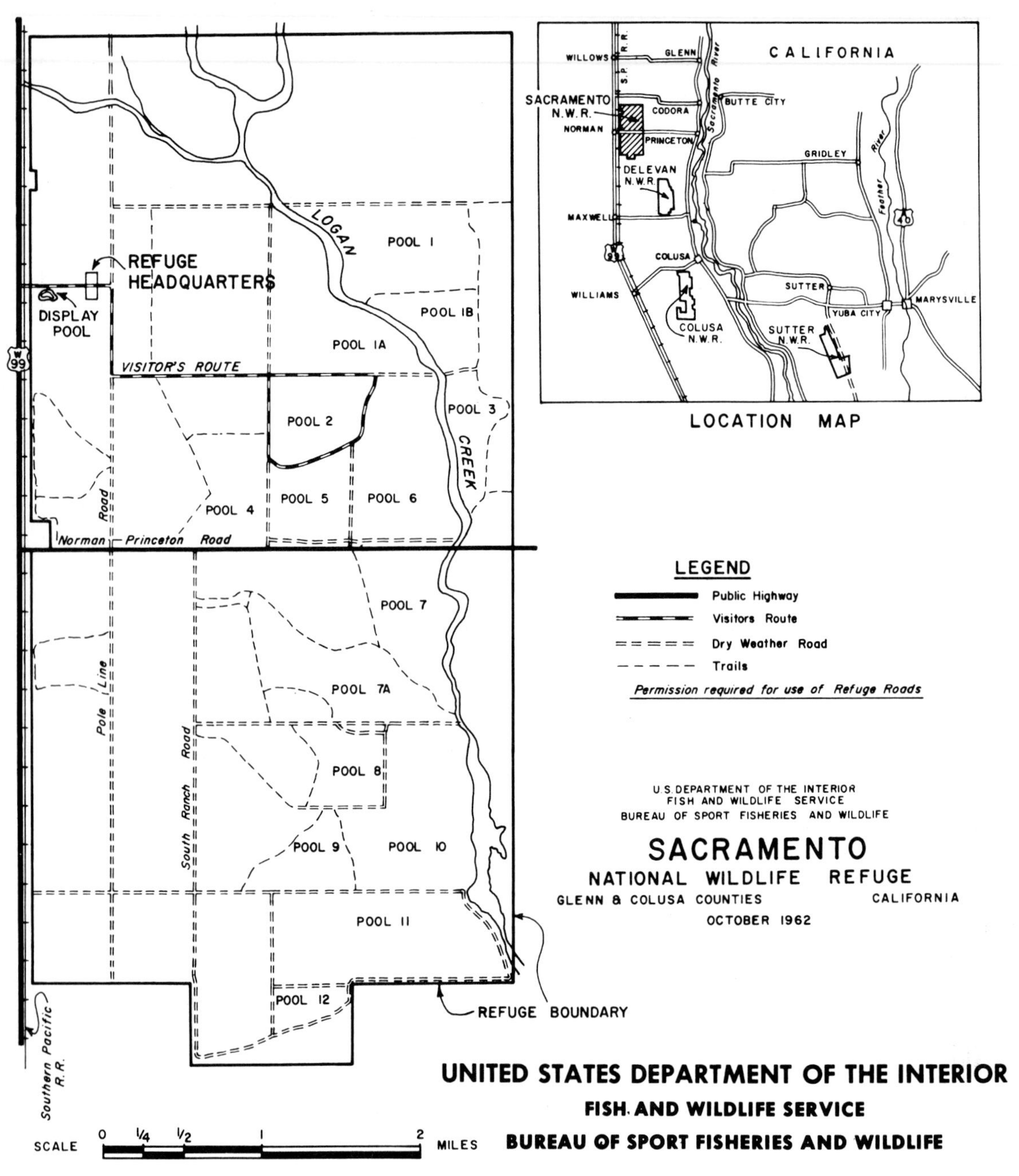

Location: In extreme southern California, 230 feet below sea level in the Imperial Valley, 10 miles north of Westmorland.
Literature Available: Information booklet, map, and bird checklist.
Address: Refuge Manager, Salton Sea National Wildlife Refuge, P.O. Box 247, Calipatria, California 92233.

SAN FRANCISCO BAY NATIONAL WILDLIFE REFUGE

Waterfowl: Mallards, gadwalls, pintails, cinnamon teal, northern shovelers, American wigeon, canvasbacks, greater scaup, lesser scaup, buffleheads, surf scoters, and ruddy ducks.
Wildlife: Mammals, birds (248 species), reptiles, amphibians, and fish.
Habitats: Salt marshes, mudflats, shallow water, and wet salt ponds.
Size: 23,000 acres.
Location: On south San Francisco Bay.
Literature Available: Information circular and maps, and bird checklist.
Address: Refuge Manager, San Francisco Bay National Wildlife Refuge, 3849 Peralta Boulevard, Suite D, Fremont, California 94536.

SAN LUIS NATIONAL WILDLIFE REFUGE

Waterfowl: Canada geese, white-fronted geese, snow geese, Ross' geese, mallards, pintails, green-winged teal, American wigeon, and northern shovelers.
Wildlife: Mammals, birds, reptiles, amphibians, and fish.
Habitats: San Joaquin River, slough, marshes, grassland, and cropland.
Size: 7,360 acres.
Location: In the San Joaquin Valley of central California, about 10 miles north of Los Banos.
Literature Available: Information leaflet and map.
Address: Refuge Manager, San Luis National Wildlife Refuge, P.O. Box 2176, Los Banos, California 93635.

SAN PABLO BAY NATIONAL WILDLIFE REFUGE

Waterfowl: Canvasbacks, mallards, pintails, American wigeon, northern shovelers, redheads, buffleheads, ruddy ducks, scaup, and scoters.
Wildlife: Mammals, birds, reptiles, amphibians, and fish.
Habitats: San Pablo Bay, salt marshes, and mudflats.
Size: 11,790 acres.
Location: North of San Francisco between the Petaluma River outlet and the City of Vallejo.
Literature Available: Information circular and map.
Address: Refuge Manager, San Pablo Bay National Wildlife Refuge, 3849 Peralta Boulevard, Suite D, Fremont, California 94536.

TULE LAKE NATIONAL WILDLIFE REFUGE

Waterfowl: Whistling swans, Canada geese, white-fronted geese, snow geese, mallards, pintails, green-winged teal, cinnamon teal, American wigeon, northern shovelers, redheads, lesser scaup, ruddy ducks, and common mergansers.
Wildlife: Mammals, birds, reptiles, amphibians, and fish.
Habitats: Tule Lake, ponds, marshes, and fields.
Size: 36,000 acres.
Location: In the Klamath Basin of northern California.

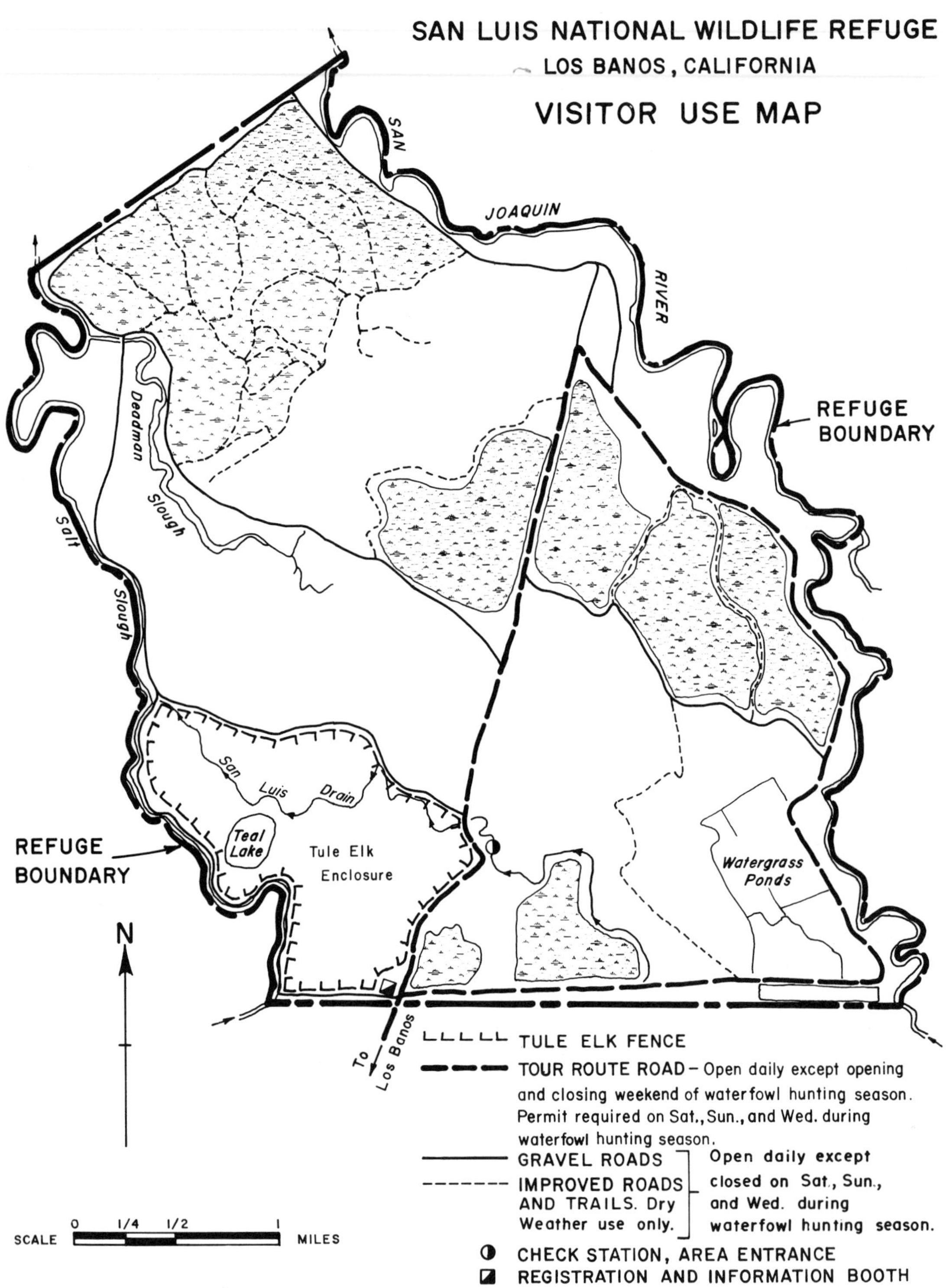
SAN LUIS NATIONAL WILDLIFE REFUGE
LOS BANOS, CALIFORNIA
VISITOR USE MAP
SAN
JOAQUIN
RIVER
REFUGE BOUNDARY
Deadman
Slough
Salt
Slough
San
Luis
Drain
Teal Lake
Tule Elk Enclosure
REFUGE BOUNDARY
Watergrass Ponds
N
To Los Banos
SCALE
0
1/4
1/2
1
MILES
TULE ELK FENCE
TOUR ROUTE ROAD – Open daily except opening and closing weekend of waterfowl hunting season. Permit required on Sat., Sun., and Wed. during waterfowl hunting season.
GRAVEL ROADS
IMPROVED ROADS AND TRAILS. Dry Weather use only.
Open daily except closed on Sat., Sun., and Wed. during waterfowl hunting season.
CHECK STATION, AREA ENTRANCE
REGISTRATION AND INFORMATION BOOTH

Snow geese resting along the edge of Lower Sump on Tule Lake National Wildlife Refuge, California. Photo by David B. Marshall / U.S. Fish and Wildlife Service.

Literature Available: Information circular and map, and bird checklist. *Address:* Refuge Manager, Klamath Basin National Wildlife Refuges, Route 1, Box 74, Tulelake, California 96134.

Alaska

Many of the wildlife refuges in Alaska are among the largest and most spectacular in the entire national wildlife refuge system. Because of their remote locations, however, many are extremely difficult to visit. In some cases airfields are located within military defense zones that require advance clearance for visitors. Full details usually can be secured from the managers of the various refuges.

ALEUTIAN ISLANDS NATIONAL WILDLIFE REFUGE

Waterfowl: Canada geese, brant, emperor geese, green-winged teal, greater scaup, common goldeneyes, buffleheads, oldsquaws, harlequin ducks, Steller's eider, common eider, king eider, white-winged scoters, black scoters, and red-breasted mergansers.
Wildlife: Mammals, birds, and fish.
Habitats: Over 200 mountainous volcanic islands, many with streams, lakes, rocky cliffs, sand, and boulder beaches.
Size: 2,720,235 acres.
Location: A chain of islands (mostly uninhabited) extending 1,100 miles westward from the Alaska Peninsula tip to within 500 miles of the Soviet Union's Kamchatka Peninsula.
Literature Available: Information circular and map, wilderness study booklet, and bird checklist.
Address: Refuge Manager, Aleutian Islands National Wildlife Refuge, Cold Bay, Alaska 99571.

ARCTIC NATIONAL WILDLIFE RANGE

Waterfowl: Whistling swans, brant, green-winged teal, oldsquaws, Steller's eider, common eider, king eider, spectacled eider, white-winged scoters, and surf scoters.
Wildlife: Mammals, birds (139 species), and fish.
Habitats: Mountainous ranges including the Brooks Range, Mt. Chamberlin (9,131 feet), Mt. Michelson (9,239 feet), deep valleys, the Yukon River Basin, lakes, oxbow sloughs, meadows, muskegs, spruce and cottonwood groves, marshy shoreline, and coastline.
Size: 8,900,000 acres.
Location: In extreme northeastern Alaska, the southern boundary 100 miles north of the Artic Circle. Access is by airplane, generally from Fort Yukon, Arctic Village, or Barter Island. There are no visitor facilites in this vast, untouched wilderness. Contact the refuge manager for full details about visiting the area.

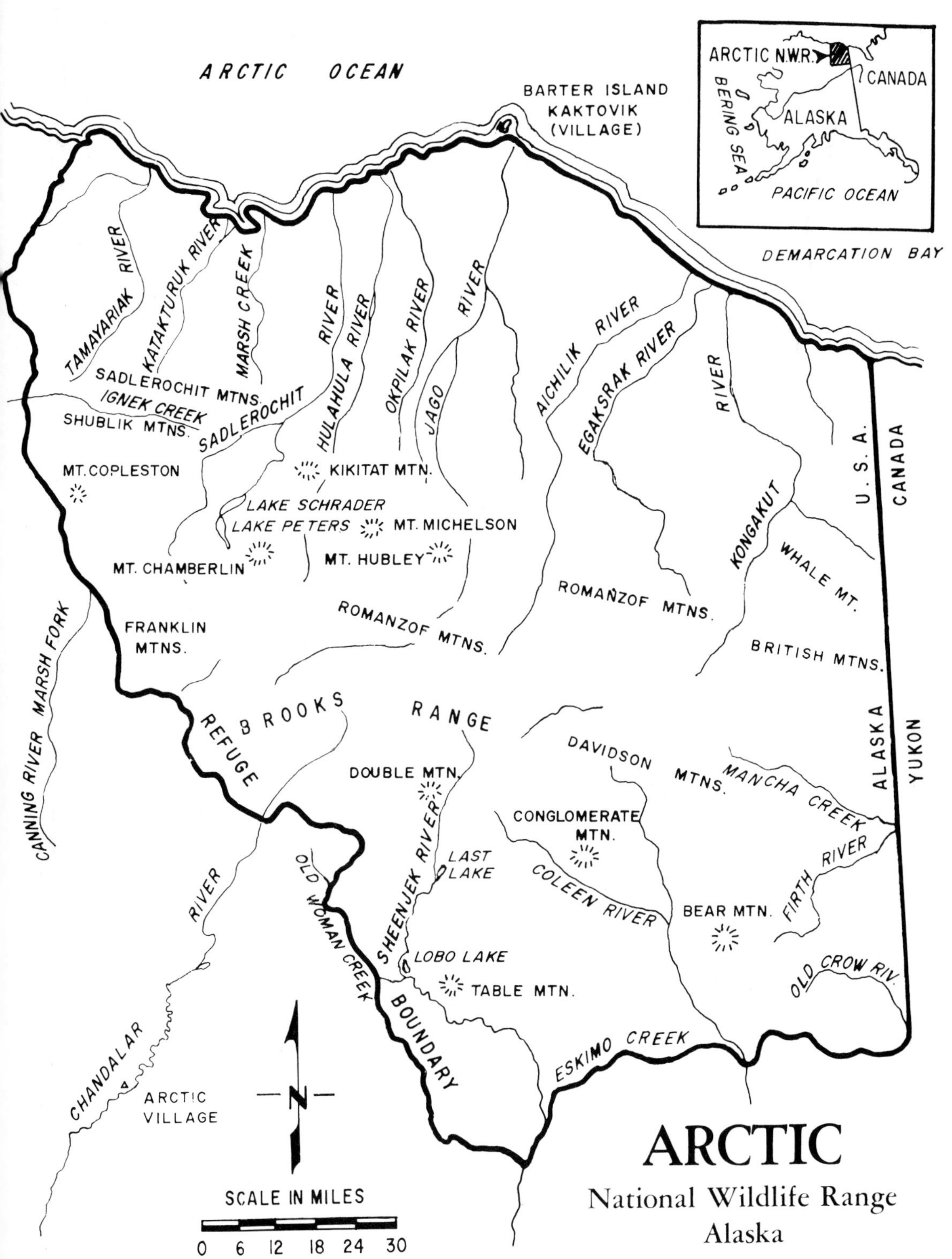

ARCTIC
National Wildlife Range
Alaska

The Canada geese of the Aleutian Islands are small birds with distinctive white collars. The subspecies is now very rare. Photo by M. Glen Smart / U.S. Fish and Wildlife Service.

Literature Available: Information circular and map, bird checklist, and camping circular.
Address: Refuge Manager, Arctic National Wildlife Range, 1412 Airport Way, Fairbanks, Alaska 99701.

BERING SEA NATIONAL WILDLIFE REFUGE

Waterfowl: Pintails, oldsquaws, harlequin ducks, common eider, and red-breasted mergansers.
Wildlife: Mammals, birds, and fish.

Habitats: Ridges, low valleys, lakes, dormant volcanoes, tundra, and sea cliffs.
Size: 41,113 acres.
Location: In the Bering Sea, 250 miles west of mainland Alaska. The refuge consists of three isolated, uninhabited islands—St. Matthew, Hall, and Pinnacle.
Literature Available: Information booklet, map, and bird checklist.
Address: Refuge Manager, Bering Sea National Wildlife Refuge, Box 346, Bethel, Alaska 99559.

CLARENCE RHODE NATIONAL WILDLIFE RANGE

Waterfowl: Whistling swans, Canada geese, brant, emperor geese, white-fronted geese, snow geese, American wigeon, greater scaup, oldsquaws, common eider, king eider, spectacled eider, and black scoters.
Wildlife: Mammals, birds, and fish.
Habitats: Lowland tundra, more than 50,000 ponds and lakes, and coastal areas.
Size: 2,800,000 acres.
Location: In southwestern Alaska, in the Yukon–Kuskokwim Delta, 500 miles west of the end of the road at Anchorage. Refuge headquarters is in Bethel.
Literature Available: Information circular and map, and bird checklist.
Address: Refuge Manager, Clarence Rhode National Wildlife Range, Box 346, Bethel, Alaska 99559.

IZEMBEK NATIONAL WILDLIFE REFUGE

Waterfowl: Canada geese, brant, emperor geese, mallards, pintails, green-winged teal, greater scaup, common goldeneyes, oldsquaws, harlequin ducks, Steller's eider, common eider, black scoters, and red-breasted mergansers.
Wildlife: Mammals, birds (142 species), and fish.
Habitats: Mountains with glaciers, low rolling valleys, tundra, streams, lakes, upland meadows with grass, heaths, and sedges, lagoons, and bays.
Size: 415,000 acres.
Location: In southwestern Alaska on 45 miles of the northern tip of the Alaska Peninsula. The headquarters, on Cold Bay, is reached via commercial air flights from Anchorage or by private air charters.
Literature Available: Information circular and bird checklist.
Address: Refuge Manager, Izembek National Wildlife Refuge, Cold Bay, Alaska 99571.

KENAI NATIONAL MOOSE RANGE

Waterfowl: Trumpeter swans, Canada geese, mallards, pintails, green-winged teal, American wigeon, northern shovelers, greater scaup, Barrow's goldeneyes, and harlequin ducks.
Wildlife: Mammals (especially moose), birds, and fish.

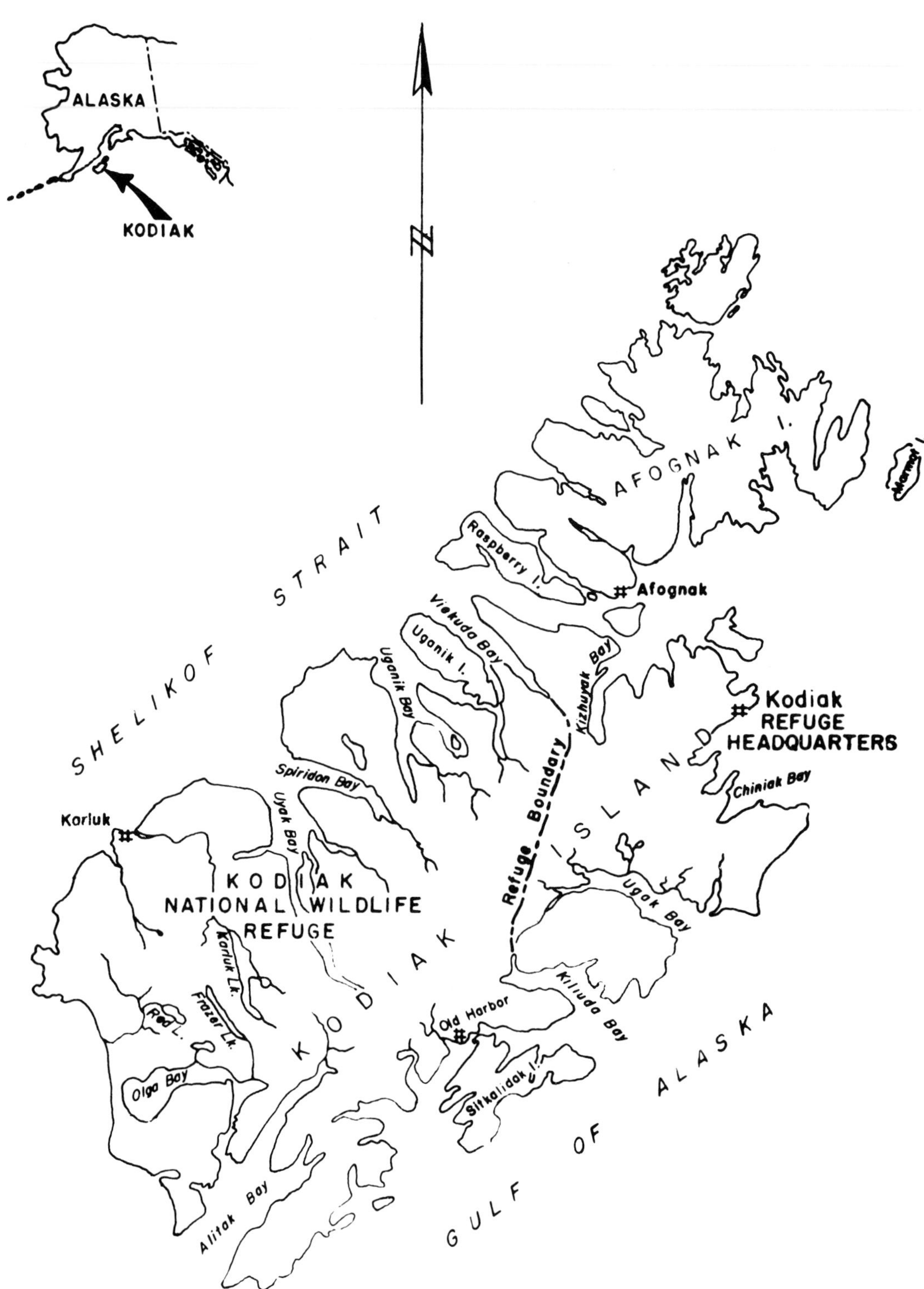

KODIAK NATIONAL WILDLIFE REFUGE

Habitats: Mountains, valleys, rivers, lakes, bogs, and spruce forests.
Size: 1,730,000 acres.
Location: In southern Alaska, 110 miles (by road) south of Anchorage.
Literature Available: Information circular and map, common bird checklist, and canoeing guide and maps.
Address: Refuge Manager, Kenai National Moose Range, Box 500, Kenai, Alaska 99611.

KODIAK NATIONAL WILDLIFE REFUGE

Waterfowl: Mallards, gadwalls, pintails, American wigeon, greater scaup, common goldeneyes, Barrow's goldeneyes, buffleheads, common mergansers, and red-breasted mergansers.
Wildlife: Mammals (including Kodiak bear), birds (116 species), and fish.
Habitats: Mountains, rolling tundra, lakes, potholes, saltwater bays, and shoreline.
Size: 1,815,000 acres.
Location: On Kodiak Island in the Gulf of Alaska, 25 miles from the base of the Alaska Peninsula. Access is by airplane or boat; there are no roads on the island's refuge. Air flights are available from Anchorage.
Literature Available: Information circular and map, bird checklist, and tourist leaflets.
Address: Refuge Manager, Kodiak National Wildlife Refuge, Box 825, Kodiak, Alaska 99615.

NUNIVAK NATIONAL WILDLIFE REFUGE

Waterfowl: Canada geese, brant, emperor geese, snow geese, oldsquaws, harlequin ducks, Steller's eider, common eider, king eider, surf scoters, black scoters, and red-breasted mergansers.
Wildlife: Mammals (including introduced muskox), birds, and fish.
Habitats: A tundra-covered island in the Bering Sea with ancient volcanic cones, lowland meadows, lakes, shoreline, sand dunes, and sea cliffs.
Size: 1,109,388 acres.
Location: In the Bering Sea, off western Alaska, west of Bethel.
Literature Available: Information circular and map, and bird checklist.
Address: Refuge Manager, Nunivak National Wildlife Refuge, Box 346, Bethel, Alaska 99559.

APPENDIX 1

Accidental Waterfowl Sightings

In addition to the species described earlier in this book, a few others have been observed accidentally in North America during this century. None has been seen on the continent more than ten times. They are birds that occurred here unexpectedly and are outside their normal geographic ranges. If some of these species occur in North America again, they are likely to do so only at infrequent intervals.

BEWICK'S SWAN *Cygnus columbianus bewickii*
This distinctive Old World subspecies has been recorded in Oregon and California.

BEAN GOOSE *Anser fabalis*
Noted only in spring, since 1946, on St. Lawrence, Pribilof, and Aleutian islands, Alaska.

SPOT-BILLED DUCK *Anas poecilorhyncha*
Photographed on Adak Island, Alaska, in 1970–71.

WHITE-CHEEKED PINTAIL *Anas bahamensis*
A West Indian species noted in Florida, Virginia, and Wisconsin.

BAIKAL TEAL *Anas formosa*
Noted in Alaska, on Swan Island, North Carolina, and at Ladner, British Columbia.

GARGANEY *Anas querquedula*
Observed in Alaska, Alberta, Manitoba, and North Carolina.

COMMON POCHARD *Aythya ferina*
Noted in the Pribilof and Aleutian islands, Alaska.

SMEW *Mergus albellus*
Noted once in upstate New York, and once in Rhode Island.

APPENDIX 2

National Wildlife Areas in Canada

Under the provisions of the Canada Wildlife Act the national government of Canada has purchased and established a number of national wildlife areas that are of primary importance for waterfowl conservation. Full details about these areas are not yet available; nevertheless, they are of sufficient importance and interest to warrant listing here in brief. For more specific details, contact the Canadian Wildlife Service in Ottawa.

Nova Scotia

CHIGNECTO NATIONAL WILDLIFE AREA: 1,435 acres of John Lusby Marsh near the town of Amherst, and 1,065 acres of Amherst Point 2 miles west of the town of Amherst in Cumberland County.

MARGAREE NATIONAL WILDLIFE AREA: 165 acres in the Gulf of St. Lawrence in Inverness County.

SAND POND NATIONAL WILDLIFE AREA: 1,285 acres in Yarmouth County.

WALLACE BAY NATIONAL WILDLIFE AREA: 1,104 acres on Northumberland in Cumberland County.

New Brunswick

PORTAGE ISLAND NATIONAL WILDLIFE AREA: 1,114 acres in Miramichi Bay.

SHEPODY NATIONAL WILDLIFE AREA: 2,041 acres in Albert County.

TINTAMARRE NATIONAL WILDLIFE AREA: 3,041 acres near Sackville.

Quebec

BAIE DE L'ILE VERT NATIONAL WILDLIFE AREA: 305 acres in the Gulf of St. Lawrence, Rivière du Loup.

CAP TOURMENTE NATIONAL WILDLIFE AREA: 5,190 acres near the town of St. Joachim in Montmorency County.

ILES CONTRECOEUR NATIONAL WILDLIFE AREA: 565.99 acres in the Gulf of St. Lawrence downstream from Montreal.

ILES DE LA PAIX NATIONAL WILDLIFE AREA: 299 acres at Lac St. Louis.

LAC ST. FRANCOIS NATIONAL WILDLIFE AREA: 2,868.5 acres near the town of Dundee in Huntingdon County.

MADELEINE NATIONAL WILDLIFE AREA: 1,892.02 acres in the Gulf of St. Lawrence.

Ontario

BIG CREEK NATIONAL WILDLIFE AREA: 1,852 acres at Long Point, Lake Erie.

DOVER MARSH NATIONAL WILDLIFE AREA: 620 acres at Lake St. Clair.
ELEANOR ISLAND NATIONAL WILDLIFE AREA: 2 acres in Lake Muskoka.
MISSISSIPPI LAKE NATIONAL WILDLIFE AREA: 580 acres in Lanark County.
WELLER BAY NATIONAL WILDLIFE AREA: 100 acres at Trenton.

Manitoba

POPE RESERVOIR NATIONAL WILDLIFE AREA: 77 acres 50 miles northwest of Brandon.

Saskatchewan

LAST MOUNTAIN LAKE NATIONAL WILDLIFE AREA: 14,984 acres 80 miles northwest of Regina.
STALWART NATIONAL WILDLIFE AREA: 1,620 acres 70 miles northwest of Regina.
TWAY LAKE NATIONAL WILDLIFE AREA: 240 acres 50 miles southeast of Prince Albert.

Alberta

BLUE QUILLS NATIONAL WILDLIFE AREA: 240 acres 90 miles northeast of Edmonton.

British Columbia

ALAKSEN NATIONAL WILDLIFE AREA: 669 acres at the western tip of Western Island in the municipality of Delta.
CRESTON NATIONAL WILDLIFE AREA: 367 acres in the Kootenay Valley.
LITTLE QUALICIUM NATIONAL WILDLIFE AREA: 73 acres.
ROSEWALL CREEK NATIONAL WILDLIFE AREA: 31 acres on Vancouver Island.
VASEUX-BIGHORN NATIONAL WILDLIFE AREA: 1,804 acres in the Okanagan Valley 3 miles south of Okanagan Falls.
WIDGEON VALLEY NATIONAL WILDLIFE AREA: 308 acres 25 miles northeast of Vancouver.
WILMER MARSHES NATIONAL WILDLIFE AREA: 1,165 acres on the west bank of the Columbia River at Wilmer.

* * *

There are a number of migratory bird sancturaries that are Crown property in the Northwest Territories, which are important waterfowl nesting areas.

AKIMISKI BIRD SANCTUARY: 1,300 square miles of Akimiski Island. An important Canada goose and duck nesting area. Attawapiskat, Ontario, is the nearest settlement.
ANDERSON RIVER BIRD SANCTUARY: 418 square miles near the mouth of the Anderson River. An important nesting area for whistling swans, Canada geese, white-fronted geese, snow geese, brant, and many ducks.

BANKS ISLAND NO. 1 BIRD SANCTUARY: 7,922 square miles in the southwestern part of Banks Island. The refuge protects large numbers of snow geese, brant, and king eiders.

BANKS ISLAND NO. 2 BIRD SANCTUARY: 55 square miles including part of the Thomsen River area and Castel Bay.

BOATSWAIN BAY BIRD SANCTUARY: 69 square miles located about 30 miles north of Rupert's House, Quebec. Provides refuge for Canada geese, snow geese, black ducks, green-winged teal, and pintails.

BYLOT ISLAND BIRD SANCTUARY: 4,200 square miles located off the northern coast of Baffin Island. It serves as the principal nesting ground for the greater snow goose, which winters along the Atlantic Coast of the United States.

CAPE DORSET BIRD SANCTUARY: 100 square miles on three islands near Baffin Island. The refuge was established in 1958 to assist in the development of an eiderdown industry.

DEWEY SOPER BIRD SANCTUARY: 3,150 square miles located between Bowman Bay and the Koukdjuak River. Provides vital nesting ground for the blue phase of the snow goose, lesser snow goose, brant, and small Hutchins' subspecies of the Canada goose.

EAST BAY BIRD SANCTUARY: 450 square miles on the east coast of Southampton Island. Protects large numbers of nesting snow geese and brant.

HANNAH BAY BIRD SANCTUARY: 115 square miles located partly in Ontario and partly in the Northwest Territories. Provides refuge for Canada geese, snow geese, black ducks, green-winged teal, and other ducks.

HARRY GIBBONS BIRD SANCTUARY: 575 square miles located at the mouth of the Boas River southwest of Southampton Island. It serves as a nesting ground for snow geese, Ross' geese, and brant.

KENDALL ISLAND BIRD SANCTUARY: 234 square miles in the Mackenzie River delta. It serves as nesting ground for whistling swans, snow geese, white-fronted geese, and brant.

McCONNELL RIVER BIRD SANCTUARY: 127 square miles at the north of the McConnell River on the western shore of Hudson Bay. Snow geese and other waterfowl nest here.

MOOSE RIVER BIRD SANCTUARY: 5.6 square miles at the mouth of the Moose River where it enters James Bay. Large numbers of Canada geese and snow geese stop here in September and October.

QUEEN MAUD GULF BIRD SANCTUARY: 24,240 square miles. Most of the world's population of Ross' geese nests here along with Canada geese, snow geese, white-fronted geese, and brant.

APPENDIX 3

Waterfowl Conservation Organizations

In addition to various federal and state wildlife agencies that devote considerable time, effort, and money toward waterfowl conservation and management, there are many private organizations and individuals working toward these same goals. Those listed here are national or international in scope and have played important roles in advancing the wildlife endeavor.

Ducks Unlimited, Inc.
P.O. Box 66300
Chicago, Illinois 60666

Ducks Unlimited (Canada)
1495 Pembina Highway
Winnipeg, Manitoba R3T 2E2
Canada

Ducks Unlimited de Mexico
Apartado Postal 776
Monterrey, N.L., Mexico

National Audubon Society
950 Third Avenue
New York, New York 10022

National Wildlife Federation
1412 16th Street, N.W.
Washington, D.C. 20036

The Wildfowl Trust
Slimbridge, Gloucestershire GL2 7BT
England

Wildlife Management Institute
709 Wire Building
Washington, D.C. 20005

World Wildlife Fund
1319 18th Street, N.W.
Washington, D.C. 20036

BobHines

APPENDIX 4

Homes for Wood Ducks

Anyone who has seen a male wood duck will be quick to agree that these splendid birds are among the most attractive of all ducks. As more and more woodland is lost to man's activities, however, these secretive birds frequently are faced with a lack of enough woodpeckerlike holes in hollow trees to serve as nest sites. Fortunately wood ducks readily accept artificial structures in which to nest, and effective projects can be developed to provide local wood duck populations with adequate numbers of artificial nest boxes. Indeed, state and federal wildlife agencies throughout much of the United States have successfully established such projects in numerous areas.

Homes for Wood Ducks

Habitat

Anyone wanting to begin a wood duck nest box project must first select a site that contains suitable habitat for raising the young. Streams, ponds, or lakes must be located close to the nest boxes, and those aquatic areas must provide sufficient food and protective cover so that the ducklings can survive the weeks before they are able to fly. Most state and federal wildlife agencies are willing to provide site evaluations and recommendations.

Nest Box Requirements

When making wood duck nest boxes, the most important requirement is *do it properly or not at all.* Careless construction or placement of these structures can result in the death of the birds or loss of eggs through the activities of predators (snakes, raccoons, opossums, mink, and rats) or competition with other birds and mammals for use of the box. The following are some key considerations:

1. Generally erect boxes on metal or wood posts. Occasionally trees can be used.
2. Always protect boxes from below by using a metal shield extending at least 18 inches from the support post.
3. Place the boxes over or along the edge of a body of water, approximately 10 feet above the water or ground surface. The metal shield or guard must be 3 feet or more above the high water level.
4. Place a 3-inch-deep layer of wood shavings or sawdust on the bottom of the nest box. This will provide the female with a safe place onto which she can lay her eggs.
5. Clean and repair the nest boxes and replace the nest material every January.
6. Place nest boxes in clusters of two or more on the same support post. Wood ducks will tolerate such close nests with other wood ducks.

Standard Nest Boxes

The standard nest box illustrated here is constructed of unplaned cypress, cedar, or other weather-resistant lumber. Do *not* paint or otherwise treat the wood. Place the oval-shaped entrance hole with the broadest measurement horizontal. A strip of hardware cloth or screen tacked inside the box beneath the entrance hole will aid the ducklings in leaving the box. Use rustproof nails and screws. To discourage bees and wasps from using the box, spray the interior with a disinfectant such as Lysol.

Predator Guards

Cone-shaped, sheet-metal guards or shields must be used to protect all nest structures from predators. The illustration shows how to make three guards from a 3×8-foot sheet of 26-gauge galvanized metal. Cut along the solid lines, and overlap the cut edge to the dotted line when installing the guard.

A variation in the method of mounting nest boxes on posts, and in the construction of predator guards, also is illustrated.

Additional Information

Most state wildlife agencies have wood duck nest box plans and information available upon request. In addition, the U.S. Fish and Wildlife Service has available Wildlife Leaflet 510, "Nest Boxes for Wood Ducks," from which this appendix was prepared. Some private conservation organizations also have plans available for the construction of wood duck nest boxes.

STANDARD WOOD DUCK NESTING BOX

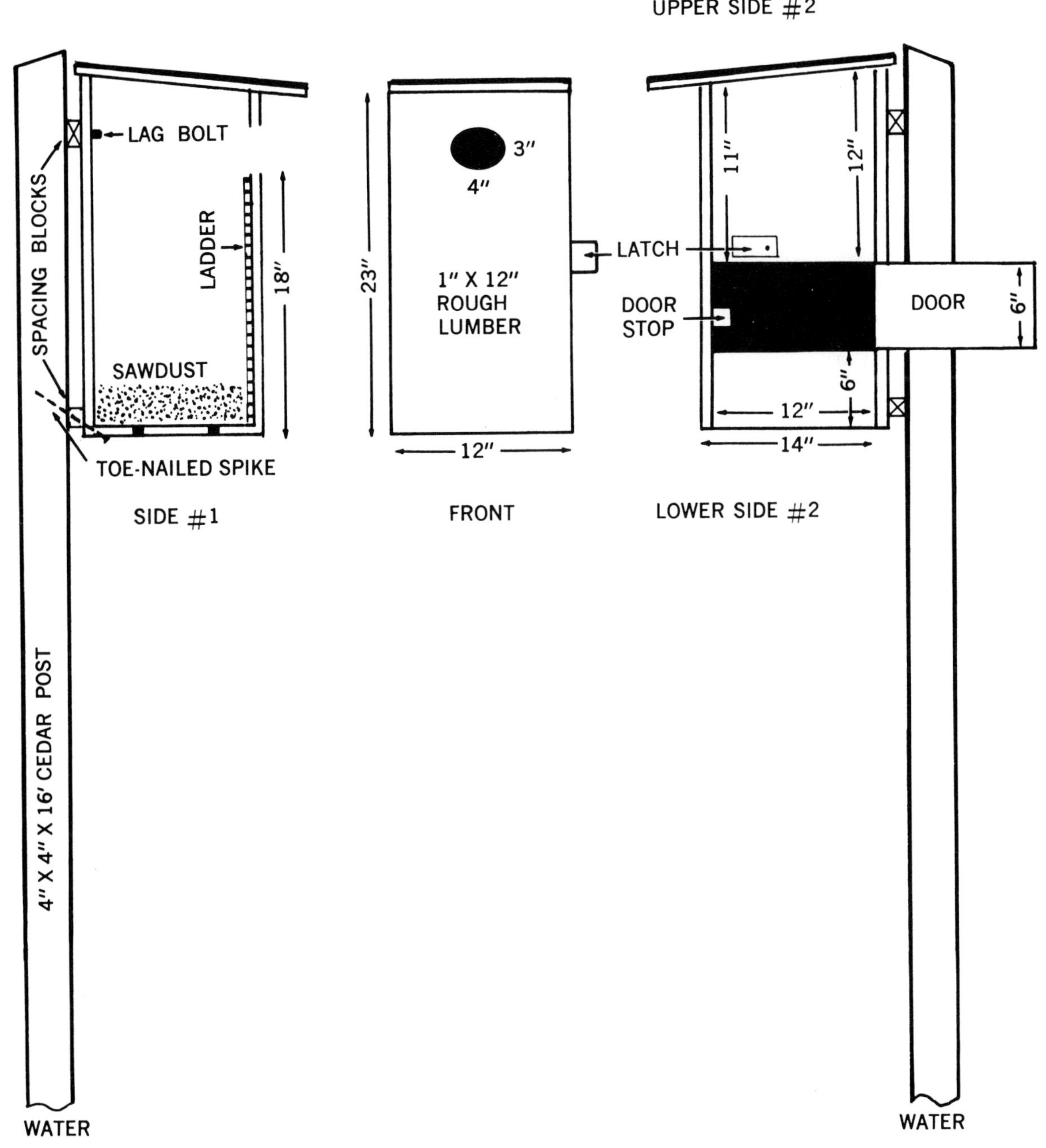

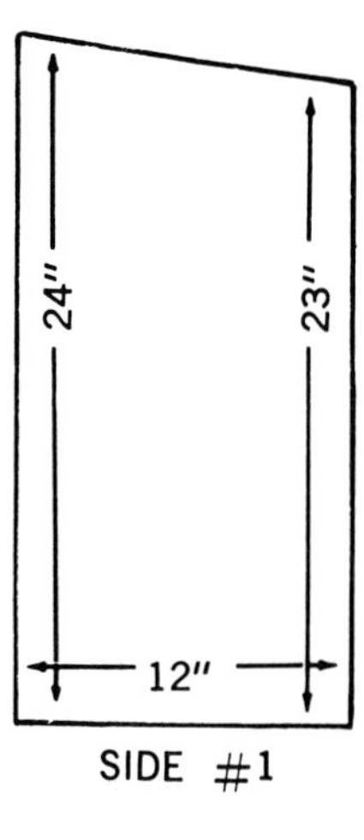
24″
23″
12″
SIDE #1

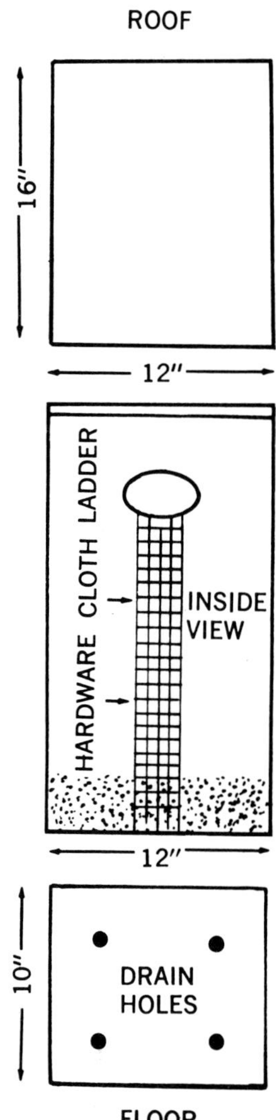
ROOF
16″
12″
HARDWARE CLOTH LADDER
INSIDE VIEW
12″
10″
DRAIN HOLES
FLOOR

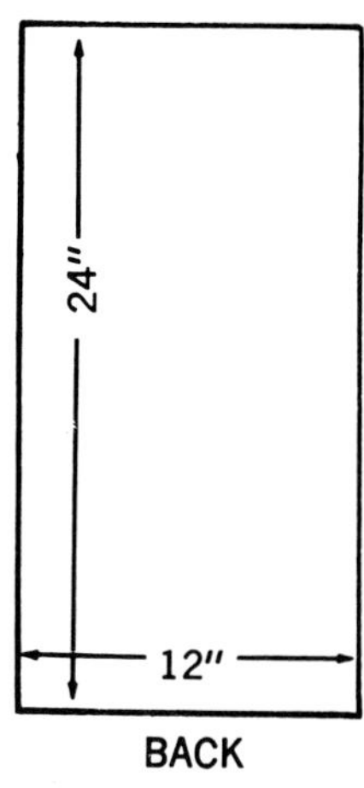
24″
12″
BACK

MATERIALS

Nails........................25—8 or 10-penny, zinc-coated.

Spike........................1—4+ inch.

Lag bolt........................1—¼-inch, 6 inches long.

Hinge........................1—3-inch cabinet + screws.

Hardware Cloth ....18-inch strip cut at least 3 inches wide. (All sharp ends should be bent under.)

Post........................1, 4″ X 4″, 16 feet long. (Should be cypress, cedar, or a preservative-treated wood.)

Plus........................Enough sawdust, wood-chips, or crumbled rotten wood to form a 3-inch nest base in each box.

Use rust-proof screws or nail that are long enough to hold securely despite rough handling and weathering.

Bore four ¼-inch drainage holes through the floor.

Tack a strip of ¼-inch mesh hardware cloth cut about 18″ X 3″ from the bottom of the box to the hole. This is necessary in order for the ducklings to be able to climb out the nest.

Spray the inside of the box with lysol or other disinfectant prior to the nesting season to discourage wasp and bees from moving in.

Wood ducks will nest in close proximity, but for the best results, the boxes should be grouped in clusters of half-a-dozen or so spaced so that each is no less than 50 feet from any other.

Each nest box must be cleaned and replenished with sawdust or wood chips each January.

10 LINEAR FEET OF 1′ X 12″ ROUGH LUMBER

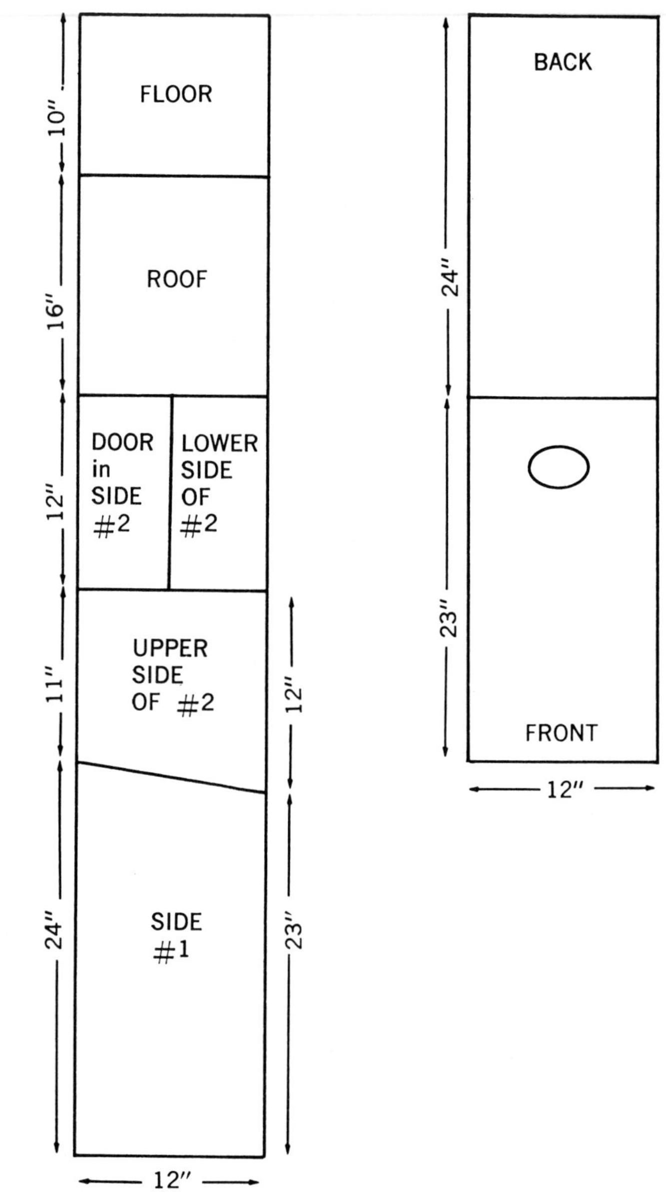

PREDATOR GUARD

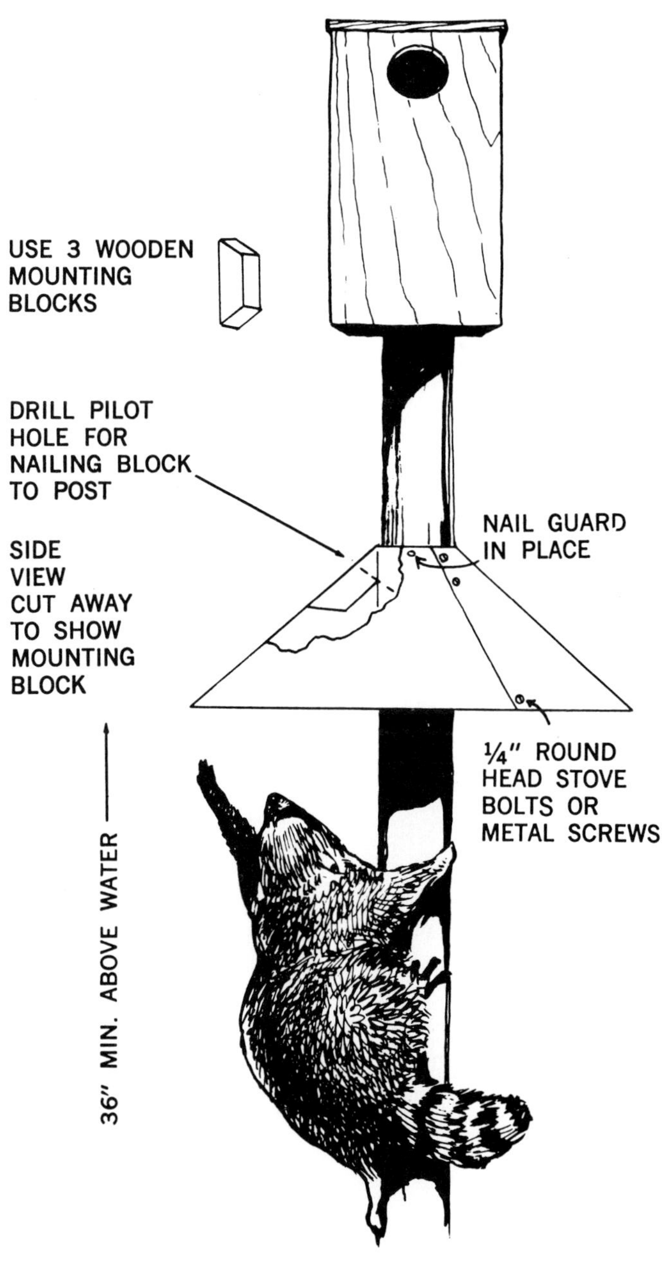

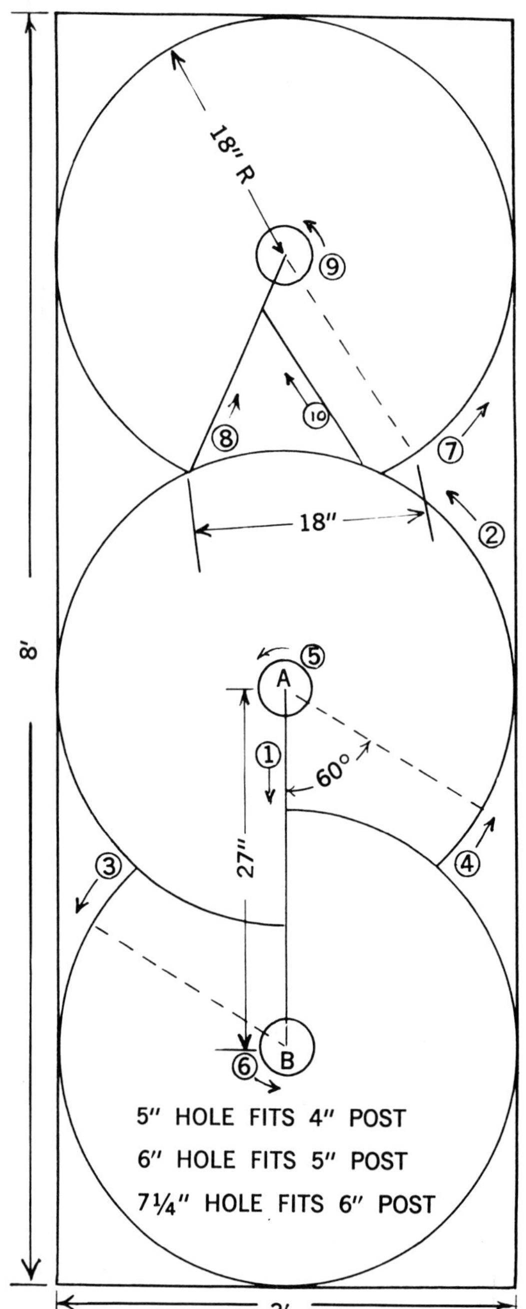

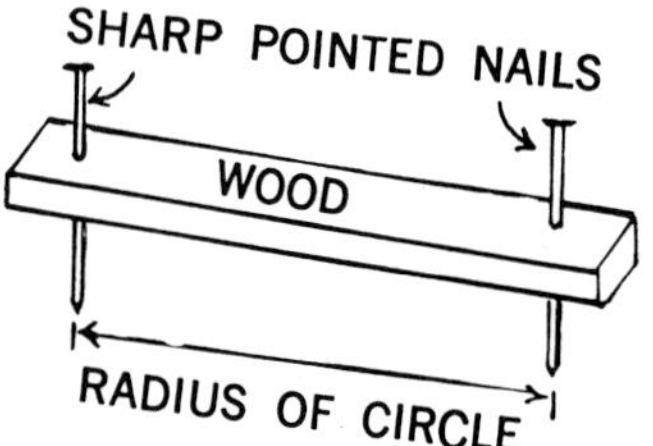

HOME MADE COMPASS
FOR SCRIBING METAL

STOVEPIPE NESTING SHELTER

The horizontal, starling-proof box, should be mounted on a channel-type steel fence post as shown below. Removal of the first and fourth prongs leaves holes about 9 inches apart. The lower hole is used for attaching the box to post with a stove bolt. The upper hole is used for fastening the ends of two support wires which are hooked through the opposite side of the nesting cylinder near each end. The box should be tightly attached to post to prevent wind from tearing it loose.

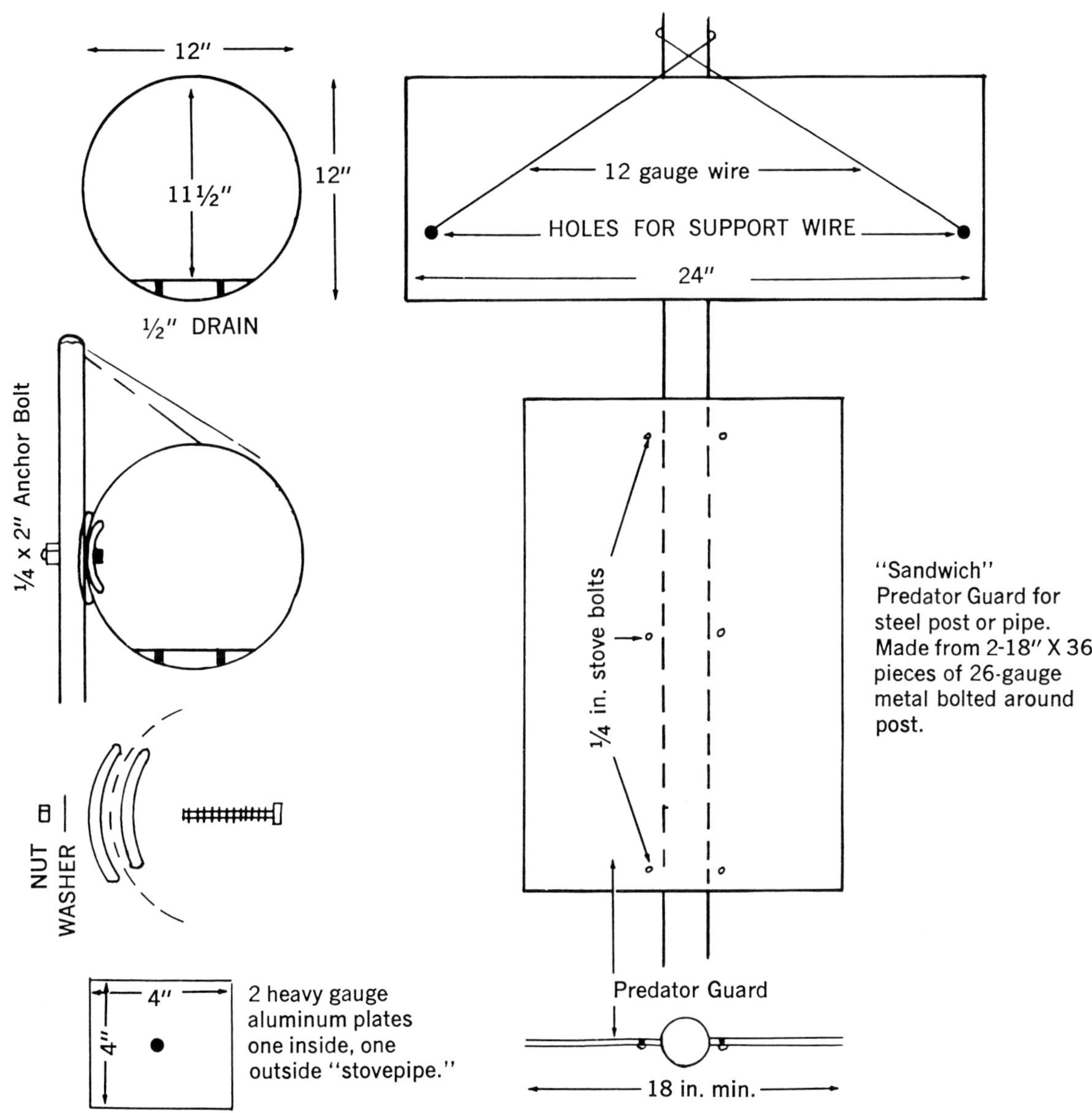

MATERIALS

Metal	2, 18″ X 36″ min. pcs. of 26 gauge metal + 8¼″ bolts for sandwich predator guard.
"Stovepipe"	1, 12″ diameter galvanized furnace pipe, 24 inches long.
Wire	10 feet of 12-gauge galvanized wire.
Nails	2 dozen, 10-penny.
Wood	Can be rough, 1—1½ inch mill ends. One (for back) 12″ wide. Other, 8″ X 12″ (for front).
Fittings	1, ¼″ X 2″ stove bolt and nut, 2 heavy gauge metal plates which have been bored out for the bolt and shaped to fit curve of furnace pipe, and 1 lock washer.
Steel post	1, 8–10 feet long, with ¼ inch hole bored about 18″ from the top for anchor bolt.

Suggested Reading

The volume of literature on waterfowl is enormous and scattered widely in books, periodicals, and other special publications. The books mentioned here are available in many libraries and provide a wealth of waterfowl information beyond that which could be included in this book.

Banko, W. E.
1960 The Trumpeter Swan. *North American Fauna No. 63*:1-214.

Bellrose, F. C.
1976 *The Ducks, Geese & Swans of North America.* Stackpole Books, Harrisburg, Pa.

Bennett, L. J.
1938 *The Blue-winged Teal, Its Ecology and Management.* Collegiate Press, Ames, Iowa.

Bent, A. C.
1923 Life Histories of North American Wild Fowl. Part one. *United States National Museum Bulletin* 126: 1-250. (Reprinted by Dover Publications, New York, N.Y.)
1925 Life Histories of North American Wild Fowl. Part two. *United States National Museum Bulletin* 130: 1-376. (Reprinted by Dover Publications, New York, N.Y.)

Burk, B.
1976 *Waterfowl Studies.* Winchester Press, New York, N.Y.

Day, A. M.
1949 *North American Waterfowl.* Stackpole and Heck, Harrisburg, Pa.

Delacour, J.
1954–64 *The Waterfowl of the World.* Four volumes. Country Life, London, England.

Einarsen, A. S.
1965 *Black Brant: Sea Goose of the Pacific Coast.* University of Washington Press, Seattle, Wash.

Erskine, A. J.
1972 Buffleheads. *Canadian Wildlife Service Monograph Series No. 4:* 1-240.

Hanson, H. C.
1965 *The Giant Canada Goose.* Southern Illinois University Press, Carbondale, Ill.

Hockbaum, H. A.
1955 *Travels and Traditions of Waterfowl.* University of Minnesota Press, Minneapolis, Minn.
1959 *The Canvasback on a Prairie Marsh.* Second Edition. Wildlife Management Institute, Washington, D.C.

Johnsgard, P. A.
1965 *Handbook of Waterfowl Behavior.* Cornell University Press, Ithaca, N.Y.
1968 *Waterfowl: Their Biology and Natural History.* University of Nebraska Press, Lincoln, Neb.
1975 *Waterfowl of North America.* Indiana University Press, Bloomington, Ind.

Kortright, F. H.
1953 *The Ducks, Geese and Swans of North America.* Stackpole Co., Harrisburg, Pa.

Palmer, R. S. (Ed.)
1976 *Handbook of North American Birds.* Volumes two and three. Yale University Press, New Haven, Conn.

Phillips, J. C.
1922–26 *The Natural History of the Ducks.* Houghton Mifflin Co., Boston, Mass.

Ripley, D.
1957 *A Paddling of Ducks.* Harcourt, Brace, New York, N.Y.

Scott, P.
1968 *A Coloured Key to the Wildfowl of the World.* The Wildfowl Trust, Slimbridge, England.
1972 *The Swans.* Houghton Mifflin Co., Boston, Mass.

Sowls, L. K.
1955 *Prairie Ducks.* Wildlife Management Institute, Washington, D.C.

Williams, C. W.
1967 *Honker.* Van Nostrand, Princeton, N.J.

Wright, B. S.
1954 *High Tide and an East Wind: The Story of the Black Duck.* Stackpole Co., Harrisburg, Pa.

Wylie, S. R. and S. S. Furlong
1972 *Key to North American Waterfowl.* Livingston Publishing Co., Wynnewood, Pa.

INDEX

Agassiz National Wildlife Refuge (Minn.), 131
Aix sponsa, 28
Akimiski Bird Sanctuary (N. W. T.), 215
Alamosa National Wildlife Refuge (Colo.), 162
Alaksen National Wildlife Area (B. C.), 215
Aleutian Islands National Wildlife Refuge (Alaska), 206
Anahuac National Wildlife Refuge (Tex.), 175
Anas acuta, 20
americana, 26
bahamensia, 213
clypeata, 27
crecca, 21
cyanoptera, 24
discors, 23
falcata, 21
formosa, 213
penelope, 25
platyrhynchos, 16
peocilorhyncha, 213
querquedula, 213
rubripes, 18
strepera, 19
Anderson River Bird Sanctuary (N. W. T.), 215
Ankeny National Wildlife Refuge (Ore.), 188
Anser albifrons, 5
caerulescens, 6
canagicus, 8
fabalis, 213
rossii, 7
Aransas National Wildlife Refuge (Tex.), 175
Arapaho National Wildlife Refuge (Colo.), 162
Arctic National Wildlife Range (Alaska), 206
Arrowwood National Wildlife Refuge (N. D.), 147
Audubon National Wildlife Refuge (N. D.), 147
Aythya affinis, 34
americana, 30
collaris, 31
ferina, 213
fuligula, 35
marila, 33
valisineria, 32

Back Bay National Wildlife Refuge (Va.), 105
Baie de L'Ile Vert National Wildlife Area (Que.), 214
Banks Island No. 1 Bird Sanctuary (N. W. T.), 216
Banks Island No. 2 Bird Sanctuary (N. W. T.), 216
Baskett Slough National Wildlife Refuge (Ore.), 188
Bear Lake National Wildlife Refuge (Idaho), 195
Bear River Migratory Bird Refuge (Utah), 160
Benton Lake National Wildlife Refuge (Mont.), 142
Big Creek National Wildlife Area (Ont.), 214
Big Lake National Wildlife Refuge (Ark.), 126
Big Stone National Wildlife Refuge (Minn.), 131
Binoculars, 54
Bitter Lake National Wildlife Refuge (N. Mex.), 171
Blackwater National Wildlife Refuge (Md.), 104
Blinds, 56
Blue Quills National Wilife Area (Alberta), 215

Boatswain Bay Bird Sanctuary (N. W. T.), 216
Bombay Hook National Wildlife Refuge (Del.), 102
Bosque del Apache National Wildlife Refuge (N. Mex.), 171
Bowdoin National Wildlife Refuge (Mont.), 142
Brant, 12
Branta bernicla, 12
canadensia, 9
leucopsis, 13
Brazoria National Wildlife Refuge (Tex.), 177
Breton National Wildlife Refuge (La.), 127
Brigantine National Wildlife Refuge (N. J.), 96
Browns Park National Wildlife Refuge (Colo.), 164
Bucephala albeola, 38
clangula, 36
islandica, 37
Buffalo Lake National Wildlife Refuge (Tex.), 177
Bufflehead, 38
Bylot Island Bird Sanctuary (N. W. T.), 216

Camas National Wildlife Refuge (Idaho), 195
Canvasback, 32
Cape Dorset Bird Sanctuary (N. W. T.), 216
Cape Romain National Wildlife Refuge (S. C.) 111
Cap Tourmente National Wildlife Area (Que.), 214
Carolina Sandhills National Wildlife Refuge (S. C.) 111
Charles M. Russell National Wildlife Range (Mont.), 142
Chassahowitzka National Wildlife Refuge (Fla.), 120
Chautauqua National Wildlife Refuge (Ill.), 138
Chignecto National Wildlife Area (N. S.), 214
Chincoteague National Wildlife Refuge (Va.), 105
Choctaw National Wildlife Refuge (Ala.), 118
Cibola National Wildlife Refuge (Ariz.), 170
Clangula hyemalis, 39
Clarence Rhode National Wildlife Range (Alaska), 209
Clear Lake National Wildlife Refuge (Calif.), 198
Columbian White-tailed Deer National Wildlife Refuge (Wash.), 182
Columbia National Wildlife Refuge (Wash.), 182
Crab Orchard National Wildlife Refuge (Ill.), 140
Creeks, 82
Crescent Lake National Wildlife Refuge (Neb.), 156
Creston National Wildlife Area (B. C.), 215
Cross Creeks National Wildlife Refuge (Tenn.), 107
Cygnus columbianus bewickii, 213
columbianus columbianus, 2
cygnus buccinator, 3
cygnus cygnus, 4
olor, 1

Decoys, 56
Deer Flat National Wildlife Refuge (Idaho), 195
Delta National Wildlife Refuge (La.), 129
Dencrocygna autumnalis, 14
bicolor, 15
Des Lacs National Wildlife Refuge (N. D.), 147
DeSoto National Wildlife Refuge (Iowa), 158
Dewey Soper Bird Sanctuary (N. W. T.), 216
Dover Marsh National Wildlife Area (Ont.), 215
Duck, American Black, 18
Harlequin, 40
Masked, 49
Ring-necked, 31
Ruddy, 48
Spot-billed, 213
Tufted, 35
Wood, 28
Ducks Unlimited (Canada), 217
Ducks Unlimited de Mexico, 217
Ducks Unlimited, Inc., 217

East Bay Bird Sanctuary (N. W. T.), 216

Eastern Neck National Wildlife Refuge (Md.), 105
Eclipse Plumage, 63
Eider, Common, 41
King, 43
Spectacled, 44
Steller's, 41
Eleanor Island National Wildlife Area (Ont.), 215
Erie National Wildlife Refuge (Pa.), 100
Eufaula National Wildlife Refuge (Ala.), 118

Flint Hills National Wildlife Refuge (Kan.), 165
Flyways, 66
Atlantic, 66
Central, 70
Mississippi, 68
Pacific, 72
Fort Niobrara National Wildlife Refuge (Neb.), 156
Franklin Island National Wildlife Refuge (Maine), 86

Gadwall, 19
Garganey, 213
Goldeneye, Barrow's, 37
Common, 36
Goose, Barnacle, 13
Bean, 213
Canada, 9
Emperor, 8
Ross', 7
Snow, 6
White-fronted, 5
Grays Lake National Wildlife Refuge (Idaho), 196
Great Meadows National Wildlife Refuge (Mass.), 90
Great Swamp National Wildlife Refuge (N. J.), 100

Hagerman National Wildlife Refuge (Tex.), 177
Hannah Bay Bird Sanctuary (N. W. T.), 216
Harris Neck National Wildlife Refuge (Ga.), 113
Harry Gibbons Bird Sanctuary (N. W. T.), 216
Hart Mountain National Antelope Refuge (Ore.), 188
Hatchie National Wildlife Refuge (Tenn.), 107
Havasu National Wildlife Refuge (Ariz.), 170
Histrionicus histrionicus, 40
Holla Bend National Wildlife Refuge (Ark.), 127
Horicon National Wildlife Refuge (Wis.), 135
Hutton Lake National Wildlife Refuge (Wyo.), 153
Hybrids, 63

Iles Contrecoeur National Wildlife Area (Que.), 214
Iles de la Paix National Wildlife Area (Que.), 214
Imperial National Wildlife Refuge (Ariz.), 170
Iroquois National Wildlife Refuge (N. Y.), 95
Izembek National Wildlife Refuge (Alaska), 209

J. Clark Salyer National Wildlife Refuge (N. D.), 147
J. N. "Ding" Darling National Wildlife Refuge (Fla.), 120

Kenai National Moose Range (Alaska), 120
Kendall Island Bird Sanctuary (N. W. T.), 216
Kern National Wildlife Refuge (Calif.), 198
Kirwin National Wildlife Refuge (Kan.), 165
Klamath Forest National Wildlife Refuge (Ore.), 190
Kodiak National Wildlife Refuge (Alaska), 211
Kootenai National Wildlife Refuge (Idaho), 196

Lacassine National Wildlife Refuge (La.), 130
Lacreek National Wildlife Refuge (S. D.), 151
Lac St. Francis National Wildlife Area (Que.), 214
Laguna Atascosa National Wildlife Refuge (Tex.), 177
Lake Andes National Wildlife Refuge (S. D.), 151

Lake Ilo National Wildlife Refuge (N. D.), 148
Lakes, 79
Lake Woodruff National Wildlife Refuge (Fla.), 120
Last Mountain Lake National Wildlife Area (Sask.), 215
Las Vegas National Wildlife Refuge (N. Mex.), 171
Lewis and Clark National Wildlife Refuge (Ore.), 190
Little Creek State Wildlife Area (Del.), 102
Little Qualicium National Wildlife Area (B. C.), 215
Long Lake National Wildlife Refuge (N. D.), 149
Lostwood National Wildlife Refuge (N. D.), 149
Lower Klamath National Wildlife Refuge (Calif.), 198
Loxahatchee National Wildlife Refuge (Fla.), 122

Madeleine National Wildlife Area (Que.), 214
Malheur National Wildlife Refuge (Ore.), 190
Mallard, 16
Margaree National Wildlife Area (N. S.), 214
Mark Twain National Wildlife Refuge (Ill.), 141
Marshes, 82
Martin National Wildlife Refuge (Md.), 105
Mason Neck National Wildlife Refuge (Va.), 106
Mattamuskeet National Wildlife Refuge (N. C.), 10
Maxwell National Wildlife Refuge (N. Mex.), 172
McConnell River Bird Sanctuary (N. W. T.), 216
McNary National Wildlife Refuge (Wash.), 182
Medicine Lake National Wildlife Refuge (Mont.), 145
Melanitta deglandi, 45
  nigra, 47
  perspicillata, 46
Merced National Wildlife Refuge (Calif.), 200
Merganser, Common, 51
  Hooded, 50
  Red-breasted, 52
Mergus albellus, 213
  cucullatus, 50
  merganser, 51
  serrator, 52
Merritt Island National Wildlife Refuge (Fla.), 122
Middle Creek Wildlife Management Area (Pa.), 100
Migration Seasons, 72
Mingo National Wildlife Refuge (Mo.), 167
Minidoka National Wildlife Refuge (Idaho), 196
Missisquoi National Wildlife Refuge (Vt.), 88
Mississippi Lake National Wildlife Area (Ont.), 215
Modoc National Wildlife Refuge (Calif.), 201
Monomoy National Wildlife Refuge (Mass.), 90
Monte Vista National Wildlife Refuge (Colo.), 164
Montezuma National Wildlife Refuge (N. Y.), 96
Moosehorn National Wildlife Refuge (Maine), 86
Moose River Bird Sanctuary (N. W. T.), 216
Morton National Wildlife Refuge (N. Y.), 96
Muleshoe National Wildlife Refuge (Te.x.), 178
Muscatatuck National Wildlife Refuge (Ind.), 141
Museums, 57

Names, Waterfowl, 58
Nantucket National Wildlife Refuge (Mass.), 90
National Audubon Society, 217
National Wildlife Federation, 217
Necedah National Wildlife Refuge (Wis.), 135
Noxubee National Wildlife Refuge (Miss.), 124
Nunivak National Wildlife Refuge (Alaska), 211

Okefenokee National Wildlife Refuge (Ga.), 117

Oldsquaw, 39
Ottawa National Wildlife Refuge (Ohio), 141
Ouray National Wildlife Refuge (Utah), 162
Oxyura dominica, 49
jamaicensis, 48

Pahranagat National Wildlife Refuge (Nev.), 197
Parker River National Wildlife Refuge (Mass.), 90
Pea Island National Wildlife Refuge (N. C.), 110
Petit Manan National Wildlife Refuge (Maine), 86
Pintail, Common, 20
White-cheeked, 213
Pixley National Wildlife Refuge (Calif.), 201
Pochard, Common, 213
Polysticta stelleri, 41
Pond Island National Wildlife Refuge (Maine), 88
Ponds, 79
Pope Reservoir National Wildlife Area (Man.), 215
Portage Island National Wildlife Area (N. B.), 214
Presquile National Wildlife Refuge (Va.), 106
Prime Hook National Wildlife Refuge (Del.), 103
Pungo National Wildlife Refuge (N. C.), 110
Pymatuning Waterfowl Area (Pa.), 101

Queen Maud Gulf Bird Sanctuary (N. W. T.), 216
Quivira National Wildlife Refuge (Kan.), 165

Rachel Carson National Wildlife Refuge (Maine), 88
Ravalli National Wildlife Refuge (Mont.), 145
Redhead, 30
Red Rock Lakes National Wildlife Refuge (Mont.), 145
Reelfoot National Wildlife Refuge (Tenn.), 107
Reservoirs, 79
Rice Lake National Wildlife Refuge (Minn.), 131
Ridgefield National Wildlife Refuge (Wash.), 184
Rivers, 82
Rosewell Creek National Wildlife Area (B. C.), 215
Ruby Lake National Wildlife Refuge (Nev.), 197

Sabine National Wildlife Refuge (La.), 130
Sachuest Point National Wildlife Refuge (R. I.), 92
Sacramento National Wildlife Refuge (Calif.), 201
Salton Sea National Wildlife Refuge (Calif.), 201
Salt Plains National Wildlife Refuge (Okla.), 173
San Bernard National Wildlife Refuge (Tex.), 180
Sand Lake National Wildlife Refuge (S. D.), 151
Sand Pond National Wildlife Area (N. S.), 214
San Francisco Bay National Wildlife Refuge (Calif.), 203
San Luis National Wildlife Refuge (Calif.), 203
San Pablo Bay National Wildlife Refuge (Calif.), 203
Santa Ana National Wildlife Refuge (Tex.), 180
Santee National Wildlife Refuge (S.C., 113
Savannah National Wildlife Refuge (Ga.), 117
Scaup, Greater, 33
Lesser, 34
Scoter, Black, 47
Surf, 46
White-winged, 45
Seacoasts, 82
Seedkadee National Wildlife Refuge (Wyo.), 153
Seney National Wildlife Refuge (Mich.), 138
Sequoyah National Wildlife Refuge (Okla.), 173
Shepody National Wildlife Area (N. B.), 214
Sherburne National Wildlife Refuge (Minn.), 133
Shiawassee National Wildlife Refuge (Mich.), 138

Shoveler, Northern, 27
Slade National Wildlife Refuge (N. D.), 149
Smew, 213
Somateria fischeri, 44
mollissima, 41
spectabilis, 43
Species Problem, 61
Squaw Creek National Wildlife Refuge (Mo.), 167
Stalwart National Wildlife Area (Sask.), 215
Stillwater National Wildlife Refuge and Management Area (Nev.), 197
St. Marks National Wildlife Refuge (Fla.), 122
Streams, 82
St. Vincent National Wildlife Refuge (Fla.), 124
Swan Lake National Wildlife Refuge (Mo.), 167
Swan, Bewick's, 213
Mute, 1
Trumpeter, 3
Whistling, 2
Whooper, 4
Swanquarter National Wildlife Refuge (N. C.), 111

Tamarac National Wildlife Refuge (Minn.), 134
Teal, Baikal, 213
Blue-winged, 23
Cinnamon, 24
Falcated, 21
Green-winged, 21
Telescopes, 55
Tennessee National Wildlife Refuge (Tenn.), 110
Tewaukon National Wildlife Refuge (N. D.), 149
Tinicum National Environmental Center (Pa.) 102
Tintamarre National Wildlife Area (N. B.), 214
Tishomingo National Wildlife Refuge (Okla.), 173
Toppenish National Wildlife Refuge (Wash.), 184
Trustom Pond National Wildlife Refuge (R. I.), 92
Tule Lake National Wildlife Refuge (Calif.), 203
Turnbull National Wildlife Refuge (Wash.), 184
Tway Lake National Wildlife Area (Sask.), 215

Umatilla National Wildlife Refuge (Ore.), 190
Union Slough National Wildlife Refuge (Iowa), 158
Upper Klamath National Wildlife Refuge (Ore.), 192
Upper Mississippi River Wild Life and Fish Refuge (Minn.), 135
Upper Souris National Wildlife Refuge (N. D.), 150

Valentine National Wildlife Refuge (Neb.), 156
Vaseux-Bighorn National Wildlife Area (B. C.), 215

Wallace Bay National Wildlife Area (N. S.), 214
Wapanocca National Wildlife Refuge (Ark.), 127
Washita National Wildlife Refuge (Okla.), 173
Waubay National Wildlife Refuge (S. D.), 153
Weller Bay National Wildlife Area (Ont.), 215
Wheeler National Wildlife Refuge (Ala.), 118
Whistling Duck, Black-bellied, 14
Fulvous, 15
White River National Wildlife Refuge (Ark.), 127
Wichita Mountains Wildlife Refuge (Okla.), 175
Widgeon Valley National Wildlife Area (B. C.), 215
Wigeon, American, 26
Eurasian, 25
Wildfowl Trust (England), 217
Wildlife Management Institute, 217
Willapa National Wildlife Refuge (Wash.), 184
William L. Finley National Wildlife Refuge (Ore.), 194
Wilmer Marshes National Wildlife Area (B. C.), 215
World Wildlife Fund, 217

Yazoo National Wildlife Refuge (Miss.), 124

Zoos, 57